The Voices of Robby Wilde

The
Voices of
Robby
Wilde

Elizabeth Kytle

Foreword by Robert Coles

The University of Georgia Press
Athens and London

Published in 1995 by the University of Georgia Press
Athens, Georgia 30602
© 1987 by Elizabeth Kytle
Foreword © 1995 by the University of Georgia Press

The paper in this book meets the guidelines for
permanence and durability of the Committee on
Production Guidelines for Book Longevity of the
Council on Library Resources.

Printed in the United States of America

99 98 97 96 95 P 5 4 3 2 1

Library of Congress Cataloging in Publication Data

Kytle, Elizabeth.
    The voices of Robby Wilde / Elizabeth Kytle ; foreword by Robert
Coles.
      p. cm.
    Originally published: Washington, D.C. : Seven Locks Press, 1987.
    ISBN 0-8203-1715-2 (pbk. : acid-free paper)
    1. Paranoid schizophrenics—United States—Biography. I. Coles,
Robert. II. Title.
[RC514.K96 1995]
616.89′82′0092—dc20
[B]   94-33591

British Library Cataloging in Publication Data available

Foreword

Robert Coles

In the late 1950s I was working in a mental hospital as a resident in psychiatry, learning to practice a particular branch of medicine. Until that time I had experienced no great difficulty in conversation with patients. Indeed I loved those clinical encounters that began in the third year of medical school—such a satisfying and instructive contrast, for me, with the first two years, not to mention the premedical course regimen: a harrowing nightmare, so some of us thought, or at best, a taxing, unavoidable hurdle, irrelevant in so many respects to a future professional life. Yet when I began working with the largely "psychotic" population I would meet early in my residency years, I had serious second thoughts about one more hurdle—for I had envisaged my psychiatric work to be, eventually, with children, with adolescents, with youths in trouble, all right, but not "out of their minds," a colloquial expression that all too fittingly applied to the kinds of men and women I was seeing then.

I can still remember one of my first psychiatric patients and how forbearing he was: ready to help his young, inexperienced physician learn the ropes of a new kind of work. Hal was his name, and he pointedly told me I was not to call him Harold, ever, and also, not to remember his last name at all (it was a fancy old Yankee one). I knew to drop all that introductory matter; and I also knew that in telling me to forget his (important) last name, Hal was in fact emphasizing it, etching it thereby more strenuously on my gray matter. I sat hour after hour, in a seemingly unchallenging kind of passivity—listening with all my might, trying to be the interested student, making even occasional efforts, at the behest of one or another wise supervisory older doctor, to avoid pronouncements and yes, even those clever interpretations all of us in psychoanalytic psychiatry find so tempting: a measure of our vanity, a measure of our humanity.

Once I spent an hour with Hal in absolute silence—his. I tried to initiate conversation; he listened but refused me all words. He would not even nod or shake his head. His eyes stared directly at mine, without so much as a blink, or so I thought. I was devastated and made to feel anxious, even fearful. He had a diagnosis similar to that of the man whose life unfolds in *The Voices of Robby Wilde*: "paranoid schizophrenia" (how well I remember thinking of those two words as I vainly tried to engage him and thereby prove myself to be of some competence). As I got up, prepared to leave, he gave me a final look and surprised me by thanking me—I had not the slightest idea why or for doing what. He must have seen the puzzled inadequacy that I felt on my face, because he offered me these hard-to-forget words: "I was just listening to a lot of my own voices, so I couldn't pay attention." As my teacher Dr. Paul Howard (such a gifted, thoughtful psychiatrist and psychoanalyst) would later remark in his characteristically terse, incisive, ironic manner, "Quite a productive hour you two had!"

In fact Hal was getting ready to tell me about himself what Robby Wilde, with the extraordinarily talented, persevering, and thoughtful assistance of Elizabeth Kytle, lets us know about his mental life—its complex, haunting, scary, melancholy nature. Hal, like Robby, had been living with voices that are not to be confused with the voice ordinary folks call their very own. To be sure, we all have our odd sides and moments; but psychosis, the torment of paranoia, the anguish of a mind split asunder with thought rendered irrational and incomprehensible to others (and to oneself as well) is a special fate indeed for someone to carry through his or her allotted days. A year later, as Hal and I were able to talk more openly—about his worries and doubts, his terrible suspicions, his all too extravagant convictions that amounted, in their sum, to a continuing sense of extreme vulnerability and jeopardy, to say the least—he could offer me this observation: "I'm shadowed all the time, no let up." (I had learned by then that as we were concluding a talk, it was time for a casual, brief comment that would later be recognized by Dr. Howard and me as compellingly illuminating, even shattering in its revelatory power.) I nodded; by then, I knew.

On one of these occasions, as we were both leaving the room a few seconds later, Hal uncannily challenged what I have just said about myself to the reader: "You can't really know—you can only try to know." Silence from me; I knew, I guess, not to reach fearfully, self-protectively for words of agreement, for words given the shape of questions. In a way he was right, though I did want to qualify; to some extent, so it goes for all of us as we try to connect with others. Still there are degrees—and sometimes quantitative differences mount so high they do become qualitative. Put differently, we all have had our moments of doubt and despair, have even known a skepticism, an outright mistrust of others, have even given such times a kind of inner expression. Yet the "voices" that are given the life of a strong, affecting narrative in this book (the story of a life—one hurt, yet one of substantial honor and dignity) are of another order.

The Voices of Robby Wilde enhances our capacity to understand a particular human being—his driven, painful journey, his determination and resourcefulness, as well as his jarring collapses, turns for the worse, blind spots, and dead ends. A life is rendered, given to others to contemplate; thereby we get to know not only Robby Wilde, but ourselves, what we can take for granted, what we have been spared, as well as what others, not a few others, in all parts of the world, of all classes and races and nationalities, have to consider their particular lot: a mind all too fragile and all too reluctant to let the world be, and for reasons still (the question of etiology) inscrutable.

To the memory of a friend, the real person who is called Robby in this book, with admiration and affection.

Author's Note

The Voices of Robby Wilde is a true story of a real person afflicted with paranoid schizophrenia.

It started with a phone call from a man, a friend of mine, whose paranoia had long ago wrenched his life out of whatever would have been its natural shape. "I want you to write a book about me," he said. "A book like *Willie Mae*." *Willie Mae* is my first-person biography first published in 1958. In it the intent was to show what it was like to be a black woman who was born in the South in the first part of this century and who spent her whole life there. My friend craved a similar effort in his behalf. His request transcended the personal, for, like Willie Mae, he was one of a large group, and his malady, common though it was and is, even yet meets with deplorably little understanding.

In random conversations, I have heard that people with paranoid schizophrenia are weak-willed victims of themselves; that their impairment is curable; that few are stricken; that most are violent; that they could straighten themselves out if they would "grow" and "learn." Actually they are victims of an irresistible force; the disease is at best treatable. More than a million and a half Americans are suffering from it; more than a million of these are hearing voices every day. Those so impaired are as a group less given to violence than the rest of us, and nobody has yet grown or learned the way out of paranoid schizophrenia.

The request came more than twenty years ago. Finally, *The Voices of Robby Wilde* is my effort to do what my friend asked. I have done it in his memory, too late to be for him; for myself because the subject is close to my heart; and for all whose lives are thus cruelly blighted.

My friend was brave enough and boldly enterprising enough to attempt the impossible, i.e. to fully confide and express what it was like for him to exist as prey to hallucinations that ravaged his life though leaving his mind intact. By attempting the impossible, however, he achieved something substantial. Thanks to his rare insight into his own condition and to his anguished and angry longing to be understood, he succeeded in large measure. He was able to tell me enough to enable me to produce a genuine likeness if not a finished portrait.

Out of respect for the privacy of the living and the dead, I have changed the names of all people here involved in Robby's life and that of his hometown. In the twice-told episodes, Robby's accounts of life experiences are made from what he told me; necessary changes in others' narrations include incidents unrelated to his sickness. In every instance these narrators accurately reflect the characters, attitudes, and behavior of the real people they stand in for. I learned of these attributes and some events from Robby, from persons both he and I knew, from one who knew him in his younger days in North Carolina, and from some who told me of incidents in which both he and they figured.

I hugely regret that I was unable to write this book while the real Robby lived. I share the view of one of its characters that he acquitted himself with more courage every day of his life than most of us are ever even called on to try to summon. Sadly, in most instances, due to the nature of his affliction and the limitations of others, vastly different perceptions registered. It was his hope and is mine that what comes out in these pages will shed some light of respect, insight, and compassion on a human condition usually looked at through flawed and dark lenses.

The two poems were written by the real Robby.

—*Elizabeth Kytle*

Who has seen the wind?
Neither I nor you.
But when the leaves hang trembling
The wind is passing through.

—Christina Rossetti

PART ONE
1920-1935

I
ONE

The first "voice" I ever heard assaulted me when I was a third-grade schoolboy. I was in an uneasy frame of mind because I had told a lie to get out of going to school. I was at home, on the landing between two flights of stairs that led to the second floor. This landing was a favorite place of mine. There was a blackboard there, and a window with a windowseat, and it was a cozy spot for me to go with my books. I was sitting there, reading, the house was perfectly quiet—and of course *I always* was quiet—and I heard the voice.

"I've got you."

The voice was plain as broad open daylight and terrifying as pitch black night. It was a man's voice—not one I recognized—and its quality was appallingly definite. I didn't then know words like sinister and ominous, but it was both of these to an unbearable degree. It wasn't a loud voice, not at all a loud voice; but it was harsh and emphatic, and the sound told me that it was the voice of a man who hated me and would surely get me. And I knew with the most chilling certainty that for a man with a voice like that to get me, I'd be done for. It spoke just the once. "I've got you."

I sat stock-still, absolutely incapable of moving a muscle. I guess this lasted just a moment or so, and then I leapt up and hurled myself down the stairs. Momma was somewhere downstairs, and I was frantic to get to her. By the time I was halfway down, my own voice returned and I started screaming bloody murder. When I found Momma, I told her somebody upstairs had said, "I've got you." She was concerned when she first saw me, because of the screaming; but when I told her this, she brushed it right aside. She said, "Oh, no. You heard somebody outside, talking to somebody else."

From that moment until my early middle years, I never told anybody about that voice or any of the other voices that have bedeviled me with very brief letups. I saw no reason to tell anybody, and every reason not to tell. I thought I was hearing real voices, and I attached them to persons present or within earshot when I was hearing them. Why should a boy or a man tell anybody about accusations being made to his very face, some by people who knew him? Loss of what few friends I had would have been a certainty. If they had heard these voices themselves, I surely wasn't going to bring it up. If they hadn't, I certainly wasn't going to tell them. This kept me off balance all the time and with everybody. I naturally thought that the voices could be heard by anybody present when I heard them, and I continued to think this for many years. The voices attacked me in every public or social situation I was ever in, and finally in seclusion too. This evolved into a condition of stark aloneness. No matter how many people were around me—friends, acquaintances, strangers—I was always alone, in the most desolate sense of the word.

When I was between three and four, two things happened that I still wonder about. One was the broken leg.

One late afternoon Zaida was minding me because Momma was sick in bed. She took me across the street. We had strict instructions not to leave our house, but there was a hammock over there and she liked it. We were in the hammock together. It tipped over, we both fell out, and Zaida piled up on top of me with my leg twisted under me. The pain was fierce, and I screamed. This scared her, I realized later, because she didn't want anybody to know that she had taken me away from the house. She snatched me up and said, "Hush up, hush up right this minute!" She said, "And when we get home, you be *quiet*. If you cry *one bit*, Momma will *die*!"

Not long before that, one of our uncles had died and they had his funeral from our house, the way they used to do then. Somebody had lifted me up so I could look at him in the coffin, and I saw them carry him away and they told me he could never come back; so I had some idea what "die" meant. And Zaida said it again. "If you cry *one bit*, Momma will die!"

I stayed all night without making a sound. The next day my father came home and saw my leg all purple and swollen, and we found out it was broken. Nobody could understand how I went through the night and the next morning without crying.

When they took me to the doctor, I was in a terror. I wanted somebody to come and stand by me while this man did whatever he was going to do, and I begged him to get Willene, my oldest sister, but he just muttered something. They left me alone with him. I know now that the doctor wouldn't let anybody in, but then I interpreted it to mean that none of them gave a hoot what happened to me. If any of them had cared, they'd have been in there with me, I thought.

It was around this time that I started having what they later termed fits. This is a hard thing for my mind to put its finger on. It may be I had nightmares, because I'd always be asleep when it happened and I'd wake up screaming.

I'd wake up screaming and feeling that I was smothering. No, this isn't right. I didn't really have the feeling that I was smothering. I've told psychiatrists that I did, but I didn't, really. The trouble is that I can't describe it. I've tried and tried, and every time it comes out "suffocating." But that isn't exactly the feeling I had.

The only thing I can possibly liken the feeling to is of seeing in my mind something that was seething and boiling near me. This thing in itself didn't bother me. It was something like seeing Niagara Falls close up. It's awesome, but you're not actually afraid. If you thought you were going to get mixed up with it, that would be horror. The horror in my mental picture was that I knew this thing was going to have its effect on me. I felt I was going to get overwhelmed by this thing. I don't know what it was. It was just there, and I was inescapably going to be struggling in it. This is what it amounted to: a *mess*, that I would be drawn into—not be swallowed up and disappear, but be caught by it—and I'd smother in it. I'd keep on screaming after I woke up, because the fear stayed with me.

As soon as I'd calm down, the family would make a *joke* of it. I was always afraid to ask, "What did I do? What happened?" What I wanted them to do was to *hush*. When they'd talk about it so flippantly right in front of me, without my ever knowing a thing about what had gone on, I'd keep saying silently, "Don't *go on* about it! Don't *talk*. If you keep on talking, you'll tell something I don't want to hear."

I was nearly five when the thing about Floride happened. She was a young married woman who lived near us, and I thought she was the most ravishingly beautiful creature. Frequently I'd just sit and stare at her. I don't know whether anybody noticed or not. They often didn't notice me, and I never told Floride or anybody else that I was so smitten by her looks. I never told anybody anything.

One night Floride was at the house, and I guess I'd been staring at her. I don't know why this thing happened, because that night was one of the few soothing, peaceful times I can remember. My father was home just then, and he was picking

6

his banjo and singing. He was telling about how he used to tease Momma before they started courting. He used to sing a very old song, not to her but right in front of her, making her think he was singing to her but able to deny it. This of course left her unable to make any kind of reply. He'd sing it to us.

> *I guess you think, my pretty little pink,*
> *That I could not live without you.*
> *Well, I've just come by to let you know*
> *That I don't care a fig about you.*

They were all talking and laughing. I remember lying on a bench behind the table and listening to Poppa sing,

> *You reap the oats*
> *And I will be the binder.*
> *Lost my true love,*
> *And I can't tell where to find her.*

I was quite drowsy when Floride came and sat on the bench. The last thing I heard was her voice, in a song that generations of Southern children have been sung to sleep by.

> *Hushaby, don't you cry,*
> *Go to sleepy, little baby.*
> *When you wake you shall have*
> *A coach and six fine horses.*

Listening to Floride's song getting faint and far off, I heard,

> *Dum-di-dum, dum-di-dum,*
> *All those pretty little horses,*

and I dropped off to sleep.

Then I had one of those spells. After it, I heard Momma or Poppa or somebody talking about it. They said I'd said, "Let Floride take my thing out and hold it." I don't remember saying that. I don't remember anything but crying and screaming after whatever happened. But I remember hearing them say I said that.

That was the last I ever would let myself hear of their talk. From that night on, whenever there'd be a spell and I'd hear somebody mention it to somebody else, this thing in me would fly up like a billboard: I DON'T WANT TO HEAR. And I didn't hear. I don't know how much or how little they talked about these spells in front of me later. As soon as they'd start, this barrier would rise up, and, then and later, it served only too well. In later life it was to my disastrous disadvantage that my barrier was always just how farmers wanted their fences—man high, bull strong, and hog tight.

I felt terrible about Floride. I felt that I'd done or said something awful and that I was somebody horrible and I just wanted to hide. I had nothing more to do with Floride. She didn't behave any differently toward me, but then she'd never behaved any particular way toward me anyhow. I'd had no friendship with her; it was only that there was this lovely face and I stared at it.

I turned to her sister, an older and rather plain woman. This too became a joke to the family. I guess it actually was kind of funny, because I didn't really care about Laura Lee; I turned to her because she was available. I was so embarrassed about Floride that I wanted to get out of that situation; so I did the only thing I knew to do and that got me into another. I made a big thing out of Laura Lee. I carried on about how pretty her hair was. It wasn't anything special, but it was long, and at that time men were supposed to like long hair—woman's crowning glory, they called it. She liked hominy, and I planted some corn so I could have hominy for her.

When she bobbed her hair—they said it was sapping her strength—I pulled my corn up. I don't know why either, because I didn't feel a thing about her. I was doing all of this totally outside myself. There I was, planting corn, pulling it up—and I really wouldn't have cared if she never had hominy and shaved her head.

So the family had another big joke. They talked about my pulling up the corn, and they told it and told it and ran it into the ground the same way they did later about Mrs. Owen's legs. This time I had a different feeling, though. This time I thought, "Well, aren't they stupid! They think I'm wild in the head about Laura Lee, and I don't care whether she comes or goes."

My bad leg finally made me give up farming, and I went to guarding at that prison camp for all those niggers. Since then I'm gone from home nearly all the time, and I haven't seen much of my youngest. I like to fell out when he raised that infernal racket last night. One of the few nights I *am* home, and he pitches a fit. I reckon it was a fit. If he didn't have a fit, he just as good as had one. All that kicking and squalling, and then, "Let Floride take out my thing and hold it." I be damned. Mamie and myself raised four head of children before Robby, and no other child of ours ever did anything like that.

When the older ones were coming up, I was growing tobacco and at home and I feel more easy with them. But the least one, I don't know him from the other side of sole leather. He never has been like other children. Not even when he was a baby. He stayed a lap baby when he should have been trying to walk. I keep telling people how he never crept, how when we'd put him on the floor he'd sit bolt upright and pull himself along, and I can't find a living soul ever heard of any other baby that did that. Why, I've told people haven't got sense enough to bell a buzzard, and even none of *them* ever had a baby that did that.

Robby pulled himself along on his heels all the time any

other baby would have been creeping and toddling. Then one evening he stood right up and started walking. Great day in the morning! I was so glad that I grabbed up a twist of tobacco and held it out to him. I wanted to hold out something to him to keep him walking, and it was the first thing I could get hold of. 'y God, if he didn't take that twist of tobacco and chew it. Now his mother tells me he's been chewing tobacco leaves ever since that night he stood up and took his first step.

My daddy used to say, "There's always some damn botheration," and it's the dying truth. *Now* Robby commences having fits. They tell me it happens every now and again. His mother and the others don't appear to pay it much mind; they just laugh it off. Maybe it *is* comical. In a way. He sure is a sight in this world, kicking and screaming and taking on when he's not having an ache or a pain. I reckon he has bad dreams or wants attention, one.

And this thing about Floride—. No telling what he'll take it into his head to do next. Sometimes I wonder what kind of man he'll make. Poor devil, he's already like that dern sensitive plant that shrivels up as soon as you touch it. Damn the luck. What can you expect of a baby that chews tobacco?

2
TWO

During my preschool years, home to me was mostly a matter of me and Momma. There was a tremendous age gap between me and all the other children. Zaida was the nearest to me, and when I was still puzzling out which was the right shoe and which was the left—and so joyful when I learnt that either sock would do for either foot and I wouldn't have to go through *that* again—Zaida was entering high school. Later, when I was twirling broomstraws down tiny holes in the ground and chanting, "Doodle bug, doodle bug, your house is on fire," Zaida was stumbling around in her first high heels. On top of this, Poppa was away all week and most weekends, and Momma and I were alone together much of the time. I developed a powerful attachment to her. I started school a year late because I didn't want to leave her.

Little as I was, for some reason that even now I don't understand, I felt that she was in great need of affection and that it was up to me to see that she got it. I fell to and I carved out a career at taking care of Momma. It was the most lopsided thing. Not even lopsided; upside down. I never felt that I belonged to her; I felt that she belonged to me.

Maybe it had to do with her being in poor health. This was a fact. She was physically sick. At preschool age, I certainly didn't know what was wrong; and when I was older,

I was so consumed by my own ordeals that I never found out. But she saw a doctor a lot, and I was aware of this.

With just the two of us at home a good part of the time, and with the situation as I saw it, I got as protective as a watchdog. This is why, when the time came for me to start school, I simply balked.

I balked because I was afraid of what might happen to her at home all by herself. I don't think I was afraid she might die. I was more afraid she might get into some kind of terrible state and there'd be nobody there to help her. She *was* taking all those shots, and shots seemed much more of a deal than pills or capsules. Shots were scary, like telegrams or long distance phone calls.

Sometimes I think Momma thought she was giving me as much extravagant affection as I lavished on her, but who knows? It's a sure thing that, no matter what she thought, she tore me to pieces over and over. Sure as gun's iron, to use Poppa's expression. I'm confident she didn't mean to do this, but she did it. And did it and did it. She'd say really dreadful things. Maybe she did this only to bring forth demonstrations of my devotion, but the things she said were dreadful just the same and she more or less kept me all torn up. Like the first time I heard of Mother's Day. I asked her what it was. She said, "Why, that's the day when people come in trucks and carry all the mothers away." I went hysterical. I screamed, "I won't let them" until my throat was sore, and I clung to her like a sand spur. She sort of prized me off her and then she hugged me and petted me and went through all this there-there now-now routine. But she didn't seem one whit perturbed at the prospect of her being carted off on a truck, and she didn't seem to be affected by my panic either. I even had a faint feeling—just a sort of tiny stirring that wasn't strong enough to register as a feeling, but somewhere toward the edges of my mind it did register, rightly or wrongly, that she was somehow pleased by the whole thing. So, on top of being terrified, I was confused.

It's a hard thing. It's sad to say this about my own flesh and blood, but, if the truth were told, none of us has any call to be surprised at the kind of adult Robby has turned out to be. It was there for all to see, practically from the day he came into the world. He's morbid. He was *born* that way. Well, he didn't get it from my side of the family. We Millingtons always said it was a poor harp that couldn't rejoice, but that's Robby all over.

From the time he was just an arm baby, I stuck to that child like a shadow and gave him all the love a mother's heart can hold, and what do I get for it? Behavior that drives nails in my coffin. It's just like they say: When children are little, they step on your feet; when they're big, they step on your heart.

Robby has been strange right from the time he was born almost. Wilde by name and wild by nature. Everybody knows I always said it. Such a shamefaced child—"shy" the young people call it now that we're all more citified than in the old days—and just as soon cry as look at you. And so *quiet*. I declare, he must have been the only boy in the world could go around in Buster Browns and make you feel like he was wearing easywalkers.

When he was tiny, I hardly put him down. Once a boy came home from school with Zaida, that smart-alecky Will Dudley. He called Robby my *bichon frisé,* showing off for Zaida. All the Dudleys are like that. Well, Mademoiselle Joubert taught me a little French too, in the normal school, but I didn't know what that was. I still had my French-English English-French dictionary, and I looked it up. Curly lapdog, it said. He was one fresh kid, that Will Dudley, but it's true I did make a pet of Robby. And proud of it. I had him right with me all the time and I kept him dressed like a little doll. I washed his baby sacques and dresses, and later his little suits and shirts, until my hands were rough as cooter backs, sometimes when I should have been in bed. Why, I wouldn't let a cold breeze blow on him.

In spite of all I could do though, he didn't seem to enjoy life. He stayed tightened up like a fiddle string, but you wouldn't know one iota about it until he suddenly popped. Even as a tee-tiny child, the least little thing would set him off. And then he'd mope until I'd look for him to go into a decline. Take for instance that scene he made about Mother's Day.

He asked me what it was, and, when I saw that anxious squinched-up face, I thought he was tuning up to cry. I thought, Katy bar the door! So I laughed and guyed him a little bit. I told him that policemen or somebody came on that day and carried all the mothers off. Well, deliver me from ever passing a joking remark to a natural-born Gloomy Gus. People like that don't *want* to be cheered up. Robby cried buckets and then took on fit to wake the dead. I was sorry to see the child cry, of course, but, bless his heart, it was sweet. In a way, it made me feel that God had favored me. It's not given to every mother to be as close to her children as I was to that little one. I know it's not in good keeping to blow your own horn, but it is true that Robby loved me to distraction. He was cute about it, too. I couldn't help laughing when I told people about Robby and Mother's Day. He really was a scream. Everybody thought so, and some of the other mothers were chockablock with pure dee jealousy.

I tried every way I knew to make Robby happy. I spoilt him in a way I never did the older children. Why, I even let him stay home a whole year after he should have started school. I could tell he needed me more than he needed school. A mother knows these things.

14

Well, he's given me many a sleepless night since that Mother's Day, and I know that before it's all over he'll bring my gray hair down in sorrow to the grave. A mother is always a mother though, and I'd be only too glad to take care of him if he'd come home. He wouldn't have to move a muscle. I'd wait on him hand and foot. I keep writing him, "East or West, home is best." I don't understand why he can't settle down and be like other people, but if there's one thing I do know, it's this: No matter how sadly my poor boy has botched up his life, I have nothing to reproach myself for.

3
THREE

When I was four and for some years after, my family was moving from one little North Carolina town to another. We moved more than Okies or Methodist ministers, seventeen times in one short period. People tend to think of the depression as a thing of the thirties, but it really started before that, especially on the farms. As I learnt later, my father had had bad luck raising tobacco, and he got a job as a guard at the county prison camp. Every time the camp moved, we moved near it. We spent every other weekend at the camp. It was more or less a family affair; uncles of mine, and grown cousins, were guards too. This meant they couldn't be home, even on most weekends, so their families would go to the camp to be with them.

I never liked the guards. I did like the prisoners. The prisoners all treated me with great kindness, even though perhaps it was because I was a guard's son; so I liked them. But the guards I hated, uncles and cousins or no. They did mean lowdown things and I knew it—they made no effort to hide their treatment of the convicts—and I was afraid of them.

At that time, guards could beat up on convicts pretty much whenever it suited their fancy. They'd simply put a man over a barrel, and one guard would beat him while everybody watched—the other guards, the children, *and the women! Oh!*

16

When the prisoners had visitors, they could never be alone for a minute, not even if they were in full sight of others. It was a rule, I think, that somebody, a guard supposedly, had to stand and listen to their conversations. But the women hung around and listened too and nobody hindered them, and they got a big bang out of hearing. I believe that sometimes it must have been pretty touching, the conversations between the prisoners and their wives, because, while I don't remember anything at all of their talk, I do remember their faces. But afterwards I'd hear the women laughing and gabbing about it: "Did you hear what that one said?" and on and on in that vein.

There was a little house, "solitary" they called it, that I used to hang around. It fascinated me, for some obscure reason. One of my uncles used this little house a lot. Uncle Dillon was quite a big shot around the camp, with a name for being able to "handle" the prisoners better than anybody else. Lots of times I saw him put a man in solitary, and I know the man would have only one cracker and one glass of water a day until Uncle Dill got good and ready to let him out. This was when I started taking issues with the guards. Not openly taking issue. I never said a word about anything they did. I was too scared of them. But within myself I took issue with them and I mentally separated myself from them.

One thing they did regularly that scared me popeyed was a thing I couldn't figure out. Every Saturday they'd put a whole bunch of prisoners on a truck and take them down to Marlowe to get shots. I couldn't tell what they were doing and nobody ever explained it to me—I never asked, of course— but I knew if they were doing it to the prisoners it couldn't be good.

I suppose these were VD shots, but then I had no idea and it was very confusing to me. I knew the prisoners didn't like it. I'd see all my relatives smirking and snickering, and the prisoners hating it and not being able to do one Lord's thing about it.

Later in this same period, there was something else. It was through the guards that I found out about the Klan. One spring night Poppa took Momma and me to a field near the edge of Lumberton. To a meeting, he said. We had no sooner got there than he said he had to go do something, and left us with other women and children. Others gathered around, including men. Everybody sat on the ground. Then Klansmen began marching by, two abreast, with the white robes and hoods—just sheets and pillowcases really—shining in the near dark. You couldn't see anything under all that but their feet. At some distance they broke the lines, took up their positions, and began going through some sort of ceremony. We couldn't hear what they were saying. We could see, because, while we were sitting in something close to darkness, there were plenty of lanterns and burning pine knots over where they were.

All in a flash, a lot of men, from different spots in the crowd, leapt up as one man, rushed the Klansmen, fell on them and beat the living daylights out of them. People said later that there wasn't a man in a sheet left standing when the others bunched up, turned their collective back on the crowd, and walked slowly away. They were Lumbee Indians.

In the days that followed, I heard adults talking. They always talked as if I weren't there. They said the Klan had been "working on" the Indians for a while; so there was no discussion of why the Indians did it, but nobody could ever figure how they worked it. There had to be some prearranged signal, for all the Indians to act as one man—and, scattered through the crowd as they'd been, they really had sprung up at the same instant, as if they were all operated by the same nervous system—but everybody who'd been there said they hadn't heard the slightest sound or seen the slightest move.

Even those who had, unbeknownst, been sitting next to Indians on the ground, and the dark was only half-dark.

A day or two after the melee, I went to a neighbor's house with Momma. We found the woman of the house shaking out a Klan hood. She and her daughter were going to do some laundry, and she was saying to the girl, "No, not with the regular wash. *Cold* water for blood stains."

That weekend at the prison camp, I saw guards with black eyes and swollen jaws and split lips and lumps the size of banty eggs on their foreheads. Poppa was limping more than usual, and he had an ugly big bruise on one cheekbone. Uncle Dill had his arm in a cast. For some reason, he told me he had fallen down the stairs. I hadn't asked him what happened. I knew. And, though it was years before I knew what the Klan was, I knew from then on that it was evil.

Curiously, since I hated the guards so intensely, they were the first group of any kind I ever felt in with. I did truly detest the guards, but, when the chance came, in I went. This was because I was always on the outside of everything from the time I could remember. I felt in with the guards for only that one Sunday, and even though it left a bad taste in my mouth, I'd have been glad to be in with them again. I'm sure I must have tried more, but it never happened again.

How I came to say it, the remark that got me in, I'll never know; but one of the few times I opened my mouth, I said I didn't like my first-grade teacher because she had skinny legs. Actually, I liked her very much. She was a woman of about fifty, she'd been teaching a long time, and she understood a lot about children and was always extra good to me. Up to that time she was the kindest person I'd bumped into. But still I said this ridiculous thing, and the family laughed like fools. They thought I was quite the little rake, noticing a woman's legs at my age.

So all that day one or another of them was hauling me

around the camp, taking me to one guard and then another and asking me to tell why I didn't like my teacher. I'd say, "Because she's got skinny legs," and the guards would fall out laughing too.

That's how I had my day in with the guards. I'd rather have been in with children than adults, but two things kept me from trying this with these children. I stood in great awe of them because they weren't afraid of the guards. They could walk right up to a guard and say, "Give me a nickel." And most times the guards would. This awed me, but it also meant that the children were part of the same thing the guards were, and I didn't like them for that reason. So I couldn't be in with the children any more than I could with the adults. That one time I was in with the guards was the one time I ever felt that I had anything like credentials to be in with anybody, but being in didn't mean to me what I'd thought it would.

So I transferred my efforts to Lonnie. To some of the prisoners who were trusties too, but mostly to Lonnie because he was the cook and this made him easily available. He was always in the kitchen. I spent a great deal of time with him there, and he would give me snacks—often a big thick cold biscuit with a hole in the middle of the top half and syrup poured in. Georgia cane syrup. Maple syrup was fancy and considered a treat, but I didn't like it. I was charmed by the tin can it came in. Once I was given an empty one and I kept it for a long time. It was shaped and colored exactly like a log cabin, and you poured the syrup through the chimney. But it was too thin and runny and there was something sharp and not right about its sweetness. Georgia cane syrup was the thing.

One day I was in the kitchen, sitting on Lonnie's lap, and we were talking. The overseer came in, and when he saw us he just went up in a purple flame. "I ought to jerk a knot on you," he said, while he was grabbing me by the hand and

20

yanking me off Lonnie's lap. He dragged me out of the kitchen. He pulled me along to what they called the shanty, where all the guards and their families were. All he said was, "He was with Lonnie," but they *all* went up in a purple flame. Everybody got so upset it scared me. They were jabbering among themselves something fierce. It got awfully noisy, and they were so excitable that it was some time before it came out that all I was doing was sitting on Lonnie's lap.

That cooled things down some, and then they started in on me. "What do you want to go in there for anyhow? Why do you want to hang around the kitchen so much? If I catch you there again I'll wear you out. You don't see H.L. and Walter and the others there. Why don't you do like they do? Why don't you play with *them?*" And on and on and on. Of course I didn't have an answer for anything, but they didn't wait to see; they went right back to their big confab. One woman said to my mother, "Well, you know, they had him in Raleigh with his head shaved, ready to electrocute him." I guess she was trying to impress on my mother to keep me away from Lonnie—I believe he *was* in the prison camp for exposing himself to children—but she said this in front of me. What she said couldn't have been true, about the electric chair; and I guess I didn't believe it, because it didn't frighten me of Lonnie.

Besides the little things he gave me to eat, there was something else that endeared Lonnie to me. Another prisoner had a box. They were allowed to keep a few little things, and this box had the first combination lock I ever saw. He was so proud of it. He thought it was just the greatest thing in the world. I was playing with the lock one day, turning it forward and back, and he laughed and said to Lonnie, "He'll never open that." And, I don't know how—I was just fiddling with it—the thing flew open. Lonnie said, "You don't know what a smart boy this one is!" The truth was that it was a cheap lock and the thing practically fell open. But, oh, wow! I was a real boy that day, and I always stayed fond of the prisoners, especially Lonnie.

After I was a grown man and away from Marlowe, people in Ohio would wonder about my coming from the South but having such a feeling as I did about race. (That wasn't common in those days.) This is where it started. With the prisoners. Who were themselves so badly mistreated, and who treated me with such kindness.

That day I was in with the guards though, that had a bad aftermath. That was one of the first things that made me start feeling that I was a horrible person. I felt I'd done a terrible thing, talking about Mrs. Owen that way. When I saw her on Monday morning, this was all I could think about and I burst into tears and cried inconsolably. The more she tried to comfort me, the worse it got. I didn't tell her or anybody else about what I'd done; I just cried and cried. I was covered with shame.

◎ Every now and then I find myself thinking of the little Wilde boy I had in the first grade, wondering how things worked out for him when his family moved and he changed schools. Here, it was simply one crying spell after another.

I never could understand it. I was quite taken with him, and most of the time he gave me the feeling that he liked me. And if I've ever intimidated a child, I don't know who it was. Still, in a quarter of a century of trying to "teach the young idea how to shoot," I never had such a failure as I had with Robby.

He was a too-quiet child, painfully shy. He was also unusually pretty, with his blue eyes and black hair. There *was* just one little thing: He had circles under his eyes. They weren't dark or sunk-in, they were only faint lavender-blue shadows and they didn't mar his looks, but there were definitely circles under his eyes. A sure sign of the baby of an old mother. Not that Mrs. Wilde was an old lady; but at the time Robby was born, she was old to be having a baby.

There was more to him than looks. I sensed that there was quality there.

There were those who thought he wasn't right bright, but I thought different. Generally he acted like he didn't have two brain cells to knock together. Sometimes though, his face would be absolutely alight with intelligence, and I'd wait for him to say something insightful or impressive in some way—and I'd be disappointed every time. I *know* he was bright, but I never could get him to speak up, and he did cry and cry.

Time and time again I'd find him at recess, alone, standing at the edge of the sidewalk, looking across the street at his house and crying. He never crossed the street and went home. He just stood as if on Jordan's stormy banks and cast a wishful eye. Sometimes I could coax him back, sometimes I couldn't. But I never got him to play like the other children; no, not once.

One day I found him there at the sidewalk, crying, and nothing I could say would stop him. Finally he slowed up enough to speak, and he told me his uncle's tonsils were rotting and he ought to go home. That even topped the Windham child. Marion Windham had trouble with cavities, and he was supposed to avoid all sweets. At a checkup one day, Mrs. Windham overheard him saying to the dentist, "She *makes* me eat chocolate-covered raisins." Mentally, I gave Robby A+ for inventiveness and recognized discretion as the better part of valor. I took him to the principal's office and got permission for him to go home. He already had more absences than all the rest of the class put together. He was at home as much as he was at school.

23

One good thing. The guards' families used to go to the prison camp nearly every weekend. Otherwise these families wouldn't have been together at all. Those Saturdays and Sundays must have done *some* good for Robby. Nearly all the guards were his relatives, and it must have been something like a big family picnic on those weekends. With his father at the camp all week, I guess Robby and his mother were thrown back on each other. I used to hear people call him a momma's boy. I don't know; maybe they spoilt him.

I'll never forget the day he dumbfounded me good and proper. It was a Monday and I'd been thinking, "Well, we'll have a fresh start, Robby and school. He's had that holiday, spent Saturday and Sunday at the camp and seen his daddy and all those relatives, and at least this might get him to start off a new week on the right foot." Well, I guess the poor child didn't have a right foot to start anything on. That morning he sidled into the classroom—by himself, of course, with the others coming in by twos and threes—and he took one look at me and started bawling. He was in a state, sobbing so hard I couldn't see how he could catch a breath. I couldn't get a word of sense out of him—never got the first word of any kind out of him—and nothing I could say made the slightest impression on him. I told the principal he was sick and got somebody to take him home.

Maybe they did spoil him. Maybe I did too. But I'm afraid it went deeper than that. Something was wrong. Something was *wrong*.

4
FOUR

I have a recurrent sorrow, my childhood feelings of hovering on the outskirts of the family. As a young boy, after I began to hear voices, I somehow connected them with the family. My tenuous link with the others made the voices all the more fearsome. I didn't ever feel *of* the family. There was the family, and then there was me. I was a useless and mismatched appendage, superfluous and maybe even shameful.

The mere fact of age was one thing. There had been three children born between Zaida and me, but all three died. This made the big gap between the two of us, and of course the gap between me and those older than Zaida was enormous and hardly to be bridged at all. They were more like my uncles and aunts, not my brothers and sisters. I never had a chance at any children-together feeling.

All the others seemed to have a life and a place in the family. They were happy and they had friends. The older boys had girlfriends they'd bring to the house, and the younger ones had school chums. I was alone on the fringes of the family. The older ones with their dates didn't want a little kid around. And the ones in school, they didn't want me around either.

I picked out Zaida as the most approachable and I'd try to hang around her some, but that never got me anywhere. I think she was rather fond of me, but she was busy growing up and didn't have much attention to spare a child. Uncle Ches used to say that she was at the stage where a girl didn't know from one minute to the next whether she wanted a brassiere or a baseball bat. Zaida must have passed through this stage quickly, because the way I remember her she was way beyond wanting a ball bat. She was very girly.

She had worked up a slight friendship with a substitute teacher, a hero-worship kind of thing. She had a crush on Miss Kitty and hung around her whenever she got a chance. She thought everything Miss Kitty did was glamorous, and I can understand that. This young woman was really lovely. She was fair, the only natural blonde I ever saw to have brown eyes. Zaida pointed out that her legs were so long and well-shaped that they even looked good in the flat-heeled patent leather pumps she wore to school. And she was engaged.

Zaida said to me once in a self-satisfied way that she had "learnt so much" from Miss Kitty. Here's what she had learnt: How to apply lipstick (with a brush); and how to put on a brassiere (lean over). All I really understood at the time was that Zaida was very busy with herself and that none of her activities had any place for me.

For a short time I used to look forward to the weekends we didn't go to the prison camp. I thought that then she might take up some time with me, but I was soon disabused of that notion. She'd shut herself up in her room all morning with Golden Peacock Bleach Cream plastered over her face, and she wouldn't open the door to anybody for love or money. She said she had to do this on Saturday mornings. Momma had made her quit doing it at bedtime because the cream had been ruining the sheets and pillowcases. Zaida was really neurotic about those few freckles. Once I said, "But Flora Urquhart has freckles, and you think she's pretty." She snapped at me, "Flora's freckles are *beige*!"

In the afternoon, she and her girl friends would reach for those dark blue cologne bottles, douse their hair with Evening in Paris, and troop down to the drugstore. They'd spend hours at a table, drinking dope with lime, reading the druggist's movie magazines without buying one, and pretending to be surprised that boys were loitering there too, doing the same things. Sunday afternoons she'd either be visiting other girls or she'd have two or three in our kitchen making great pots of chocolate fudge. They'd gorge themselves on fudge and drink ice water until they were too sick to eat supper.

There was a great deal of chattering and giggling, but at the same time they took fudgemaking seriously. Those girls were as snobbish about fudge as their mothers were about fruitcake. When they talked about a box supper and one of them said Reba Harris packed such-and-such in her box, and such-and-such, "and some of that grainy fudge she makes," I knew Reba had been put in her place. So when they made fudge, they just took over the kitchen. They wouldn't be mean to me or make me go away. They didn't notice I was there.

When I was a little bit older, no longer such a small child, I began to be aware of several things. One was that Momma had not needed all the protection I had been giving her, or that I had been trying to give her. I can't remember any exact point at which I learnt this, and I don't remember that it was connected with any definite incident. It just gradually came to me.

I do remember that it was this realization that led me to look at my whole family a little more objectively. This was terrible, because then I saw that the family didn't mean what I'd always *made* it mean. I realized I had been living a complete blank. Trying to join them, trying to be part of them, trying to get in on the whole family thing—when I didn't really care, or at least I didn't care anything like as much as I had been thinking I did.

More than that. I realized that I could have held my own in the family. They would not have thrown me out. And if they did throw me out now—for not dotting some i or crossing some t—it would no longer matter to me so much. Then I started being able to go places. I wouldn't worry that if I left I'd come back and find that my precarious, nebulous "place" at home had been abolished. Then I could go to see Uncle Ches, or I could go to the Ashcrafts and stay all night. With this new freedom, I began actually wanting to get away; and as soon as I grew up and got work, I got out. Went to live at the Y in Marlowe. I wanted to get away because nothing at home any longer meant what it had meant to me. Even if I *could* get in with them, it wouldn't really matter. And I know I was right, because when I went back there the last time it was absolutely empty. There was nothing. This doesn't mean that I have no feeling for them. I care about them, I would be concerned if any of them got into trouble or were seriously sick. But as far as wanting to be *one of them,* I couldn't. I couldn't and I don't want to. But back there, at the time of Zaida and her fudge parties and her Golden Peacock Bleach Cream, when I was trying so hard to get my foot in their door, the difference between me and the others became more and more pronounced. I finally had become such a borderline member of the family that I got around to thinking that Poppa was their father but not mine. This could have been only an ordinary childish fancy except that, instead of letting it go, I carried it much farther.

There was a neighbor who was awfully good to me, and, I guess because I was so vulnerable and so alone in the family, I decided he was my real father. This was Tom Ashcraft. He'd always hold me and hug me and make a fuss over me. Sometimes I'd go to spend the night with the Ashcrafts, and

I'd always sleep with him. I learnt later that he and Mrs. Ashcraft hadn't got on well for years, that it was not a good situation with them, and that they stayed together and patched things up on the surface because of their children. At that age, however, I didn't given any thought to their having separate bedrooms.

I liked it that way. I liked everything about being with Mr. Tom. One day my shoestring came untied and I was about to trip over it. He showed me how to tie shoestrings so that they would never come undone until you wanted them undone. They stayed tied, no matter what; but they came undone just at the pull of one end when you were ready. I thought that was wonderful. I no longer think of it as wonderful, but I still tie my shoestrings that way.

He taught me to listen to the little frogs at night, and pointed out that they were singing, "Tea table fry bacon, tea table fry bacon." Right at first, this wasn't as plain as a partridge calling, "Bob, Bob White? Your peas ripe?" But once you paid attention, it was plain as day. And he told me how an older cousin of his, a railroad man in South Carolina, had taught *him* as a child in Hampton to hear what the trains said as they rushed and huffed along. They said, "Black-a-dusta, black-a-dusta, going to Augusta. Black-a-dusta, black-a-dusta, going to Augusta." I listened, and our trains said the same thing.

One moonlit fall evening when I'd gone over to spend the night, we were sitting on the porch steps way past my bedtime. We were there because Mr. Tom knew some neighbors had got up a drag hunt. He purely hated fox hunting—and this put some distance, sometimes icy stares, between him and most of the men around there—but that night he wanted to listen to the dogs. Knowing there'd be no fox, just the drag.

What the men did, they'd take a bundle of straw and put

it in a croker sack, soak it in water, and then pour on anise oil. That made this thing smell something like a red fox. Like fox urine, actually. One man would get on a horse and, with a rope, drag the croker sack along the ground and make a trail for the dogs to follow.

The men were mostly farmers and all were of modest means, but they had fine, breedy dogs and they took great pride in them. Dogs were their passion. They knew all there was to know about hound dogs. (If I'd ever been a hunter, I'd be saying "hounds." These men never called their dogs "dogs." Always "hounds.") Anyhow, the men would gather and they'd get their dogs together to form a pack. Whether it was a fox or a drag they were after, it was the dogs, not the men, that were the hunters. The pack would light out and the men would station themselves to listen. They knew where the trail went, so they could tell where to wait for the dogs to come by or to come within earshot. Some would sit around fires in fields or on hillsides. Others could stay right at home and sit on their porches or steps, or on a neighbor's steps, and listen with him. And everybody could hear the dogs at some time. Every one of the men was all ears for what they considered the music the dogs made.

Mostly, the dogs followed the trail. Though there were times when they'd take a notion not to. Then they'd act silly and chase around everywhere but on the trail, and that would be the end of that drag hunt. But some said that usually they were every bit as quick to follow anise oil as a fox. This particular night, they were. They got wildly excited, and when they gave tongue it was no ordinary yelping and yipping. It was frenzied. It sounded absolutely bloodthirsty, which it was. They didn't seem to know it was a croker sack they were trailing, and they were frantic to run down an exhausted fox and tear it to bits. The sound of them made me sick.

Mr. Tom loved animals and he never hunted anything. Which was all but unheard of. A countryman who didn't hunt was as queer a duck as I was. Even though the drag hunts were technically harmless, the dogs were thinking in other terms, used to the real thing, and Mr. Tom felt uncomfortable with himself for listening. He was always of two minds about it, he said. But that night he felt like listening. He said ruefully and rather apologetically that the dogs did sound beautiful. Not to me, they didn't. But I sat and listened because Mr. Tom was listening.

At one point he jumped up and hollered, "There's Belle Boyd! Wayne Joiner's Belle! Out in front again!" Of course I knew that you could tell one dog's voice from another's, if you could just sort them all out. I knew too that, out of all that unholy racket, each man around those fires or on those porch steps could single out at least two voices—his own dog's and Belle Boyd's. Everybody for miles around knew Belle's voice. But how could Mr. Tom know she was out in front? I asked him, and he said with great respect, "Belle never speaks except when she's out in front."

I don't believe it would ever have skittered across the mind of any member of my family that lots of people would do well to take a leaf from Belle's book. For all kinds of reasons, Mr. Tom meant the world to me.

I did wonder about one thing. I'd wake up in the night and Mr. Tom's arm would be around me, and I'd wonder why me and not one of his own boys. But it made me feel so good, and I was so enchanted with him because of it, that I decided I was one of his own boys.

She was good to me too. All us children called her Miss Loulie. Louisiana was her first name and she had several others. Her grandfather had been allowed to choose names for all her parents' children, and he said, when the first one came, he'd name them after all the states in the Confederacy, and he did. He gave the first two extremely long names, because he didn't know how many children there'd be and he wanted to use all the state names. Miss Loulie was the youngest, and even she had a long name.

I was always delighted if one of my visits came at a time when Miss Loulie was stirring up a cake. As a treat for me, then, sometimes she'd put in what she called "too much" shortening and sugar and make a sad cake. She knew I put a high rating on the heavy, nearly soggy cakes. Lots of people used to like them. I still do, but I don't think I've had a sad cake since Miss Loulie's.

And there would always be something special for breakfast—waffles instead of pancakes, or caky little muffins instead of biscuits. One afternoon I wandered my way over to their house and found Miss Loulie cracking and picking out pecans for a pie. She said, "Spend the night, and I'll save you a piece for breakfast tomorrow morning." She did that, and I was so thrilled about this that I told Momma, which was unusual for me. Momma said, "Pie for breakfast! What a Yankee thing to do!" I thought it was grand. I loved Miss Loulie because she fixed those fine breakfasts, and for many, many years afterwards breakfast meant something tremendous to me. For a long time I didn't know why, but one day it suddenly came to me.

Up until the time of his death when I was ten or eleven, Mr. Tom paid a good bit of attention to me. He even gave me spending money. I was devoted to him, and his death hit me hard. He was the only person I'd ever had such love for or from, and it chilled me to know that I would never have him any more. I did my best to hide this. I had a special reason for not wanting anybody to know how crushed I was by losing him. They already knew a lot about how much he meant to me, of course, but I still felt this way. My secret reason was that I was right at the onset of a very worrying situation.

It was only beginning to come on at the time of his death, and it progressed very slowly. It wasn't full-fledged until I was fourteen or fifteen. By the time I got up around that age, I was filled with misgivings about myself and what I might be. This made me entertain grave doubts about the nature of our mutual affection. Sometimes I wonder if my life might not have been different if I hadn't begun to look back at our relationship in this changed way. I only knew that I had enjoyed that relationship as I had no other. So I said to myself that, even though nothing had happened, my love for Mr. Tom must have been a homosexual thing.

This bothered me so much that I wouldn't get near any man or boy who seemed the least bit attractive. I wouldn't even undress and take a shower in the school locker room. There was the history teacher, Mr. Boone. He used to play tennis with me, and afterwards sometimes he'd say, "Shower time." This would send shivers all over me. I'd grab up my things and streak home straight from the court. Sometimes we played when the weather was hot enough to peel the paint off houses. I'd be dirty and dripping wet and I hated the way this felt, but oh lor', I wouldn't go to the locker room with him for anything.

It never once entered my head that Mr. Boone would make advances to me. I was afraid of my own self. Whatever my own self might be. That was the whole thing. I didn't even know what I was afraid I might do or say. I only know I feared that I'd reveal myself in some way that I didn't have figured out and that it would be awful. I couldn't be on guard against an unknown quantity, so I simply avoided men and boys as much as I could.

 I was always Robby's favorite sister, for whatever that amounted to. Maybe this was because I was the nearest to him in age. Rather, the least far from him. Robby was OK, but he was always hanging onto Momma's skirts and seemed to me he was crying a lot. If he wasn't crying, you wouldn't know he was around. I'd be doing something, and, if I'd turn around all of a sudden, I'd nearly fall over him. That's creepy. But I liked him and we got along pretty well, what little we were together. Still, excusing Momma, Tom Ashcraft was the only person I ever knew to be close to Robby.

Tom was tenderhearted. He was very fond of children, and he went out of his way to be good to Robby. I think Tom felt sorry for the child, because in a way he was without a father. Poppa was away at the prison camp nearly all the time when Robby was a baby and a small boy. Robby used to go with us to the camp on weekends; still and yet, he and Poppa hardly knew each other.

We all crossed our fingers when Robby took a fancy to Tom. All children liked Tom, and for once in his life Robby acted like everybody else. He grew to be crazy about Tom. He wouldn't go anywhere with anybody out of the family, let alone—perish the thought—stay overnight. But he'd spend the night with the Ashcrafts. Any time he got the chance. The first time Tom was at the house and asked Robby if he'd like to go home with him for the night, I fully expected Robby to have conniption fits right while we looked at him, just at the very idea. But Master Robby hopped right up and trotted off with Tom and left us all with our mouths hanging open. Robby liked Miss Loulie too, Tom's wife.

Tom died when Robby was something like eleven going on twelve. This was upsetting for everybody in our family, especially Momma. She was sad for a long time. Tom had always been a friend of the family and we'd known him all our lives. He had been good as gold to Robby for years, and Robby worshiped the ground he walked on. Or so we thought. When Tom died, we were all afraid of the same thing. We were afraid that Robby would just dry up and blow away. He did no such of a thing; he hardly turned a hair. Even when Miss Loulie gave him Tom's pocketknife for a keepsake. She was shocked, you could tell, when Robby had so near to nothing to say about that, or about Tom's death for that matter. Little monster. I never have felt the same toward Robby since.

He was always shut-mouthed and strange, even about little things. Take tennis. You might think tennis, in a small town in North Carolina at the time Robby was in high school, would be a game strictly for the country club set. But at Marlowe High, tennis was *the* activity.

It was like this. The three towns we lived near for the longest, the schools each had something special. Something important and different from all the others. It was funny, but the whys and wherefores always had to do with somebody on the school board.

Haymont was a big music town. This all had begun back around 1925, when a circus went bankrupt while it was there. The bandmaster, Gerald Fitzgerald, stayed in Haymont and taught music, all kinds of instruments. Then he worked out a plan for a music program for the whole school system and he was made the head of it. The chairman of the board had a son who was taking clarinet, and through that he got interested in Mr. Fitzgerald. From then on, everything went lickety-split. The grammar school had an orchestra and the high school a marching band, and Mr. Fitzgerald had them playing circus music, jazz, and lots of military marches. They gave the schools personality plus, and they were the pets of the whole town.

At Cedar Hill there was a great roller skating rink. Nothing like it anywhere around. This came about because the most loved member of the school board had diabetes. He said that thirty minutes or so of steady exercise raised his insulin level as much as a shot; so the town of Cedar Hill got this skating rink. It belonged to the school system, but anybody could use it cheap. It was very popular, especially in rainy weather or wintertime. And every evening there'd be Mr. Rhymes, with his iron gray hair and his maroon cardigan, bluestreaking it round and round with all the kids in Cedar Hill.

Marlowe had tennis courts, donated by Mr. Yoder, owner of the hardware store and member of the school board. He gave them in memory of his son, who had died young. The school didn't offer tennis classes, but so many played that the P.E. teacher regularly set up tournaments, one right after the other. Robby only played with whoever he drew. None of the others gave him much of a game though, and he fell into playing with Mr. Boone. They were more on a level. But would Robby even do this in a regular, easy, natural way? He would not.

The courts were on the school grounds, and the shower rooms were right there but Robby would never use them. Any half-bright human being would have. They'd play on days so hot that even indoors you'd think any minute you'd melt and run out in the yard; but still Robby wouldn't go to the locker room and take a shower. He'd come home soaking dripping wet with perspiration, and bathe there. And we didn't have a shower, which he loved. Of course he never said why. It sounds like a piddling little thing to remember, but in Robby it was noticeable. Every other way he was clean as a new pin, and it wasn't one bit like him to stay dirty any longer than he had to. It just goes to show. You never could know what he'd do or how he'd act about anything. Grandma used to shake her head and say, "Still water runs deep." None of the rest of us was like that.

5
FIVE

In the second grade, here I was in my third new school. Another move, another school, and everything new to me. This was hard on me. Two months later I still felt like a rank stranger.

There was nothing that wasn't an acute distress to me. I wouldn't do things that I could have done, because I didn't want to call attention to myself. I wouldn't answer a question in class. Of course I would *never* hold up my hand. If the teacher directly asked me a question, sometimes I'd answer it if I could, but I would never, never volunteer. I was trying not to be noticed. I wanted so badly not to be noticed, I was so afraid, that sometimes if she asked me a question and I knew the answer I'd say I didn't. That would get her off me and onto somebody else. I didn't want to talk or be singled out.

There was to be a class picnic in the park. Everybody was to bring his own dime and there'd be a picnic lunch. One boy was in charge of games. Even though I'd been there two months, I still didn't take part in anything. I don't know why, but I couldn't. When all this picnic planning began swirling around me, I got panicky. I went to the teacher and said, "Just before we moved here, I had an appendicitis operation." This was an outright lie, of course. "So," I said, "please tell Wade Wightman not to put me on a baseball team or anything."

She told Wade, and he said, "I hadn't thought about him anyhow." I'm sure he didn't say it with any malice; he just truthfully hadn't thought about me. That was even worse. It killed me to know he said that. It was what I'd feared in the first place, about this picnic, and it had happened.

Through that particular period, any time, for any reason, I could wriggle out of going to school, I stayed home. Once I was absent for something like thirty days in a school year. I made the honor roll anyhow. Not surprisingly, this had a bad effect on me. The minute I found out I could not only pass but make the honor roll without going to school any more than I had, I stayed away as if I'd been hired to do that. I'd just get the books and go off some place by myself—and make the honor roll again. It was easier for me this way, because the thing that frightened me about being in school was the thought of being there and not being accepted. And I never was. I was always an outsider.

I had a football then. It was the only football I ever owned, and it was the only football in the second grade. I'd take it to school and play with it by myself. This was worse than standoffish, but I was acting this stupid way because I couldn't bring myself to join the others enough to play with them. When they saw the ball, I thought, maybe they'd join me. It was odd, but I never remember that anybody ever asked me to let them play with my ball. Think of that. I even *had the only football,* and still they didn't want to play with me.

All this time I was eating my heart out to get in with them, be a part of things. I made one prodigious effort, but I blew it. Walking home from school, groups would take off together. One boy, three or four grades ahead of me, was something of a leader; and one day I walked on the fringe of the group around him. Always a group formed around him.

That had to be the day that the bigger boys wanted to

start a fight. I can't remember the exact circumstances, but they didn't care who fought or what they fought about or who won. They just wanted a couple of little kids to fight. Trying to become eligible to walk with them and be one of them, I fought a boy I had absolutely nothing against. We came out about even, but how it came out didn't matter to me any more than it did to the big boys. I was very much upset after this brawl.

I was so badly upset at what I'd done—fought a boy I wasn't mad with—that when the little fracas was over and everybody continued walking home, I left the group. I left the group the instant I could think of a way to do it. There was a Mrs. Dunbar who lived along the way we were going. I didn't know her very well, but as soon as I spotted her house I broke away from the boys and raced over and pounded on her door. When she answered, I said, "I've come to see you," and she let me in.

Once inside, I didn't know what to do and I had nothing to say for myself. Later in life I developed a facility for chattering nonstop in tight situations, but then I didn't have it. I stayed there though, until the group had walked on out of sight. That's how I fouled up my chance to get in with them. If I had stayed, they might very well have accepted me. But I was so aghast at what I'd done that I couldn't have stayed one more minute than I did. So there I was. I had joined the group and it hadn't worked out. My hope was dashed and that right quickly. It has never been any different with me in my whole life.

That youngest Wilde boy was full of surprises. As slightly as I knew him, once he flummoxed me twice in the space of ten minutes.

One spring day, just after school let out, I was coming in

from the yard where I'd been setting out a new cape jessamine, and I saw a cluster of children walking along home together. They stopped a couple of doors away under the Millers' chinaberry tree, and two of the least ones began to fight. One was Robby. This by itself was enough to make me open my eyes. I didn't know him or any of his family well when I lived near them, but I did know Robby was gentle as a lamb.

It didn't look like anything serious, so I went on into the house without interfering. Less than five minutes later, here came a furious banging at the door and there stood Robby, white as sugar. "I've come to see you," he blurted.

He came to see me all right, but I never could tell why. He had not one Lord's thing to say, and he looked like bears were after him. I tried and tried to talk with him, but he just fidgeted. No, he didn't want cookies, thank you ma'am. No, he didn't want lemonade, thank you ma'am. No, he didn't want anything I could think to offer him. I doubt if I could have drawn out two whole sentences if I'd put a flaxseed poultice on his mouth. Finally I asked him if I hadn't seen him fighting a few minutes ago, and he got red, simply beetified, clean down to his collarbone, and a second later he took off like a covey of partridges. "Bye," he said, and out the door he shot. He never came to see me again.

This makes him sound not right bright, but he was. I knew this from a friend's son, Harry Hackney, in Robby's class. That was the second grade; but for some reason Mrs. Wilde had started Robby to school a year late and he was actually third-grade age. Even that age seems young to do storytelling programs for his class, sometimes for classes two grades ahead of his, even in other schools, and that's what Miss Blakely had him doing.

According to Hack, there was something funny about Robby. Funny peculiar, not funny ha-ha. Seems that Robby wouldn't play with the other children. Fighting, and not playing—I couldn't understand it. Hack said Robby was the only boy in the class who had a football, and that he'd bring it to school and never let anybody else play with it. Being this hoggish about a football doesn't make sense. What's a football for but to play football with? And a boy can't *play* football by himself.

Hack said Robby would just kick the ball and then run and get it, trot around some and kick it again, and nobody ever got to play with him. I asked Hack if they ever asked Robby to let them play, and he said no. He said Robby wasn't friendly. I gathered that they let him go his own crosspatch way and keep his old football.

This puzzled me. I vow, I never took Robby for a selfish child. He *wasn't* a selfish child. I remember the time, when we lived near the Wildes, that Robby had a big bag of assorted old-fashioned penny candies—jawbreakers, licorice pipes, red-hot dollars, papers of candy buttons, wax bottles, hearts and mottoes, glass pistols, all of it. That little thing took and pawed through the whole heap, picking out all the pink ones. He brought them to me because he'd heard me say that pink was my favorite color. Now, a child who'd do a thing like that wouldn't be a hog about a ball.

Still, he *was* a hog about the ball. And he *was* fighting in the street. That much I saw with my own eyes. He may well have been one of those folks who are all honey and turtledoves most of the time but who'll one day march up and kick you in the shin. Takes all kinds, I reckon, and you can't tell a book by its cover.

6
SIX

A thing that early came to be an integral part of my whole makeup was that *I had to do something.* I couldn't just let things be; they were always too intolerable. I had somehow to make things be so that they would even let me exist. This is how I came to be such a liar.

In the second grade, I had a friend. Bubba Blankenship. Once I went home with Bubba, and we found his mother washing diapers. It was spring, it was very warm in the house, and the smell—. I was sick at my stomach. But I couldn't bear for it to be that way. Bubba was my friend. It was lovely at his house. I was forced to think that way.

That time, of course, I was only lying to myself to make something bearable. But in no time at all I was having to lie to any and everybody, to make something else bearable. And something else and something else.

One day, as on many other days, I was resisting going to school. That day my brother took me. He deposited me at the basketball court right near the schoolhouse entrance and told me to go in, and he left. When he left, I left. I went straight back home. By this time I was no longer fighting off school so I could look after Momma. It was by now me. I didn't want to go to school.

The next morning I did go, and the teacher said that the principal wanted to see me. I went to his office, scared stiff, and he said, "Explain yourself. You were absent from school yesterday, but you were seen on the basketball court." I said, "No, sir. Not me." He decided that Miss Blakely had sent him the wrong boy, so he told me to go on back to class and I went, still terrified.

At recess, Miss Blakely had a chance to talk with the principal. Later, in class, she said, "Bubba. Robby. Come with me." And the three of us trooped into the principal's office. It was Bubba who had seen me and told. I was shocked down to the marrow of my bones. We were such buddies. We were always together at recess. We always shared. If there was only one apple, we cut it half in two. But he was the one who put the finger on me. My friend.

I stood there with my heart sinking down in my shoes, terrified of the teachers and the principal and crushed because it was Bubba who had done this to me. Shock and betrayal notwithstanding, I had to say something. I said, "I was sick. If you don't believe me, ask my mother."

I had no idea what Momma would say if they asked her, but I was trying to brazen this thing out because I was desperate. The principal said, "All right, Robby. You come by my office this afternoon, and we'll go talk to your mother about this." I sat under the fire escape that afternoon until I knew it was too late for him to go, and then I went to his office. He said we'd have to attend to it another time. I hoped against hope that by the next day he would have forgot, and I guess he had. Nobody ever mentioned it again.

After that I had nothing to do with Bubba. We didn't have words; I just didn't have a friend any more. Bubba was the first and only friend I ever had during my school days.

During this same school year another thing happened, and it drove me deeper and deeper into habitual lying. I was lying in self-defense, and I discovered I had considerable agility in doing it. The new thing was storytelling. Miss

Blakely asked me to read a story, any story, and then tell it to the class. There's no knowing why, but, instead of reading one, I made up one. I presented it as one I'd read.

After I told it in my class, Miss Blakely sent me to the fourth grade to tell it. Then to another school. It got worse and worse by the day. There were three schools involved before it was over with. Nobody at home ever knew about this, because I didn't want the family to know I was lying.

I had these two things constantly with me: guilt and lying. Guilt because everybody at school thought I was telling a story I'd read, and guilt because by not telling them about it at home I was lying there too. This double guilt stayed with me relentlessly. It was always on my mind. I was lying every day—lying out loud at school, lying by silence at home, and the whole thing just fanned out all over the place.

Even if guilt hadn't been in the picture, the storytelling in itself was a bad thing for me. It made me even more noticeably different from the others. Being taken out of the classroom and carried somewhere else for an hour or so made me conspicuous, a thing I mortally dreaded. Distaste for being conspicuous was a normal enough thing. We all felt this. The quickest way to get somebody to stop doing something or to pipe down was to say in an undertone, "You're attracting attention." Or "Lower your tones." That would do it every time. In me though, this distaste had become grossly exaggerated.

And then there was still another thing: I couldn't figure out why people didn't like me. For some time I'd been thinking that people disliked me. Everybody. Every single person who came along. I think it was somewhere in here that I first knew I had to have a defense, a defense against all these things, that nobody else was going to defend me and I had it to do myself or go down undefended. I had to defend myself against things that I was afraid of, things that were far bigger than I was. Just because they were bigger than I was, the only way I could think of to defend myself was to put up some kind of front. This line of thought, if not in these words, continued and developed steadily.

As I grew older, a large part of my front was the preservation of an impassive manner and facial expression. As an adult now, every time I see a newspaper account of a crime and there's a comment on the convicted criminal or the suspect, "He showed no emotion," my heart goes out to him. Because I know how many times I have "showed no emotion" when inside I was volcanic.

In the second grade, however, I was a beginner at this. By grammar school, I had developed other defensive stratagems. There, I had the teacher, the other children, the whole kit and caboodle, thinking I had a heart condition. I could get up and walk out of class any time. Simply leave. The teacher never questioned this. Of course I never had a note to the teacher from a doctor, which usually would have been required. I had only told her myself. When I think of it now, it amazes me that she would have accepted such a story from a child. But she did.

Nothing in my life was easy or simple. Everything was difficult and complicated and fraught with anxiety. Because of the family's many moves and my many schools, school was a continuing trial. At the time I started this heart thing, we had moved from Marlowe to the country, and the school was organized differently from the one I'd just left. In Marlowe, we changed rooms for different classes and we had different teachers. Here it was all day in one classroom with one teacher. Mrs. Glover.

As it always happened, at this school they were more advanced in some subjects than I was and behind me in others. Either way I was out of step. This just couldn't be. I couldn't stand to be out of step everywhere. Being out of step was being conspicuous. Being out of step was not belonging. Here at the new school in the country, I wasn't with it and I was never comfortable. I was nervous and agitated, inside, and I had to do something. Of course, in my childish clumsiness and inexperience, what I thought of to do made me far more conspicuous. I thought of the heart condition.

There was only one snag, but it almost threw me. Mrs. Glover's husband was my father's insurance agent. When I told Mrs. Glover about my "heart condition," she began wondering about others in my family. She questioned me closely on this, but I maneuvered all around and I think I managed to convince her that I was the only one. Lucky for me at home, she never had her husband to investigate.

With this development, however, my fears were aggravated and rose rapidly to terror. It became almost impossible for me to go to school. When I did go, I *had* to use this fictitious heart condition. I used it whenever things got out of hand, and this happened rather frequently. It happened frequently because it didn't take much to bring it on. Usually it would be when we were on some subject I was behind the others in.

"Go to the board." That would do it. I couldn't go to the board in arithmetic class not knowing what she might tell me to do. Not knowing how badly I'd mess up. I'd be disgraced, stared at, held up to ridicule, made even a worse kind of outsider than I already was. So I'd say, "I'm not well. . . I shouldn't have. . . My heart. . ." And I'd get up and walk out.

Even earlier that same year another deplorable development showed up. I somehow formed a firm belief that everything bad that happened would be blamed on me. One day at school somebody broke a windowpane, threw a ball through it, and I was sure I'd get the blame and I didn't know *what* might happen then. I got physically sick. The nurse took me home that day. She said I was running a fever. It's easy enough now to see that if I had broken the window, nobody was going to kill and eat me. I don't know what I thought anybody might do, but I couldn't have been much more frightened.

The fact that nobody ever accused me of breaking the window didn't help a bit. Didn't teach me a thing. I can't explain this particular fear, because I don't have a history of being unjustly blamed. Nonetheless, I had this feeling very young and it grew and grew, and until I was way up in my forties I still thought I'd be blamed for whatever awful thing happened anywhere around me. Of course, by that time the voices had long been tirelessly telling me that I would be blamed.

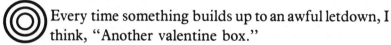 Every time something builds up to an awful letdown, I think, "Another valentine box."

Poor Miss Coates. She was my third-grade teacher, and she tried to do something nice for us by having a valentine box. She got a grocery carton from the Piggly Wiggly, and she let me help her fix it up because I was the youngest girl in the class.

We cut a slot in the lid, covered the box with thick creamy white shelf paper, and glued red construction paper hearts all over it. Miss Coates brought it out nearly a week before Valentine's Day. As we got our valentines addressed, we'd bring them to school and drop them into the box. The box was the center of attention.

We had done a good job, and the box was pretty. But the plan was jinxed from the word go. With the box out for a week before Valentine's Day, we had plenty of time to get worked up about it. I think even the boys were more concerned than they let on. They pretended to think the whole thing was too silly for words, but the girls were on pins and needles. We worried about how many valentines we'd get, and who might get more than we would, and, when the big day finally came, nothing worked right.

Johnnie Mae Weston didn't get but one valentine. Later, we wondered if she hadn't sent it to herself to make sure she'd get at least one. If we had thought about her for one minute, we'd have known that she wouldn't get many, maybe not any. And if a one of us had had a scrap of decency, somebody would have put a card in the box for her. If we ever got kind at all, we did it when we were older.

I felt almost as sorry for myself as I do now for Johnnie Mae. This was because of the way Robby Wilde acted about the valentine I sent him. I sent that boy a twenty-five-cent valentine. Then, you could get nice cards for a dime, perfectly beautiful ones for fifteen cents. This twenty-five-cent card was a sight in this world. I can see it right now. It was a huge square card with a great big red tissue paper heart inside that spread out when the card was opened. It was like those old-fashioned red paper Christmas bells that came folded flat and opened up to three dimensions. When I saw it in the bookstore, I couldn't keep my hands off it. If I hadn't been so crazy about it, I never would have spent a quarter and done such a thing as I did.

Nobody in the class had ever got or sent such an expensive valentine. When Robby took it out of its envelope and opened it and that big red heart spread out like *that,* it caused some excitement, let me tell you. Everybody crowded around him. They couldn't decide which to stare at the most, the valentine because it was so big and beautiful, or Robby because he was somebody who got such a valentine. You'd think Robby would have been tickled pink, but he wasn't. He was very grumpy about letting a few people hold it and see it up close, and then he grabbed that gorgeous thing and stuffed it into his bookbag. *Ruined* it. Bent it all up and ruined it.

Scotland Frazier was furious. She sent a whole handful of valentines to Roddy Wentworth—put them together from a kit. She had written, "Guess Who???" on each one, the same way everybody "signed" valentines. Soon as he opened them though, Roddy said, "Scotland, you put these together wrong." Right out in front of the whole class. She was ready for the earth to open up and swallow her. I don't know whether Roddy thought she'd like to know, or what, but he plowed ahead and kept trying to show her how she had pasted the little tabs on wrong. She *had* pasted them on wrong, but Roddy should have had sense enough not to let her know he knew she had sent the valentines to him. Let alone let the rest of the class know; I don't know which was worse. She hated him after that.

The Johnson twins behaved about as usual. They liked to gang up on people. If you don't think two is enough to gang up, that's because you never knew Eunice and Rena Johnson. They sent lots of funny valentines, and everybody who got one (or more) was mad and embarrassed. And not a one of us had thought to send a valentine to Miss Coates. All in all, the valentine box caused more trouble than it was worth.

I was purely disgusted with Robby. I nearly cried when I saw that beautiful twenty-five-cent valentine being bent up and ruined, and nobody knows how hard I wished I had my money back. For a while I had thought Robby was cute as new shoes. That was before he acted so ugly about that valentine.

Robby could be hateful in some ways, I knew that. He was sometimey. He used to be thick as thieves with Bubba Blankenship in the second grade. Crazy about him. Then, all in a minute, he wouldn't have prayed for rain if Bubba's clothes were on fire. Nobody knew them to have a fuss. Robby just suddenly had no use for Bubba and was never caught speaking to him again. Bubba never spoke to Robby either, but he tried. It's hard to speak to somebody looking through you like a fresh washed windowpane.

My candid opinion is that Robby was stuck up. I think it started with all that going around to other classes and telling stories. Miss Blakely took on over how well he did that, even sent him to other schools. I think it went to his head. Give the devil his due though: Robby never put on airs the way some people do. Like Rosella Redwine's big sister, Grace. She went to visit their aunt in Atlanta and came back calling supper "dinner" and spelling her name G-r-a-y-c-e. Even calling lightning bugs "fireflies." In Atlanta they said lightning bugs, same as we did; Grace just got fancy after she'd been there. Robby never did anything like that. Could be he was feeling bad a lot of the time; he did develop some kind of heart trouble. That may have had something to do with how he acted.

While I'm giving the devil his due, I'll say this much more for Robby: He always told the truth. I was in his class for at least two grades, and sooner or later most of us would story about something. But Robby always told the truth.

PART TWO
1935-1950

7
SEVEN

As I look back and try to map out how my troubles began and developed, there are two things I keep dwelling on. I can't get them out of my thoughts; and no wonder, because their conflict colored my whole life. These were the craving to belong and the compelling need, in most situations, to be as nearly invisible as possible.

There isn't a day I can remember when I wasn't wanting, more than anything else on earth, to belong. It was probably at the same time, however, that same indeterminate time when this started, that there rose in me an irresistibly powerful feeling that *I must not be conspicuous*. Not in any way at all. I had some of this all along, but it grew and became the overriding element in my behavior. All of it happened and I was painfully aware of it long before I was old enough to put it into words. The way I remember always feeling is that I must at all times be as quiet as possible and not draw any attention to myself, or They—and I never have learnt exactly who They are—would do something terrible. Whoever I was around would call Them and They would come and throw me out or—. Well, to be cast out was and is the worst fate I can conceive of.

I can't overstate how deep this went with me. Even when I was a little shaver with this fantastic notion that I didn't belong to Momma but that she belonged to me and I had to take care of her in some sense, I had it about her. Even her. I felt that at any moment I didn't toe some unseen and unknown mark she could stop this thing like *that*. Or *any of them*, anybody in the family. They could get along very well without me. I couldn't get along without them.

It was so ingrained, ingrown may be more like it, the feeling that I couldn't afford to offend anybody in any degree, that I wouldn't even ask for specific things for Christmas. Once I did get bold and I hinted around for Kipling's *Just So Stories*. They gave me a Bobbsey Twins book. Now the Bobbsey twins weren't a barrel of fun even if you weren't too old for them and if you hadn't had your mouth set for "How the Elephant Got Its Trunk." Although I knew painfully well I was walking a tightrope, I hadn't quite got the hang of it— my front was in its earliest forming stage—and I slipped up. I didn't show open disappointment—I never would have dared—but I did let it show that I wasn't overjoyed. They were irritated with me and they couldn't understand. I wanted a book and they gave me a book, didn't they? I never made *that* mistake again. Whatever I got was just what I wanted; yes, sir, even if I couldn't stand the sight of it.

As I moved into my late teens, alcohol became a factor in the overall hurly-burly. In high school, there was the matter of the junior-senior prom. I was simply yearning to be a part of this thing, and yet I couldn't have gone unless somebody held a gun to my head. Caught in this kind of net, I compounded the confusion of being misunderstood. I began purposely doing things to make me appear other than I was.

There was a place called the Wagon Wheel not too far from the school. It must have been at least a mile and a half away, else they couldn't have sold beer. One day at lunch time I went there with Byrdine Brown, who amounted to the school prostitute, and we came back smelling like beer. In addition, I took care to help get the word around, and this solved my prom problem. It made it impossible for me to go. Many years later, in Ohio, somebody said, "Robby does have a way of burning his bridges before him." It went back this far. After I went off that way with Byrdine, none of the other girls would have gone to the prom with me if I'd asked. Those who saw us come back from the Wagon Wheel had looked holes through us. There wasn't any girl I particularly wanted to take to the prom. I just wanted to go and be a part of it. But I didn't dare. I don't know why. I just didn't dare.

Later, alcohol played a different part in my frantic struggle and the complications of all the protective coloration I took on. When I had just finished high school, I was still living like walking between two eggs, making people think I was something that I wasn't at all. We had a married neighbor with two attractive younger sisters. This woman brought her sisters into the neighborhood, and either she or they wanted me to date them. Of course this was because I had somehow contrived to give the neighbors the impression that I was the best dancer and the most frolicsome person around. They'd never seen me dance, of course. I didn't know *how*.

At Easter time, which was a big deal around home, these girls wanted me to go with them to the Wagon Wheel. To dance. I was petrified. How could I do anything like that? But I had put on such a braggadocio act that I couldn't get out of it. So we went.

They had liquor, and I had my first drink. This did something. All of a sudden, I found myself on the dance floor. I felt less afraid, there was the music, and my feet did move, and, hard to believe, I got along pretty well.

This was a milestone. I had found a way I could do things. I'd take several drinks, and then I could manage. This was expedient, but in the long run it only scrambled my situation further. Most of the things that happened later that attracted attention seemed to people to happen because I was drinking. It was generally the opposite. The outlandish things I did that made me unpleasantly conspicuous were done when I was stark staring sober. The times when I appeared to be blending into a group and all seemed well—*those* were the times when I was drinking. And those were the times when people came the nearest to accepting me.

Drinking worked then, but I paid dearly for this. When I was drinking and doing things that were not only socially acceptable but desirable, I achieved some outward appearance of what I wanted people to take me for. I was simultaneously feeling cheated out of the real thing and burdened with guilt because I was offering something false.

Nobody knew that when I was more or less acting like everybody else I was only pot valiant. But I knew I was a fake, and to know I was a fake was scorching my very hide. I kept on doing it anyhow, because it was the only way I *could* do. Thanks to this masquerade, there was a period when I was eighteen or nineteen when I was tremendously popular with the set that frequented the Wagon Wheel. I tried to protect myself from girls by getting thick with a set of young married couples.

Others in Marlowe had a term for people like these couples. It was "the vulgar element." (All the others weren't necessarily morally superior, but their trappings weren't vulgar.) But it wasn't my friends' lack of refinement that would have upset my sister Willene the most. Practically everything they did, Willene was dead set against—card playing, dancing, drinking, low-cut dresses, Sabbath breaking. And much more.

My pals really were a wild bunch. They lived for the moment, like their world was peachy-creamy and there was no tomorrow. Saturday night was the big deal. Each Saturday that rolled around, everybody had to go out and dance and drink and carry on. In several cases there was gossip about me—and I think I got some satisfaction out of that—to the effect that I might break up this couple, or I was seeing too much of that wife, and so on.

Sometimes, many times, I did see the wives separately. Two in particular; Lurleen Johnson and Willise Grady. While this did cause some talk, it made no trouble with the husbands because I kept on a friendly level with them as couples. There was also the possibility that the husbands were fooling around and prepared to look the other way if maybe their wives were having some fun on the side. As for other people, I deliberately led them to think that my involvement wasn't so innocent. As talk got around, it improved things for me; I became more sought after by other people too. The talk pleased me, because I felt this was what I should be but certainly wasn't. I was trying hard to belong to *something,* even something I didn't admire and didn't really want in the first place. Like the guards when I was little.

This was, I think—oh, what's the use? I don't think; I know. During this period I definitely came to the conclusion that I would never belong to either sex. I knew this beyond any possibility of doubt, and it was a desperate thing. People weren't supposed to be this way. You were supposed to be one or the other. You were supposed to be something. Rationally, I can think now that if it happens the way it happened to be with me, there's nothing evil about it. But even now I can't often really feel that way. Way back then, of course, the horror and shock of full discovery was fresh upon me. I don't like "discovery." That sounds so abrupt, and it wasn't abrupt at all. It was slow—oh, slow. It crept along in such imperceptible stages that I hardly could mark moving from one degree of awareness to the next. Finally I did make another imperceptible move and went into the stage from which there was no going any further, because I was *there.* I was there and I knew it. As gradually as I came to know this about myself, the ultimate knowing was as unsettling as if it had hit me all at one blow.

I was reeling from the impact of this relevation as I went into a frenzy of sustained exertion to hide my shameful shortcomings. The best I could do was to assume this deceptively rakish appearance. I had some vague idea of what people were supposed to be, especially men, and I seriously set about building my false front. I fabricated a personality like what I thought people should see in a young man, because I didn't want them to see what they'd see if they *did* see me, my real self. I don't know what I was so petrified of having them see, I never have known, beyond the awful business of belonging to neither sex.

For the time being, my false front was a rousing success. With everybody but me. No matter what kind of gay-blade picture other people had of me because of my calculated actions, I didn't fool myself. Not for one moment. I never gave a thought to this masquerade in terms of fairness or unfairness to anybody. It was a matter of my survival, and I did it.

I lived in desperation. Many, many years later, I read in something of Aldous Huxley's about "the reassuring banality of everyday existence." This was something I always longed for. I'd hear people complaining about being bored. I would have been so glad to be bored. It would indeed have been reassuring. But there was never any easing of my desperation. I had to keep it up all the time, this struggle to continue to survive. Just to exist, I had to keep pushing myself.

Things even went this far: One night at the Wagon Wheel, a married woman, Myrtice Carter, went out to a parked car with me. She was quite forward. Actually "forward" wasn't in it; she was what the boys used to call hot as a fox in mating season. She was very aggressive, and things got pretty steamy in that car. I really was in a fix, but somehow I did manage to crawfish out of it. *But.* I left the car seats all out of place, tumbled looking, so that some of the others would be bound to notice and to talk slyly and knowingly about us.

All I wanted was to be comfortable. I loathed going through all this sleight of hand, but it was the only way. In my eagerness to be accepted—by anybody, anybody at all—I had got into this wild bunch, and this was simply the only way I could manage with them. By now I was a little older and I had a good job at the Convoy Motor Freight Company, and that gained me some respect too. I was the youngest of this group I'd got into, the youngest and the only single person. I was managing it right well, and the only snag was that it seemed I was always getting into situations with the others. Twice it was with men.

The men were no trouble. I made it plain that I wasn't interested, and they let it drop right there. It was the women who gave me a hard time. Mercifully, they lived at this nice suburban level, where, in those times, people didn't talk much to one another about themselves in this kind of thing; so I was able to keep everybody like five balls in the air at the same time. When I'd get into a situation with one girl and squirm out of it, she'd think, "Well, I must not be attractive to him, and Lurleen is." Lurleen would be thinking the same about the others. I believe they didn't talk because they figured this wasn't very flattering to them.

Lurleen and I got into one perfectly horrendous mess. She had been after me and after me, and of course I'd been a little bit after her too in my camouflaging way, and a time came when I found myself going off to a motel with her. Oh, Lordy. I thought maybe I could *make* it work, or seem to her to work, and I went with every firm intention of going through with it. I almost made it. I writhe at the memory, but what happened was that we got right up to the real business and at the crucial moment I froze. I was cold as ice and utterly confused. It almost came to a thing of my pushing her away before she could believe it wasn't some sort of game I was playing.

It was horribly embarrassing for both of us, and we went through an awkward sort of untangling procedure, getting straightened up and out of the motel and all, with both of us so torn up we couldn't look at each other. She said she wouldn't tell anybody though, so I thought I was at least safe from being a public disgrace and a laughingstock.

Some safe. This was the time of my life when the voices really went to work on me, and they've never stopped. For an entire week after the motel incident, the voices were at me. Out loud. "—making all those people think what he wants to, *but I know*—So you didn't run through all those red lights— or set that fire at the hardware store—*or anything*—I can make everybody think you did, and you'll get every bit of the blame—preying on a girl like that—fake, fake, fake—rotten filthy fake—every bit of the blame—" And I knew They could get me blamed too, for everything, because of the picture I'd painted of myself. It's easy enough to see now that the picture I'd painted of myself was not that of an arsonist, but then that didn't even occur to me.

Of course I didn't know that the voices were hallucinations. I thought they were real voices, because at that time They only spoke to me or about me when other people were around, when they could have been real voices. Somewhere in the course of all this bombardment, it got so bad that the voices hounded me even when I was alone. By the time that happened I was so far gone and so demoralized that I didn't even notice the change when it took place.

 One young man I'll never forget if I live to be two hundred is Robby Wilde. He was younger than the rest of us—not much more than a boy, really, but he used to chase around with me and Bill and several other married couples. He had a light foot on the dance floor and he was quite a party boy, a good sport. We all liked him. He was known to be something of a devil with the girls, but we certainly weren't the ones to be put off by that. It was an added attraction more than anything else.

I'd heard something about him before we knew him, something my younger sister told me. He had scandalized the whole high school by tootling off to our own favorite spot, the Wagon Wheel, in the middle of a school day, for pity's sake. All the other kids were buzzing about it, my sister said.

Byrdine Brown was with him. Byrdine's older sister was a real tramp, and either she followed in her sister's footsteps or else she had inherited her reputation and had the name without the game; I never was sure which. Anyhow, Byrdine had kind of a name, and she and Robby went off, bold as brass monkeys, before the whole school, and came back smelling like a brewery.

Later on, when we knew Robby, this was ancient history. It was nice to have an extra man in the bunch, and we didn't much care what his habits might be. There were people in Marlowe who thought we were wild as bucks ourselves. We did do a lot of drinking and tearing around, but we were just out for a good time.

Robby was good-looking and full of life, and a flirt. This was fun. The girls enjoyed the attention, and no harm done. But then things began to seem a little more complicated with me and Robby. I thought he was cute as a speckled pup, and sometimes at dances we'd go outside and do a little mild courting. For a good while that was all there was to it. I knew there was gossip getting started about us—and about him and other girls in our crowd too, for that matter, but who cared? It just added a little spice to life, and if the busybodies hadn't been wagging their tongues about us it would have been about somebody else. None of us paid them any mind anyhow.

It was after Bill got a traveling job that things began to change. Bill was gone a lot, and I used to have a lonesome time of it. I'd go right on to the beach parties and the Saturday night dances with the rest of the bunch, but I felt sort of like a fifth wheel. More and more I got paired off with Robby. This was natural, with Bill away and Robby the extra man. I got involved with him more than I'd meant to, and once we got into a reckless mood and planned to go to Windermere, about twenty miles from Marlowe, and spend the weekend. I knew this was asking for trouble. But I was tired of being lonely with Bill gone—and how did I know what *he* was doing all those evenings?—and Robby was right there, and, after all, you're only young once, and why not?

We had a couple of drinks and dinner somewhere on the way. After we got to the motel we had another drink, but neither of us was drunk, not in any way, shape, or form. Before long we were in bed. Everything went smooth as silk off a reel right up to the very last minute. When we got right up to the main event, Robby stopped cold.

It took me a minute or two to catch on. At first I only knew something had gone wrong, but I didn't dream how wrong, and I got nervous and giggly and I tried to get us going again. But that was it, i-t it. Robby had signed off. I got terribly upset. I felt like I might fly to pieces, and I was mad and mortified and every other thing at once. I didn't know whether to bark or faint. I did cry. I remember crying. I have never been so humiliated in all my born days. And then that jerk had the nerve to ask me not to tell anybody.

Hell! How could I?

8
EIGHT

The only thing really important to me about the Little Theater was that it led to my first encounter with a therapist. God knows I've had a catholic experience of therapists since. Theron Hearn was the first.

In my year of college I'd been in only one play, but I'd done a good deal with the drama club in high school. Actually I'd excelled in it. Twice I won first place at the District Meet. Once for reading "A Message to Garcia," an old chestnut not of my choosing, and once Henry Grady's "The New South." All this seemed beneficial—partly, I imagine, because in a role I could more or less lose myself. People, including a good many professional actors, have often said that actors hide in roles or find a transient identity in them. I felt more that a role was a way to get away from myself. Maybe it's six of one and half dozen of the other. At any rate, I could pretend with all my might that I was this character, and that shook me loose from myself for the time being. This was good. There was a bad part too, though. I was always scared pea green and pop-eyed when I had to face an audience.

Acting might seem strange in light of my horror of being conspicuous, but it was entirely sensible and simple. There was no personal contact. I was up here and the audience was out there and, while I hoped there was a connection, there was no close contact. Entirely different from being conspicuous in a life situation.

I had met some of the Little Theater people in Marlowe, and they'd invited me in and I'd had some sort of association with them for a good while. At the time I speak of, there had been several unnerving incidents to go through. On top of that, I was drinking heavily. But the Little Theater was doing a play and I was taking a part. What drove me to try out, I don't know, except maybe, without being fully aware, I thought it might help me. Anyhow, it was my habit. I'd always try out for parts. I'd get them and then I'd make a fool of myself.

I'd make a fool of myself because sometimes the voices would get to me, and sometimes the Little Theater people would get to me. Sometimes both. For people who don't know these groups, it would be an eye-opener to watch them practice what they liked to call their craft and see how disgusting they can get. They're so arty you could screech, and they're so impressed with themselves—oh, they're the world's greatest. As good as Broadway, you understand. So pretentious. So self-important. Such straining for effect. I can hear them right now: "Just let me take that line again—I want to give it more—." Somebody was always bleating, "But what's the *motivation*?" Some of them were so hung up on motivation they'd want to be given reasons to move a muscle. They could drive a director crazy.

The director they had was Ann Tindall Roberts, a retired speech and drama teacher, and she was excellent. I don't believe she'd have stomached this group if she hadn't needed the money. But she did, and she did well by them. She was very good at getting the most out of people, and often this group really did do creditably.

From time to time one member, without doing a fool thing about it himself or herself, would get to be a fad within the group. I remember one in particular. She was a nice girl, but she wasn't the brightest or the prettiest either. But she was the moment's belle of the ball. When she did something really stupid, this was charming and "zany." While she was riding the crest, she was *"jolie laide."* When her hour was over, she was "plain."

They were so stagestruck, and they knocked themselves out behaving the way they imagined professionals behaved. I don't know; maybe they were right. If they were, actors are pills. Mostly they were warmly supportive of one another. Often they dished out flattery so gross that it was a scream to see the others gulp it down and gawp for more. But they also had spells of sniping.

One that sniped at me took me by surprise, because ordinarily it was the players who did this and she had never been one of them. This May Belle Coker had been in the Little Theater for a long time and she was a valued member, but the necessary things she did didn't include playing parts. So I wouldn't have expected sniping from that quarter. She did take several potshots at me though, and it didn't take much to throw me off balance. I began to think maybe I had no business doing this major role. She got to me so much that I even mentioned it to Kirby Northrop.

I don't know what possessed me. I hardly knew him. He was a leader in Marlowe's cultural life, and rich and social, and I only met him by accident. He was a friend of Ann Tindall's, and occasionally dropped by when we were rehearsing. I suppose I told him because he was at hand when I reached the point of having to tell somebody and he looked understanding. So I told him how May Belle was undermining me. And a blessing I did, because he helped me enormously.

He said, "Forget it. For-get it." He said, "I've known May Belle for a long time, and in general she's a pleasant person. But you don't need to attach any weight to her opinion in this instance. Ann Tindall tells me you have a reliable instinct for what's right, and I know May Belle has what you could call very ordinary taste and responses. She was in high school with my sister, and I don't think she's changed a bit. Once, way back then, I asked Charlotte what May Belle was like. Charlotte thought for a moment and then she said, 'She's got a dog named Rover and a cat named Spot, and she always wants to put marshmallows in the fudge.' *Now*, are you going to worry about what May Belle thinks?''

Well, when he put it that way, May Belle did seem like one worry I could shed. It would be hard to believe how much this simple thing helped restore my shaky self-confidence. (I did have some self-confidence in this one area.) She told me once, later, that I never would amount to anything because my handwriting was so legible. (*She* wrote in that pugnacious progressive-school way that looks like bad printing.) I ignored this. I no longer cared for a split second what Missy May Belle thought of me. It flat didn't matter. Kirby Northrop had made me feel eminently acceptable.

Vashti Powell made me feel acceptable too. I first knew Vashti as part of the studio crowd, but she didn't paint. Writing was her thing. She had been a widow since she was a relatively young woman, and her one child was long since grown and living in another state, and she had lots of time for friends and clubs. She was real arty, in a sort of old-fashioned way. She didn't burn candles in bottles, but she was always going around with broken fingernails and stringy hair, and somehow this was regarded as part of her being creative and "honest." She looked nice when she dressed up but she usually dressed up in something odd. She had a necklace—I never did look at it too closely, but I think it was made of teeth.

In spite of this foolishness, she really was talented. She wrote poetry, and frequently she'd be invited to give readings before local clubs or school groups. She'd been published in local papers and in several regional magazines. She was a good deal older than most of the members of the Little Theater, and one of the most popular and looked up to of the whole shooting match. I thought she was terrific. She took a keen interest in young people, and they flocked around her. She was something of a den mother to all the budding young talent around Marlowe.

There was another Marlowe poet—a middle-aged man, a smart dresser and very social. Guy Cameron Fairlie. He didn't move in our circle of hopefuls; he was way beyond us. He had had several volumes published by New York houses. He was our community celebrity. It was amazing to us in the Pen Club how he could have had so much success with the kind of poetry he wrote. We never tried to deny that he had talent, but his work really was slight. For years he had been writing about ships and lips, and it didn't seem like enough. His romantic verses were always graceful and refined, and he was great with descriptions of nature, but Vashti's work was far superior. There was more substance and strength in it. We all thought that, and it wasn't blindfolded loyalty and affection; she truly was better than he was.

Still, he was the one who had made something of a name and she was almost local. I remember once she was asked to speak before my old college's creative writing class. She did this for free, as requested. At the close of the reception that followed the program, one of those bubbleheaded students came up and burbled at her. "Oh, Mrs. Powell! We can't thank you enough for what you've done for our English Club! We've been saving up, and, now that we sold tickets tonight, we have enough money to get Guy Cameron Fairlie next time!"

I thought three names were too many, even for a nationally published poet; but, to his credit, he was known to all as Cam. It was generally agreed that he was homosexual, but he was discreet and he never invited criticism. He was meticulous about keeping up appearances. He was more than welcome everywhere on Marlowe's social scene; he was much sought after. Lots of prominent people were his friends.

Vashti had formed the Pen Club and I was in it. Oh, I really did want to write. I think from time to time I did have some good ideas; it was only that I didn't have the equipment to develop them. So I went to the Pen Club religiously. I got on fine there. I was well thought of and respected. A couple of times there was a little to-do about something I wrote. One of the men had written a short story about a girl, a white girl, who had been raped by a young Negro. It was pretty gruesome, the way he ended it. The boy was going to be electrocuted, and the narrator ended the story by saying he would get his gun and do the execution himself.

All the next week, the whole enduring week, I wrote furiously. So I could take my story to the next meeting. What I wrote didn't help my own cause any, but I didn't think about that at the time. I wrote a first-person thing. I was the girl the Negro had "raped." I had made the first move and I had led him on, and then when he followed through, I had yelled rape. This wasn't so imaginative of me. In real life it was not an unheard-of situation. I read this thing at the next meeting, and it caused some small commotion. When this was all over, I had the feeling that they didn't go along with me but that they had a reluctant respect for me.

I depended on that group for support, but there was nobody in it like Vashti. She was a rock. There was, however, one extremely disturbing thing that came out of the Pen Club. That's where I met Lamar Ratliff. He was some older than I was, and he wasn't especially interested in writing; he played piano. But he had met Vashti and he was facinated with her.

One Saturday afternoon, he and I were with Edmonia. She was my mother's first cousin once removed, and I sometimes took art lessons from her. How she got in on this thing I can't remember. We all three rode over to Vashti's apartment in Lamar's car. He had said he wanted to talk to her, and she asked me and Edmonia to go into the bedroom so they could talk privately. And then—we couldn't help hearing—there was Lamar in the next room weeping and saying "I'm in love with him and he doesn't know I even exist." Edmonia and I had been talking a little, but the walls were paper-thin and when we heard this we stopped talking. We heard Vashti say, "You said 'him." And Lamar said "Robby."

I don't know exactly how I felt. I only know I left the apartment right that minute. Shot through the door from the bedroom to the hall and didn't have to see Vashti or Lamar. I didn't know where I was going; I just lit out. Later, Edmonia kept bringing this up and she'd go hysterical every time. She was unstable, she really was.

Lamar had never made the faintest suggestion of this to me, and he never did. We saw a lot of each other later on, and he never did and I never let him know I'd overheard. After I knew him better, I decided that this was the way he was. He loved to talk about himself and his problems and to cry on somebody's shoulder. I decided—I know this sounds mean, and it's not the kind of thing I often think about people, but I really believe it about Lamar—I decided that he liked the "misery" and the crying on shoulders much more than he was worried about whatever the problem was. I don't believe he was in any real distress when he talked with Vashti. I also think he may have known that he was letting Edmonia think she was his unresponsive love, and that maybe he enjoyed that a little.

But none of that lessened the jolting blow that this was the first time I'd heard such a statement as his made about me. In my own mind I had been wrestling with the whole idea of gender, and I was still quite afraid to be around men too much. But this thing about Lamar was the first time I'd come into real contact with the problem, if that could be called real contact. Always before it had been only imagination and worry. But here was something concrete, and it was very disturbing. Worse. It totally knocked me off my feet. When I flew out of Vashti's apartment, I was so unhinged that I rushed around aimlessly for a while. Then I went to Momma's at Bentley's Creek. I heard later that Edmonia had left Vashti's right after I did, but that Lamar had spent the night there—and I guess talked or cried at her all night. I didn't go back in to town for two months.

When I finally got back to the Pen Club, Vashti was still a rock. It had been my habit, in times of trouble, to go to her apartment. I did this often. She seemed to have no idea what my problem was. Apparently she had thought of that outburst at her place as Lamar's problem, not mine. After all, he had said, "He doesn't know I exist," and I could see how she'd take it that way. She could easily see that I was in deep distress, but she attributed it all to "artistic temperament."

Sometimes I would go to her place and stay all night. Her whole way of life was so casual that I didn't have to feel guilty about waking her up at some ungodly hour or anything like that. She even seemed to welcome this. I think it meant a lot to her that a troubled young person would come to her. I think if she had known the root of my disordered comings and goings, it might have upset her.

But she didn't know, and in the Pen Club I was her fair-haired boy. I believe this was because the dissension that I sometimes stirred up did have a livening effect on the group. So, all during my period of wildness, when I was drinking and dancing and carousing all night, especially Saturdays, I had Vashti and her refining influence too.

Earlier, outside looking in, I had noticed how the Little Theater people all seemed so happy with themselves and with one another and with what they were doing. I had envied them and wished I could be one of them. But whenever I'd get right in there with them, I couldn't stand them. I really could not stand them. All the same, the Little Theater was a temporary escape for me, and I was in it a lot during one prolonged period of turmoil.

This was when we were rehearsing *Light Up the Sky.* I was the sensitive young playwright whose play is all botched up by the people who are doing it. To steady myself and to help me bear up under all that "artistic" posturing all over the place, I'd always take a bottle to rehearsal. The director always had her bottle too, but she could handle it; I was messing up. I'd get there and I wouldn't know my lines. I had known them in advance, but I'd go up in rehearsals. I'd bungle so many lines, people were getting worried. They were actually saying, "What are we going to *do?*" Besides these living voices of real living people, there'd be the ones out in the wings or behind the flats, my voices. "*Look* at him! Trying to make people think he knows what he's doing. Just wait 'til opening night. Wait 'til he gets out on that stage before that audience. *Then* they'll know all about him. That's all it'll take—for him just to walk out on the stage. Rotten creep anyhow. Went out of the house in the middle of the night and *left* that old lady. Drinks like a fish. Runs around with queers. And other men's wives. Queer himself. Started when he was almost a *baby.*"

In the meantime, while all this was churning, I had met Theron Hearn. He was a psychiatrist. He had been at a private hospital for a while, but then he moved to another town—Highfield, I think—and now he was back in Marlowe. I don't know what impressed me so much with him. Maybe it was a kind of calmness about him. I think that was it. I couldn't really say, but I did feel something where he was concerned.

So one badly troubled night during rehearsals—. In fairness to the others, I *was* behaving a little strangely. I knew my lines now, always, but I couldn't do my part along with the others. This upset me and it upset the whole cast, and before rehearsal was over each night I'd be soused. I would drink because then I could do a little better. This one particularly troubled evening I called Theron Hearn and asked him if I could come over, and he suggested a time.

I went. He was the traditional lying-on-the-couch type, but I didn't know this when we went into his little room and I just sat on the couch. We talked about nothing that really mattered, and at the end of the session I asked him when I should come back. He said, "Whenever you like. Just call and make an appointment. I haven't decided whether or not you need long-term therapy." This made me feel a little better about him.

There were people in Marlowe had the idea that he was hot after the money, and he did give them reason. One of his theories, and he'd tell you this right off the bat, was that he would not accept GIs under their Bill of Rights. With the government paying. He would only counsel when the client paid. So of course people had talked about his money grubbing, and I'd thought they were right; but when he said he didn't know whether or not I should go into therapy, I reconsidered. I thought, well, at least he wasn't trying to pull me right in. Which he would have if money was all that mattered.

Next week I went back, and of course I told him about rehearsals and what I went through with them and how I was drinking. He still didn't suggest regular appointments. The third time I went, my forehead was bandaged, and he didn't say one word about this. I didn't tell him what happened and he didn't ask me. And still no regular appointment.

The bandage was just two days off my head when the play opened. We had a very clever makeup artist—we were all artists, you understand—and she covered the fresh scar so it hardly showed. I hung on and, if I do say it myself, I stunned Marlowe audiences. Somehow I got a grip on myself. I had a mysterious surge of energy and control, and I sailed through the entire run of the play without a bobble. After opening night the reviewers on the two Marlowe papers had brutal things to say about everybody but me. One had a headline, ORCHIDS TO WILDE.

There was this peculiar thing: during the performance on opening night, I knew I was doing well. After the performance, I knew I had done well. Everybody was talking about it. Still, instead of going to a party for the cast, I slipped away and left the theater unobserved. Why I did this, I don't know. I don't know.

I cut the reviews from the papers and mailed them to Theron Hearn, and what followed has always seemed mighty strange to me. He sent me a very nice note, and at the end he said, "You do need intensive therapy." What he had picked up from the clippings—or from the performance if he had been at the play, which he very well could have—or from what he'd been mulling over earlier—I can't imagine, but something. To hold off on a decision as long as he did, and then to decide bang as soon as the play opened and the reviews came out. I never knew what to make of that.

There was no possibility of finding out, because I never saw him again. I know why, too. In a way. As long as there had been doubt in his mind, I could keep saying to myself that things weren't all that bad with me. But when he firmly decided, this scared me. And, really, made it hard. The first time I went to him I had got myself all set to go right into a once-a-week deal. But his delay chipped away at my resolve, and that made it too hard for me. By the time he told me to come, I couldn't go. This is one reason it took me so long to get to a psychiatrist in years to come.

Of course, *always*, in the back of my mind, I knew things

were far from right with me. But it was always my way to try to make things work. Things could be glaringly impossible, but I'd try to make them work. Every time. As a small child I did this. That day I went home with Bubba, my buddy, and his mother talked common as pigtracks and the house had that awful diaper smell, I told myself everything was lovely. I did it with Lurleen. I did it later with Kirby. And here I was, trying to do this, trying to make things work, when anybody with half an eye could see that they wouldn't.

I'd keep saying to myself, "Well, Theron Hearn is wrong. It's only one man's opinion anyhow. I can clean this thing up, and let's don't fool with doctors." Of course I had some of the old prevailing notion that psychiatrists—. Well, attitudes have changed. Back then though, there was the opinion that if you went to a psychiatrist, you were off. You were going over the edge. Which, of course, was exactly what I was doing.

None of us knew Robby very well when we asked him to come to our Little Theater tryouts. We had a feeling about him though, and definitely thought he had something to offer. We were right. In time, he added a lot to our prestige in the community. But he did nearly give us one giant collective nervous breakdown when we did what turned out to be his swan song, *Light Up the Sky*.

He was so unprofessional. Of course none of us was an Equity member, but we'd been in little theaters for some years and we didn't feel like outright novices. We weren't frivolous about Little Theater. We tried to behave like professionals. Robby never would. He showed up at rehearsals, but he never, never, never knew his lines. Once in a while he'd do better and we'd begin to breathe again. Then he'd fall right back. There were times when he'd come and volunteer—he knew we were worried—that he had his part down pat. Then he'd go up in his lines. Just in a single rehearsal he'd do this so often that if we hadn't got well into production I do believe Ann Tindall would have replaced him.

He had a sparkling record in his high-school drama club, but we didn't know anything about behind-the-scenes circumstances. He hadn't had the experience most of us had, and he wasn't inclined to go very deeply into any part. He was mostly skimming the surface of his roles. As time went by, we got the strong feeling that he thought we'd do well to be more on the surface. This was mostly an impression; Robby had very little to say. He did break down once and chime in. He said he didn't talk about working, the way we did, because he didn't have anything to say. He said he believed what an actor had said long ago—that an actor's job was to know his lines and not bump into the furniture.

Well, we'd heard that too, but it didn't set too well with those of us who were trying to create character. My idea was that you'd want to know whole heaps more about your character than the lines. After all, the lines weren't anything but black marks on paper until we brought them to life. For every role I played, I worked out a mental picture of the character—the shape of her hands, what she liked to eat, how she got along with her family, what color her hair was, what kinds of clothes she wore, countless things that certainly didn't appear in the lines. I'm sure Robby thought this baroque of me. Things we took for granted seemed to him farfetched and foolish. I even caught him cutting his eyes around when I mentioned that Mary Margaret Worsham changed her name to Margot Worsham after she left us amateurs and joined the Stratford Players.

Another thing. Before I move, I need to know why. I simply cannot traipse all over a stage without knowing why

I'm doing it. Our director was experienced and highly skilled, but she was bad on motivation. We'd have to plead with her. She'd generally comply and be gracious about it, but you could tell she was humoring us. That rankled for a while, but we got used to her and we liked her and we'd just dig it out of her. After all, we had a right. We weren't green kids. We weren't treading the boards for the first time. We had done some things that New York audiences needn't have sneezed at. Our sphere was circumscribed, but within it we had reputations to uphold. Robby didn't have this to consider. He had only his high-school productions behind him. He'd be great at tryouts, and then he'd bumble around and foul up at every rehearsal. He never once asked the director for motivation.

With *Light Up the Sky* his state of ghastly unpreparedness was still unchanged when we were right under the wire. We were throwing up our hands in holy horror. We kept saying to one another, "Bad dress, good opening," but we were whistling in the dark.

On opening night we were all shaking in our shoes, of course, and it wasn't simply opening night nerves. We were so terrified of what Robby would do or not do that we couldn't pay proper attention to our own natural fears of the kind any artist worth his salt does have.

Would you believe that Robby was letter-perfect? And much more than letter-perfect. He breezed through the play as if on wings of song. Did an absolutely superb job. The rest of us had the impression that we were fine too.

We had a party afterwards, an *intime* affair for cast and crew, and we were very merry. The whole cast had done a good job, and Robby had been spectacular. We could hardly wait for him to arrive, because we were all agog about his terrific performance. I say "we all," but Ann Tindall hardly took part in our celebration. Oh, she was physically present, but she very well didn't grace the occasion, as they say. Right after curtain calls she had given us whiskey-scented kisses and called us her own dears. Right stingy comment, we thought, but then we figured she'd save what she had to say for the party. She didn't join in our talk at the party at all. After we left the theater, she never said another word. Throughout the party, she just sat heavily in one place and methodically drank herself into insensibility and had to be poured into a car and carried home. Robby never showed his face. In spite of these two major defections, all the rest of us went to our respective homes feeling no pain and savoring a sense of accomplishment.

The morning paper put an end to all that. It panned us unmercifully. All but Robby. Him, it praised to the skies. He deserved this; we all gave him credit; but I think we deserved better than a ton of brickbats. The evening paper was no better. One of the reviewers said I gave my part "a great deal more tone than was called for." Now, that's cruel. One said the another player "clearly belonged to the Oh-God-the-pain-of-it school of acting that went out with silent movies." I won't go into this any further except to repeat that the reviewers ripped us up one side and down the other. We felt cut to ribbons; and after we'd thought we'd done well! Of course you're always twitchy about what might be said—you *have* put your head on a chopping block—but it never crossed our minds that we'd be set upon in this barbarous fashion. We never had been before.

Nobody earned his pay that day. We were phoning one another all morning. Ann Tindall called a meeting for lunch time. She was wonderfully recovered from the night before, and she somehow managed to convince us that we could go on that night. We had been half seriously doubting this; we were that crushed and cowed. She told us not to bother our pretty heads about anything those ninnyhammers on the papers had to say, people so ill informed that they frequently referred to anybody in toe shoes as a ballerina. She said it was easy and cheap to sit safely back and throw rocks at people who had the guts and the *esprit* to reveal their artistic efforts for daws to peck at. She said drama critics were often actors *manqué* and eaten with jealousy. Besides, she said, they were cowards to hack us to bits when we had no chance to reply. She said we could defend ourselves only by doing a bang-up job every night from then on. She said if we would take ourselves in hand, she knew we could give brilliant performances. She reminded us that professionals went on and gave their best shots no matter what. She said this wounding criticism was the kind of thing that separated the troopers from the dabblers. Those reviewers certainly had taken the rustle out of our silk, but somehow Ann Tindall revived us. That night we did go out on that stage and take another whack at it, and most people thought we were at least adequate and some thought better. Ann Tindall said she was proud of our turnaround. This steadied us for the run of the play. And— will wonders never cease?—Robby did as well every single night as he had at the opening.

He never offered any explanation of his bizarre behavior the night of the party, and we were so busy thanking our lucky stars that we could hold up our heads again that we didn't bother him. After the play closed he dropped from sight. We heard a stray item or two about him, something once about trouble on his job, and later we heard that he'd left town.

9
NINE

A chance meeting developed into a rare friendship. It came during the early part of my time as the Convoy cashier at Marlowe, the nearest thing to a heyday I ever had. I was living it up, spending improvidently on clothes, and going to dances all the time. Carousing, really, and riding hard for a fall. The operators at the Beauty Spot—I was going with one of them, Lonita Curtis—were the main sponsors of a big dance at the roof garden of the Cherokee Hotel. Serafina Bello was there.

She was a little older than I was. She seemed older, or more mature, to me because she was so knowledgeable and assured. At that time she hadn't been in Marlowe very long, and she was calling herself Sara Bell. Her real name, I learnt later. She was from somewhere in Connecticut, and her parents were Italian. I never knew why Fina came to Marlowe in the first place. I got an idea that she'd had some kind of jolting experience with a marriage or an affair, and also that it had something to do with her being Italian. Although of course she wasn't; her parents were. My notion is that she decided to get away and she came South—and why she picked Marlowe, North Carolina, nobody knows.

Maybe she actually did what I've had vague thoughts of doing. Sometimes in turbulent periods I used to think, "If I could just get away, go to some small town where nobody

knows me, maybe I could start all over and get along better."
I suppose it's a common enough error to fall into. Actually, I
would know that I wouldn't be one whit better off in Hot
Coffee, Mississippi, than I would right where I was. Nonetheless, I'd get into this line of thought: if I could just get to
some unlikely place—Between, Georgia, or Ninety-Six, South
Carolina—and get *organized,* on a very small scale. If I could
live in a tiny little house—and so on. And then I'd realize I
was fantasizing something that was like a child's story. I'd live
in a tiny little house, and go every day to my tiny little job, and
come home in the evenings and cook my tiny little dinner.
Crazy. Still and yet, the daydream had a certain logic. It was
my struggle to bring things down to a manageable size, to
regain some bit of control of my life.

Anyhow, I did feel that Fina came to Marlowe with the
definite idea of making a fresh start, a new life, even taking a
new name.

After the dance we saw each other around town occasionally, and we'd speak. I don't remember exactly how we
became friends except that first there was a series of casual
encounters. The earliest memorable impression I had of her
was that she was the first person I'd ever met that I thought
had the slightest understanding of me. Maybe she needed a
friend herself. In spite of her terrific appearance and all the
rest of it, I felt that she too was lonely. And our friendship
really did flower, partly because she made no demands. That
was important. Up to that point, any individual I had singled
out, male or female, wanted something of me, generally
sexual.

Fina was lively. Not overanimated, just bright and quick
and loaded with vitality. She was striking-looking, and she
had impeccable taste. To me, at my age and with my
background of simple living, she was a glittering, almost
magical, creature. I was thrilled that she took to me.

She was the first person I ever knew who habitually drank wine with her meals—to me that was glamour, that was class—and she was a splendid cook. She'd seen a lot of theater, and she loved to talk about it. She could keep me entranced for hours. I had had just one year of college, but I had read a good bit in a haphazard way, and I had at least a nodding acquaintance with many of the people and plays and books she talked about. So I could talk about them some too.

As time went by, she developed that strange sort of attitude that I later learnt she develops for anybody she greatly likes: She wanted me to be perfect. As she defined perfection. She didn't want anybody she cared about to deviate from the pattern of perfection that she drew.

For a long time I didn't mind this. The things she was telling me to do were for my own improvement, that was an actual fact, and in the beginning she told me in the nicest way. She kept at me to be more careful about my grammar, and she'd help me pick out clothes. This about the clothes was a mercy, even if at first I felt lukewarm about some of her choices. I could howl when I think of it, but I did dress worse than a racetrack tout. I had one sports coat that was light green, almost chartreuse, and just awful. And funny-looking shoes, and flashy ties, the works. I'd spent a lot on them, and now they'd cost a cow and a calf, but they were awful. Fina was the first person I ever heard talk about understated clothes. She dressed beautifully herself. Under her tutelage, I shaped up, and she reached the stage where she'd be infuriated whenever I did anything that wasn't chic and proper.

She had a bandbox of an apartment. It was only one huge room and a kitchenette and bath, but put together with the most discriminating taste. Everybody said so. She was working at a specialty shop, the Gift Horse, when I met her, but she later opened her own place. She had had some kind of legacy, so she had more to live on and maneuver with than her earnings. People would come to her apartment on Sundays, the kind of people I'd never known before. A good many of them were from the state college a few miles away in Highfield. They were in design, drama, and the college radio station, that kind of thing. Fina would coach me ahead of time. What this amounted to, she wanted me to talk old-Southern-plantation, not backwoodsy. Be fine. And if I couldn't think of anything to say, just be quiet. Be quiet and nobody will *know*. For a while, these put-downs were kind of amusing, and it was only later that a resentment built up. She *was* helping me in lots of ways, and I was enthralled. I was just floating. It sounds trite, but she introduced me to a new way of living.

Not only that, but she came to be a kind of security that I'd never had before. She would encourage me in all kinds of ways. I was trying to write, trying to draw, and she'd look at what I'd done and sometimes she'd say, "You really have got something, if you'll only get some training." I got so used to her lovely, comfortable apartment, and became so greatly dependent on her—to tell me what to do, almost. She was fond of me, she was good to me, and she helped me in many ways, and I loved being with her. I was at her place more than my own. I was there so much that we even pooled our grocery money, and, inevitably, there was talk about us.

The voices had at me. "That's what he's making people think—having an affair—but I know better—no girl would have an affair with him—" And all that. Once on a bus I distinctly heard a girl say something. I ran into this girl I'd always admired, who lived back home, out in the country at Hungry Run near Bentley's Creek, and who I hadn't seen for a long time. We were talking, and I clearly heard a girl's voice right on the other side of us say, "*Look* at that Wilde boy! I just can't stand that thing!" I kept talking like my tongue was tied in the middle and loose at both ends, and watching Noellene to see if she was hearing me or if she heard the girl. It's only in relatively recent years that I've understood that Noellene didn't hear anything but me because there wasn't anything else to hear.

When Sara opened her own shop, she went back to her real name. At the Gift Horse she had got well along the way to becoming a local institution. Then through her own shop she was taken up by the richer, more worldly people in Marlowe. She called her place Serafina's, and the shop did have a sort of flair. She had established herself in Marlowe, and people saw her in a new way. Serafina Bello was no longer an immigrant name; it was exotic. Fina, rightly enough, I think, made use of that. She became quite the rage, and whatever she said went. If she had told some of those women to wear a nest of robins in their hair, they'd have done it. I was jubilant at her success. I basked in it like a lizard in the sun.

There was another reason I was lost in admiration of her. She could be so poised and unruffled in a hotel dining room, say, when my voices where chattering like magpies. I thought she was so sophisticated and blasé that all this talk didn't make her bat an eye.

Far more important than what I took for her blasé quality, it was thanks to her that the voices bothered me a little less. They didn't stop, of course, but it became somewhat easier for me to take them. When They would be ranting and raving, I was able to think, "I don't care what *you* think about me. *Serafina Bello* thinks I'm fine." This is why I'm still so fond of Fina and always will be. Nobody in my life had ever made me feel quite that way.

And there was another thing, not of great importance but enjoyable. To a certain extent, I shone in her reflected light, and I was happy and content to be her little moon.

Once her sister came from up north to visit, and Fina tried to Pygmalion her the way she did me; but Anna Maria wouldn't sit still for it. I got the impression that this sort of thing had been a bone of contention with them before. They were as different as chalk is from cheese. Fina was intense, sometimes dramatic; Anna Maria was easygoing and sunny. Fina followed fashion. Anna Maria didn't care a fig about fashion *or* style; she wore whatever appealed to her, and it wasn't understated. Fina was really better looking. She had regular features, her head was nicely set on her shoulders, and she looked taller than she was—I think because she carried herself so well. She was smart. Anna Maria was more sort of fluffy. She was wonderfully pretty, and softer and more approachable looking than Fina.

She'd come sashaying into the shop or the apartment wearing clothes that set Fina's teeth on edge. She'd wear black skirts, in what I think they used to call waltz length, and blouses in color combinations like turquoise and fuschia or bright navy blue and chartreuse, and flowered shawls, and big gold hoop earrings, and many bracelets. I thought the colors were luscious, and Anna Maria couldn't help being pretty, but it was easy to see how the overall effect would grate on Fina.

I remember one day she came in to Fina's apartment wearing all that stuff. Fina's face took on a pained expression and then she said, "Where's your tambourine? Outside in the wagon?" That would have shriveled me up, but Anna Maria just laughed at her and said, "Cross my palm with silver and I'll tell your fortune." Other times Fina would pick out some *tiny* detail of Anna Maria's getup and compliment her on it, but this didn't faze Anna Maria either. I think they loved each other, but they didn't get along too well. Mostly this was because of Fina's domineering ways. The funny thing was that they didn't seem domineering unless they were resisted. To be resisted astonished her and she could not understand it. She simply could not bear it that Anna Maria wouldn't be glad to dress the way she told her to.

Soon enough, the time came when she shriveled me up, just the way I said she could. Entirely because of her improvement of me, I came to have a little bit of confidence in myself and to be less pliant. When this happened, she didn't fail to let me know I was still a clodhopper. It was true, of course, to a certain extent. But still. My family and I were country, but we didn't plant red verbena in the centers of old automobile tires or line the porch steps with geraniums in coffee cans painted green. Poppa had been prosperous in a modest way when he was a tobacco farmer, before my time. But he'd had one stroke of bad luck after another, including the depression and a badly broken and badly set leg that healed crooked and cut down on his activity. By the time I came along, he had come down to being a guard at a prison camp. I always got the impression that my mother's family felt that she'd married beneath them. At any rate, Fina needn't have been so haughty and high-heeled with me. We were country, but we weren't Dogpatch. Not by a long shot.

Fina also didn't scruple to say quite a lot about the "tacky" people I used to hang around with. (She picked up a lot of Southernisms.) As she pointed out more than one time, the operators at the beauty shop were the kind of people who entered beauty contests. And one had gone to Luray, Virginia, to be married in the caverns there, and this was all over the Marlowe papers. It certainly wasn't any classy group I used to be in, but I had eased away from it. This wasn't a conscious decision on my part, but I realized later that I had done it. Mainly because I had found something that interested me more: Fina, and the way she lived and the people she knew. Again to her credit, she did lift me out of that wild bunch. That was the trouble with them—that they were wild, not that they were tacky. If it hadn't been for Fina, I would have gone to the dogs fast, at the rate I was going when I met her.

Fina had one bad failing. She had a violent temper. It

was this, plus the resentment that was churning in me, that finished us. Right at this time in our friendship, I became deeply troubled and I would get drunk on wine. I drank a lot, and wine was the cheapest. When I was drunk, sometimes I'd needle Fina. I'd say things I didn't even think or mean. I'd get drunk, she'd get irritated, and *then* I'd needle her. I got vicious about this. I did it because it tore me down a lot in my own eyes, the degree to which I was dependent on her.

I surely didn't want to break with her. I had got used to what was for me a plush life, in material comforts and in new acquaintances, both of which she shared with me. I couldn't painlessly have gone back to doing without all that. But far more than that, Fina was *somebody for me*. I felt that if I didn't have her I would simply go down the drain. I would resent this so much that when I was drinking I'd give her a hard time.

Then she'd curse me in Italian, and this made me come all over queer. It was a lot more blistering than if she'd used English. It sounded like she was saying ten times more than she really was, and all that quantity got to me. Besides, she'd prowl around the room while she was loosing that torrential outpouring on me and, I swear, it was like I had stuck my head through a hole and she was chunking firecrackers at me. I'm aware that English has its "short ugly words," but I love English. I'm awkward with even a few words in a foreign language. (Fina said this was provincial of me.) To me, anything in German sounds like unloading coal in the basement, and Fina's Italian tirades were scalding and they always unnerved me.

One evening she had made some kind of plan for me. She would do this frequently, make a plan for me if she were going to be occupied elsewhere. This was to keep me from doing something with my tacky friends. I resented this too, and besides that I wouldn't be with my tacky friends. I'd be with somebody who would make her elegance look like mighty small potatoes. This one evening, whatever her plan for me was, I went just opposite. When I went by her apartment, as I always did before I went home to my room, I had shopped at an all-night market and I brought several bags of groceries. I just plunked them down on a kitchen counter and didn't put anything away. Then I sprawled on the sofa with my feet up on it. So there were two things that I knew would get her going. And I had to get her going, because if she wasn't mad I couldn't needle her. When she came in then, there was this situation ready-made for an explosion. She got thin-lipped and hard-faced and immediately started putting away the groceries. I braced myself for what would happen next.

It was more than bracing myself against her anger. There was this evil thing in my head. It was to get at her, to get at that facade she had that I didn't have. And batter it down, I guess. I sensed strongly that she was having some inner troubles of her own, but still she could put up an impressive front and I couldn't. It festered in me that my turmoil was sticking out all over me (at least to her it was, I thought), and that hers was camouflaged beyond detection. It wasn't fair. With my problems front-and-center and with her not even conceding that she had any, she could be condescending. I wanted to tear the cover off at least some of her misgivings or whatever she had smoldering. Then we could be more on the same plane and she couldn't be condescending to me *all* the time.

I waited until she was mad good and proper, and then I said something. I don't know exactly what, I was drunk and I don't remember exactly, but maybe something like, "What a rotten thing, to call yourself Sara Bell so people wouldn't know you're a wop." I don't know that I said this. I could have. If I said it, it was only to say something that would gouge into her; I never called anybody a wop in my life.

Whatever I said, it touched a nerve. She was handling the groceries and, without missing a beat, she grabbed a jar of kumquats—the first thing she could put her hand to—and threw it at me with all her strength. It wasn't a direct hit, it was a glancing blow, but it laid my forehead open just parallel with one eyebrow and not much above it. I had to be taken to the emergency room and get it stitched up. And this was less than a week before I had to appear in a Little Theater production. The doctor said if, when I "fell down the stairs," I'd had the blow just a smidgin lower, he could never have saved my eye.

Fina had carried me to the hospital right away, and back to my room after I'd been sewn up. She had the palest, saddest face I ever saw—she looked just killed—but she didn't talk at all about what had happened. Neither of us ever has. I simply quit going to her place and she didn't ask me to come back. We'd be pleasant to each other when we'd meet by happenstance, but it was all gone, all over.

I think of her often. She was a lifesaver, and I do think of her often and always with warm affection. I always will. Maybe not with altogether unmixed affection, but with genuine affection and a great lot of gratitude.

◎ One look into "Serafina's" any day would show the place aswarm with Marlowe's elite. I groan about how I drudge away in my dress shop, and I do work like a woman possessed, but I love it. Many of the regular customers became my personal friends long ago, and I know that I'm needed and wanted in this town.

If I wanted to do it, I could go for a month without cooking or buying dinner. I have so many invitations that, together with the shop, I'm nearly always at the brink of exhaustion. When I came here, I was hardly in step with the locals, but I've made a place for myself in this community and I don't see why Rob couldn't have done this too. There was a time when I thought he was on the way. He was never the outsider I was, and he had every chance; I saw to that. Oh, well, I miss him a great deal less than I used to. I don't know whether that means I'm getting callous or mature, if there's any difference.

For a long time, Rob was a tremendous comfort and pleasure to me. Unlike the upper crusters who gradually took me up, Rob never showed any curiosity about my whys and wherefores. When I volunteered to tell him about myself is what he satisfied himself with, and I didn't volunteer anything I'd rather not. Oh, the others didn't ask any outright questions. Nothing so direct. But there were all sorts of sly little hints "let fall," as they put it. They soon gave up hinting though. They're good loyal friends to me now, and I to them. I have a capacity for making and keeping friends. I'm quite open about whatever takes place now, but I don't hand out biographical sketches. If I'd prefer to have a husband and a home but am disinclined to marry, that's my problem, not theirs. It's a private matter. I came down here so I'd be around new people. It's all so far behind me that I even kid around sometimes about how I'm such a perfectionist and so set in my ways that nobody would suit me or put up with me. It may even be true.

I've put my past behind me, and I no longer get emotional about it. What's to get emotional about? That would be a thundering bore, and I don't feel any need to talk or even think about it. I use the silver my mother gave me when we thought there'd be a wedding. Why not? Andy came and went, but silver is for life. Things happen and people get over them. If I found somebody I wanted to marry, well, maybe I'd marry him.

It was different before. I was feeling bridey and seeing

myself lighting candles and setting the table with Lenox china, just like the girls in the magazine ads. Then Andy came with his so-sorry-good-bye-please. He was going to marry the girl he left behind when he came to Connecticut. She had just happened to turn up, taking an autumn foliage tour. With his sister! That revived everything in a twinkling, apparently, and I was out of the picture. I had known there was such a person, somebody he'd practically grown up with. But I'd thought she was all over with, because Andy had thought so.

This was a violent blow. No denying that, but I don't give in easily. When I'm shattered, I'm more like mosaic than confetti. I turned to bits and pieces, but I didn't fall apart. I didn't do a song-and-dance about it, and I didn't want anybody even talking to me about it. But the others were out of my control, I found.

I knew Andy well, and he was a fine human being and we could have been happy together. If what's-her-name hadn't come along. It was my misfortune that he preferred her to me, but this didn't mean that I'd been conned. I could still grieve to some extent over Andy, except that that's in my past and I let it stay there. I don't give it a thought. No use pulling it out and picking over it. I let it lie. I didn't *want* to root Andy out of my mind, but I had to do it and I did it. Rooted him out and kept him out. I never think of him any more. Never give him a thought.

While it was happening, I didn't talk to anybody about it. It hurt too much. I silently marinated in my own juices and in time I could have cleared things up, but my family and friends wouldn't let it alone. They all leaned in the direction of high-school dramatics, and I finally got tired of having to quell so much soap opera. So I said to myself, "Basta! And to hell with it," and I cleared out. I came South, to Marlowe. I'd been here once, on my way to a Florida vacation, and liked it. I made it my home and I've never been sorry.

All this trouble was barely below the surface when I met Robby. That's why it was so important to me that he was different from the others. I think he intuitively knew that I didn't want to talk about myself much, and he never dropped the first hint. Also, sex never got its pretty high-heeled pump in the door. Robby and I didn't have that kind of interest in each other.

I had begun to get myself in hand. I wasn't the first woman in the world to be crudely thrown over, and I wouldn't be the last. To all appearances, I was myself. After a while I really was myself. But all during this difficult period, when I could use an unquestioning, undemanding friend, Rob filled the bill.

More than that. He gave me an interest outside myself, a personal and creative interest. This was separate and distinct from the shop and over and above other social contacts I was making, and he gave me richly rewarding companionship. He was a few years younger, and urban life still sat a little strangely on him—different from me to that extent. He had plenty of potential though, and he was malleable. One of the most gratifying things about the changes I brought about in him was that he was so entranced with them himself. So many simple things were new to him, like sherry in the onion soup, or meat a bit rare instead of overcooked the way so many Southerners like it. He was as fresh and delighted as a child. Both he and I took pride in his changed appearance after he got rid of those atrocious clothes.

I couldn't get my own sister to do this. I adore Anna Maria, but the way she tarts herself up affects me like Banlon sweaters. As Robby would put it, I could pinch her head off. She twirls around the place looking like Chiquita Banana or Carmen the Beautiful Cigarette Girl. Most of all, she reminds me of vintage Ginger Rogers: Beautiful herself, but "If you can't wear it, carry it." Put a well-cut pure-lined dress on

Anna Maria and one important piece of jewelry, and she
wouldn't have to take second place to anybody. As it is, she's
ridiculous. If she didn't lack all sense of humor, she'd know it.
I don't believe she owns a stitch of lingerie that isn't either
black or lace. Once at bedtime she was looking like an early
Hollywood starlet's dream of glamour, and I said, "All you
need is a white fur rug and a few yards of satin cut on the bias
and you'd look like Jean Harlow." She took that as a
compliment.

But all this is off the subject. The subject is Rob. For
months and months, everything was palmy. We cooked and
ate together, we went to shows together, he came whenever I
had company, we read many of the same books, and we talked
nonstop about it all. Then it wasn't palmy any more. Just
mezzo mezzo. The change began in slight ways, but somewhere along the line Rob began to have an air of something
like insolence about him. It was just the merest tinge and for
the merest flash and just once in a while. Then he began to be
hostile and almost defiant. But there wasn't anything to defy.
The whole thing was goofy.

In this perverse mood, he'd go to considerable trouble to
fake overly rustic ways. He'd ask for things like turnip greens
and pot likker, usually when I was having dinner guests.
More than once he took off his jacket just before guests
arrived in full fig, and met them in rolled up shirtsleeves.
He'd get backwoodsy in his talk. He'd rattle on about how he
"drug" something somewhere, and how his Aunt Wesa was a
"yarb woman" who said smoking was dangerous because
nicotine would collect in the calves of your legs. And how his
sister Willene liked to "argify" about religion. It was stupe-
fying, all the more so as not a word of it was true. The greens
and pot likker part was half true. They're nutritious foods,
and I found that plenty of smart-as-paint people kept a liking
for them, but nowhere are they considered party fare. The
rest was pure fabrication, though I didn't know it then.

Not that he ever introduced us, but I've met his Aunt Louisa now, and his sister too. His Aunt Wesa does live in the country, and she uses infusions of goldenseal and comfrey as home remedies. But the worth of herbal remedies has been rediscovered, and goldenseal and comfrey are a far cry from High John the Conqueror and the devil's shoestrings. She doesn't yearn for city life, and she isn't in the least concerned about what's in. She wears a cameo (a nice cameo) "breast pin," and at Sunday dinner she has ambrosia in her mother's cut-glass bowl. She disapproves of smoking as a "dirty and altogether unlovely habit." I'm sure she never said "yarb" in her life. Willene is offensive about her religion, because she's intrusive. As Robby says, she's too missionary to be nice. But she doesn't argify with everybody she sees, and she doesn't use words like "argify."

At the time I met Rob I had already formed a nucleus of contacts that I enjoyed. They engendered real friendships as well as helped my business. I'd gone beyond the period of adjustment and was settling in firmly. During that early time I was what Robby called breast high amid the alien corn. I had felt that. It involved things I hadn't had time to notice when I was there such a short time years ago, but for a while, I had culture shock. To begin with, there was the language barrier. I'd hear those women talking about lemon-cheese cake, and I'd think they meant cheesecake. They'd go to see relatives in Taliaferro County, Georgia, and they'd call it Tolliver. They have names like Beauchamp, which they pronounce Beecham. The first time I heard a man say he'd carry the cook home, it sounded like piggyback to me.

Sometimes they talked in an odd way that wasn't about language but about *them.* People who had never lived on a farm, people who had always been in at least medium-sized towns and who had college degrees, talked like field hands. I don't mean bad grammar, although that was sometimes in it; I mean they used field-hand expressions. A man would come into my shop dressed very sharp, and buy a designer scarf for his wife and call it a head rag. A woman in a hurry to get somewhere might say she was going to put her foot in her hand, and her hand would be sporting a ring with an impressive stone. If you took any of this talk seriously, straight, thought they didn't know any better, the joke was on you. In time I caught on to that, with an assist from Robby, and now I can talk this way with the best of them. Shoot, I reckon.

It was the same with the way they spoke of themselves. I know that lots of these people were what they'd call proud and high-heeled, but they were almost oriental in the way they deprecated themselves or what they had. If somebody working with a social-educational organization told you he'd got "a little grant," more than likely the grant would mean something big to him, and even objectively impressive enough. If you thought of it as his "little grant," just because he called it that, you'd be nowhere. I don't want to sell these people short. This wasn't exactly false modesty. Or if it was, it grew out of a horror of boasting. Robby said all along it was "just manners." When I caught on, I liked them for it. For me to say a thing like this means I've been assimilated, I think.

I believe Robby was right, that it was a matter of manners. These people were very big on what somebody called the decent hypocrisies, and it certainly smoothed everyday life. Without hypocrisy of any kind, they'd defer to one another. A you-go-first attitude was common.

But back to Robby's phony rustic routine. Right enough that before he knew me he was happy on a steady diet of pork chops and bread by the loaf. Any kind of pasty white bread. And true, Willene *was* hipped on some peculiar sect. But all his quaintly bucolic behavior was solid fake with an overlay of spite. What was he spiting me *for*?

If I complained about any of this in private, why, he

hadn't the vaguest idea what I was talking about. He'd then ramble on about how I must understand that in those parts the rural folk held their heads pretty high, and pure Anglo-Saxons, and a bold peasantry its country's pride, and God knows what else until my ears rang. Bold peasantry! Not even Daniel Boone was so rustic as Rob when he got on a country jag.

After we'd gone a few rounds of this sort of thing, he progressed to where after a few drinks he'd make cracks at *my* speech and habits. My speech was still unmistakably Yankee, he said, but its native harshness was mellowing under the influence of the Southrons. That's what he said, Southrons. He said I was beginning to use a somewhat softer version of what Samuel Johnson called "the rough, snarling letter r." Yes, indeed. Once he asked me which was right with aspirin, red wine or white.

He announced to my startled guests one night that I was so highly polished you couldn't see the grain. And there was that night he arrived late to a dinner party. He apologized profusely, and said he'd had to wait until his eyes cleared up. They'd been right bloodshot, he said, and he would have ruined my color coordination. (What he actually said was "near about ruint.") Even that wasn't enough. He didn't go on to the sneak preview with us as planned. Jesus, Mary, and Joseph. He couldn't appear in public. He hadn't had time to get his shoelaces ironed.

With this grotesque behavior, our friendship curdled. The whole thing was embarrassing for me and for my nice friends. I was thoroughly hurt and bewildered and indignant. I'd given him no cause. All I'd ever done was help him. He would come to my place reeling and lurching and reeking of the cheapest kind of wine, and start those bouts for no reason I could ever find. For a time I continued to behave in the same old way toward him—between matches—and I never left him out of anything I planned. Never slighted him in any way. I even kept on making plans for him when there were other things I had to do, to distance him from those raffish friends he used to waste his time with.

None of this did any good, and finally my patience snapped. He said such a detestable thing to me one night, such a shabby thing that I won't even repeat it, and without any provocation. Before I knew what I was doing, I had clobbered him over the head. It scared me to death, because I seriously injured him. It shocked me that I'd let him provoke me to do such a thing.

After that we went our separate ways by unspoken agreement. There was nothing else to do. Things were beyond repair. As I said, I no longer worry about what might be happening with him, but I still carry a painful memory. Sometimes I believe I think of Rob more often than Andy. After all, I know what happened with me and Andy. Anyhow, I've other things to think about and I've put Andy out of my mind.

10
TEN

Once when there was a great buildup of voices—I don't remember the exact precipitating incident, they're likely to be so similar—the place I was living became unbearable. The way all places did in time. I fled to my old refuge, the Y. Like a terrorized little animal running for its life, to its burrow.

During my toughing-out and settling-down efforts, I thought of the two months I had holed up at Bentley's Creek after Lamar had given me such a shock. During that time, Edmonia would come out there. She'd do things like go out and pick thistles and stuff the family saw every day and thought less than nothing of, and carry it all home with her. They were impressed that she could paint, but sometimes they half seriously thought she wasn't all there. At best they thought she was an oddball. "Edmonia's a case," they'd say. They couldn't imagine what I saw in her.

Edmonia was so mixed up it was pitiful. She used to halfway think she was in love with me, although she was considerably older, and she most emphatically was always thinking people, mostly young men, were in love with me. She had had a good feeling for me since I was a child. She was in chronic bad health even then; and once when she was in bed and I went to see her, I said I liked to go to the library because I liked the smell it had. She took this to mean something, and, for whatever construction she put on it, it impressed her.

When I was about twenty, she was still having an on-again-off-again life because of her health. She'd had a good bit of art training and was qualified to teach. Poor girl, she wanted to paint and teach, and every time she'd get better she'd open a little studio and it would fold up and she'd go back home and try to get together a little money and try again. Her studio was a comfortable place for me, and I used to go there a lot. This put me on the edges of Marlowe's arty crowd. Of course I didn't belong to the crowd, but through the studio I associated with these people right much. One of them was about the only person I'd really liked in the Little Theater, Vashti Powell. It was at the studio that Lamar met Vashti, and that's how that big awkward mess at her apartment came about.

After his tearful to-do at Vashti's, I never heard a peep out of Lamar, and soon he went into the Army. But Edmonia never let me forget it. It had been rough on her too. Edmonia had a problem with herself in that she was prone to think that every man loved her, couldn't resist her. So she had been telling me about how there was this poor young man in love with a woman and it was just the worst thing and she didn't know how she could help him. He had told her about this unrequited love, and she had naturally assumed that he was talking about a woman. And then we both heard Lamar through the wall at Vashti's. Edmonia was almost as upset about this as I was.

To go back to the time of my fleeing once again to the Y after a buildup of voices. The Y was my old faithful, and this time I felt a sense of release there. Maybe it was only that I was cut off from all influences. I can't account for it, but I did feel this sense of release. Sadly enough, and I suppose predictably enough, I didn't use it well.

I started running around. With nearly anybody, but mainly with Lamar Ratliff, of all people. One day—very shortly after this buildup and big explosion—I was eating at Woolworth's, and I saw Lamar. He was back from the Army. He was now a professional pianist, and he played in a jazz band. He had a degree in history, but he said he'd sooner be in a band. We chatted a while and then he said, "Couldn't we go over to Edmonia's?" For the next couple of months, he was there more than I was, because I soon left the Y and went back to Bentley's Creek and was in town only on weekends.

We were all fools—me, Lamar, and Edmonia—but this is how we got back together. I had rather shrunk from it because I didn't know how it would look to the people at the studio, Lamar coming back with me. I thought, "Everybody knows about that thing, and I don't know what they're thinking of me." The truth was that everybody didn't; it was only my uneasiness. I never heard a word out of the arty people, and of course none of the three of us ever made any reference to that old embarrassment. But it stayed on Edmonia's mind. Without ever mentioning it right out, she kept throwing it up to me. From that time on, she was a caution. She had this fix; she thought every single person was after me.

Once we went to a drugstore together and I bought cigarettes. When the boy gave me the change, he said, "Thank you very much." Big deal. Thank you very much instead of just plain thank you. Edmonia whirled around on me and squeaked, "What *is* it with you? More men than women are after you." This was typical. She would start it all up again if any man so much as looked at me.

Actually, it didn't even take that much. One evening Lamar and I were strolling around downtown—nearly all of his work with the band was on weekends and this was the middle of the week—and he went into a hotel to buy a magazine. I waited for him on the street. To my dismay Edmonia loomed up and shrilled out at me, "Has it come to this? That you wait outside hotels while he keeps his sordid engagements?", and flew off into the night. She did all this with Fred's Fruit Emporium right next to the hotel and people sitting at outdoor tables eating watermelon. I don't know but what she *was* touched. She didn't care who heard her. There was just no limit to the way she'd carry on, and it had a harmful effect on me. I was in turmoil enough without her and her ravings.

She let me know too that she was still hopping mad about having thought that Lamar was in love with her. She ranted. He had taken up all her time with this, and she had worried about it, had been so concerned for his feelings when she'd turn him down, and she had suffered so much trying to figure how to do this, and there it was me all the time. Of course by then I had lots of voices telling me I was queer. Edmonia was well-known in Marlowe, and she saw a lot of people. I figured that the voices I heard were people that she had told. She'd start this stuff right on the street or anywhere, and I figured she was just sweeping the town with it. So the voices seemed to me as logical as anything could be. Voices of people in stores, people on streets, on elevators, anywhere. I never heard Them except when people were around and could have been talking.

The only way I could think of to deal with all this, to attempt to quell what I thought was gossip going like wildfire, was to move from Bentley's Creek to Willene's. She and her husband lived on the edge of Marlowe. They didn't have room for me, but they said I could come on anyhow and sleep in the hall. So I left the farm and moved in with Willene and Orie, and I really did try to be like them. Thinking it might possibly help me. Willene was already gone on that hardshell primitive church, and I thought I'd go to church too and maybe that would help. This was against my grain, but it shows how bad off I was. I would have grasped at any straw, and this was the straw that presented itself.

Willene and Orie had a young friend, Cullen Studstill. They thought a lot of him and wanted us to be friends. Cullen had a bad stutter. He could sing or read aloud beautifully, but he stuttered when he talked. I introduced him to Edmonia, and he started taking art lessons from her. This helped her, because he was one of the few who would always pay. Cullen was a nice boy, and what happened later doesn't change that.

I didn't join the church, but I attended services with them all and I did join a Sunday School class. That was a mistake, because before long the class went to Twin Lakes for a weekend and Cullen and I were assigned bunk beds. I woke up in the middle of the night and Cullen was in bed with me. He was under the cover and he had his arms around me and I didn't know how long he'd been there.

I nearly went wild. I jumped straight up and I know I looked startled out of my wits, because I was. I don't know how I managed it, but somehow I got a grip on myself and I sort of laughed a little and said something like, "You've walked in your sleep and you're out of your bed." He went through such a frightful struggle of stuttering and trying to say something that he looked like he was having a seizure. I was sorry for him about that later, but all I could think of then was to get him away from me. I sort of snapped at him to calm down and go back to his bed. So he quit this almost convulsive effort to speak, and climbed back up to his own bunk. The next day things were pretty strained, and we were never friendly any more.

On top of Lamar and Edmonia, this was too much for me. It aggravated my self-doubt, and it made the voices worse. Cullen was working with Edmonia at the studio, and I didn't know what he might be telling her—the way Lamar had blabbed to Vashti. I don't think he ever did though.

As it worked out, I hadn't been comfortable at Willene's for long, aside from Cullen. In the very beginning it was pleasant there, because there was never a word of criticism of me from either Willene or Orie, but this was soon ruined because I felt guilty. As far as they knew, I was living the life they wanted for me, but I never felt any of it. I just went through the motions. I felt so miserable that I had to give up the effort at church. I didn't stop going because of Cullen. I stopped because the church was worse than no solution. It was no solution because of my thoughts while I was there. They would preach and I'd think, "I can't believe like that" and "That doesn't sound right at all" and sometimes I'd just think, "NO." I couldn't sit there thinking this way and looking down on the whole thing and then, after service, smile and shake hands and let them think I was like-minded. I couldn't stand it. I couldn't stand the people. I couldn't stand their church. It was absolutely no good for me. I had to drop it.

I went back to running around. Lamar still seemed to like me, and he discounted my unstable behavior as that of a brilliant eccentric, or at any rate that of an eccentric who was fitfully brilliant. This sounds ridiculous, but he had had a vastly inflated notion about me ever since he saw me in a play and read some of my things at the Pen Club. After that he thought I was quite a guy, and, whatever I did that was so odd it would have put anybody else off, he thought was just an expectable part of "brilliance."

I began to go wherever he and the orchestra were playing on Saturday nights, and this was very bad for me. Two or three of the boys in the band took Benzedrine and stuff like that, and, as I got in with them, I began taking it too. And then we'd go to nightclubs. This means black. Negro, we said then. Then the only real nightclubs in Marlowe were black, and after hours these musicians would go to them and have jam sessions. I knew I had no business taking Benzedrine, but it was a relief—just at first. Later the voices started in on this. They'd go on about it. "He associates with niggers—*Look* at him—He'll try to make you believe he doesn't, but just *look* at him—Don't have anything to do with him—Running around with that homosexual piano player—They're all taking dope—popping Bennies every whipstitch."

Well, we *were* doing all that. Those musicians taught me a terrible thing: to smash sniffers—inhalers, for colds—and chew the things in them. I heard later that each Benzedrine inhaler had the equivalent of sixty pills in the little felt thing inside. I would smash the inhaler the way they showed me, and get this whole thing out and chew it with chewing gum. It had a wonderful effect. I could be out all night and go to work the next day. The part about work was incredible. I could do a mammoth amount of work in one morning and do it right. I could work like a Trojan. I was tireless. I didn't care what the voices were saying. It was wonderful. *It was wonderful.*

There was a homosexually tinged incident, but it wasn't me and Lamar. He never ever did say a word to me about what he'd been crying to Vashti. He and the band were playing a dance at Clarksboro, and I went along. To wait until they finished, I stayed in a bar downtown. Thanks to Benzedrine, I could drink 'til all hours and never show that I had drunk a drop. I wouldn't feel drunk either; I just had this wonderful sensation. Benzedrine made me feel so good! *Nothing mattered.* It was the most enormous relief from my usual state.

This particular night I waited, as I say, in a bar downtown. The musicians came when they'd finished, and we started for the Successful Lingayen Gulf Landing Café. They said the food was good there. This was a place owned and run by a Filipino who had lived in Clarksboro for years, they told me. During World War II, when our troops were moving up from Leyte towards the northern part of Luzon, and others were landing up there and moving down to meet them, and they all were to knock out the Japanese in between, he followed this operation closely. He was thrilled when the landing party up north, where he was from, made it ashore. He was so excited he changed the name of his restaurant and hired more help and kept it open day and night. Whether or not that last part was ever true, the Successful Lingayen Gulf Landing Café was closed when we got to it that night.

On the way, we'd passed the Brimstone Pit; so we went back there and had some barbecue. When we stopped at this all-night joint, we were hungry and in a hurry to eat and Lamar parked in the wrong place. I don't know what all Lamar had taken, but he was loaded. Of course he'd been playing at some country club and liquor had been handy. I hadn't had anything at the bar but beer.

After we'd eaten, we came ouside and got in the car, Lamar and I, and a police officer appeared. He went around to Lamar's side of the car, talking about the parking violation. Then—it was the most astonishing thing—he came around the car on my side and said to me, "You come with me." He opened the car door and told me to get into his car. Well, he was a policeman. He was in uniform, the car was a police car, and he had a gun in plain view. I went around to the passenger door of his car and he walked to the driver's side, but I ran back and jumped into Lamar's car and said, "Let's go!" And we went. We went like a bat out of hell, all around the Clarksboro streets and this cop chasing us with his siren screaming.

Got me again. Didn't get Lamar. Got me. He shoved me in his car and drove out to a park at one end of town and stopped. He said, "I've had my eye on you. I've been watching you at the bar. I know what you are, and tonight it's going to be you and me." I said, "You just take me wherever you're going to." I meant the jail. I thought, no matter what he said, I was under arrest; and I put it this stupid way because I was unfamiliar with Clarksboro and I didn't know where the jail might be.

I never knew what caused his sudden switch, but, when I said what I did, all at once his whole manner changed. He was frankly scared. He started saying he hadn't meant anything by what he'd said, he hadn't planned to do anything or take me anywhere, he was just kidding. He begged me not to tell anybody. I hadn't been smart enough to figure all this, but Lamar could tell a hawk from a handsaw. He knew right away what was up, not an arrest but a plan the cop had for me. Of course he couldn't know that the cop had reconsidered.

The cop drove to City Hall and he and I walked inside. The first thing we heard was a big bellow. "My friend has been kidnapped." It was Lamar, telling the world. I went over to him and pulled him outside. He wanted to go back and do something about the whole situation, but I wouldn't. I didn't want any more. I figured there had already been more than enough. We drove away and nobody hindered us.

This was only one of many incidents in this period. On Benzedrine, I would go with crowds to the beach on weekends and get not one wink of sleep. I don't think I was eating much, either. I just breezed along and never seemed to get hungry or sleepy. And as long as I kept going like that, I wasn't troubled much by the voices, at least not to the degree that I was without the Benzedrine. Then They began to trouble me even with it. And gradually it didn't help any more. I have the feeling that bit by bit I became so unbalanced that even my beach pals didn't want to be around me.

They weren't so enjoyable either. I felt they'd all changed, gone rancid somehow. It seemed that people who had been so fun-loving and good-natured and ready for anything were getting snappish, and there was a lot of squabbling. I don't recall that I was squabbling, but I don't know what strange things I might have been doing. I don't really remember what I was like. Nearly all the others were full of Bennies too. Not just me. But I'm afraid that gradually I got either frightened or overtired or both—finally I couldn't take the pace any longer—and it made me so peculiar that they didn't like to be around me any more.

Then the Benzedrine completely played out on me. Even with it, I would keep going back to my old feelings that everybody else had something to do and somwhere to belong and somebody to count on, and I was always the lone and forlorn one. When I'd feel that way, I cared terribly. Even on Benzedrine. And the voices started coming back, stabbing clear through my dopey insulation.

Outside my room at the Y I heard all kinds of things. How I could hear women in a YMCA hallway and make it seem plausible to myself, I don't know, but outside my room I'd hear men and women talking. I was living on a shoestring and overtaxing my strength and loading up on Benzedrine and all this whole mess. Then Theo came back from the Army. My brother Theo. In some peculiar way, this got me out of the mess I was in.

Theo was drinking all the time. I don't know what was upsetting him, but he was drinking heavily. He was the childlike type, and I guess he never had anybody he could count on either. Once I found out he was in jail—on a drunk charge—and I went and got him out. So from then on, when he'd use his one allowed phone call, he'd get in touch with me somehow. Sometimes he could catch me on the phone; sometimes other people would find me for him. I'd go and get him out of jail.

Then for some unknown reason I started following him.

I'd follow him down on Commerce Street, in and out of bars, and this came to replace the running around on Benzedrine with the musicians. I wasn't trying to pretend that I was so great or noble or anything of the sort, but I did tell myself that I followed Theo to keep him out of jail. I did keep him out. I'd always go to a place that I'd seen him go in—it was quite easy to find him, wherever he was—and when they'd throw him out, I'd leave. I wouldn't join him; I'd follow him. Generally he'd go to another joint, and I'd go there too and get in some dim corner. So he wouldn't see me. Finally, when he was falling-down drunk, I'd go to him and take him home.

Somehow this gave me a sense of purpose, a mission. A reason for being, really. If I ever could feel that I had a purpose, it would pull me right together. Nothing in this world ever jerked me around and straightened me up like a feeling that somebody needed me, that I was doing something that had some worth. If I couldn't do anything fit to mention for myself, then I'd try to do something for somebody else.

At the same time I was following Theo, I began hiding from Serafina. I don't know why. I just developed a fright. This would have seemed strange to her. I would dart into places when I saw her coming. One night I saw her on her way out of a movie house with some friends, and I cracked my shirttail around popping into a doorway. Once I was standing at a shelf in the Carnegie Library and I saw her across the room. I scooted around the shelf to a spot where she couldn't see me if she looked that way. WHY? I'll never know. It wasn't that she had injured me that time. That was all over. It was just part of my generally erratic behavior, I guess. But anyway I'd have this reaction of fear whenever I'd see her.

By this time I was slowing down on the Benzedrine. Following Theo, because it gave me a purpose, helped with this. For another thing, the pure-food-and-drug people had made them take it out of the sniffers. They're still on the market, but they don't have the potent stimulant. I was still taking Bennies, but only occasionally. There was a druggist in Marlowe that the boys in the band knew and I knew him through them, and he would sell Benzedrine indiscriminately, and occasionally I bought some. But things got so bad that it didn't even occur to me any longer to get it and take it.

It seemed better to follow Theo and to be exhausted than to be stimulated, because being stimulated didn't help any more. It only kept me from getting any sleep. If I could just go until I gave completely out, then I'd be better off. I would sleep from whenever I went to bed until morning. I would hear people talking, but I would go on to sleep and not listen to them, and this condition would hold for whatever was left of the night. This seemed better to me, and that's how I tapered off and finally quit taking Benzedrine.

I think it was during this period that I began to feel anger at my lot in life. Open anger. I was fed up with the tormenting voices and the hectic, harassed way I was forced to live. This anger got progressively worse and sometimes it would make me hostile. Hostile toward everybody and without any provocation. I tried to control this hostility to unoffending people, but the generalized anger was there to stay. I know that on my deathbed I'll be angry, *furious*, at what has happened to me.

When I came home from the Army, I found Robby behaving mighty strange. Could be I might have helped him some way. I don't know. When I think how things went with him later, I've been sorry that I didn't at least try. But the truth is I was in no shape to help anybody. I was all tore up and I didn't have anything to give anybody.

I'd lived through the war, and if it hadn't ruint me it sure God hadn't done me any good. For one thing, it certainly hadn't made me feel gung ho about the U.S. of A.'s military service. There was lots more, but just one thing will show. In Australia I was with combat troops from Buna coming in to Camp Doomben in Brisbane. Falling down with exhaustion and half-starved and battle-fatigued and all the rest of it, we had to pitch our own tents before we could get a meal, let alone the rest we'd been sent there for. We were so shook by what we'd been through that, a few days after we arrived, when somebody made a sudden crash, dropped a tray in the mess, every one of us disappeared under the tables in nothing flat. That's how bad off we were. Yet all the time we had been wrestling those tents around, we looked through windows right before our eyes and saw officers sitting at tables with white tablecloths and waiters serving them food and wine. As my half-French Army buddy used to say, *merde.*

Before the Army I'd quit truck driving when I had a chance to teach auto mechanics in the Marlowe Vocational School. I hadn't had formal training, but I was ever more than qualified. When I was little, I hung around Cousin Peyton's filling station. Not around the gas pumps; in the shop. I grew up in the shop. The mechanics showed me how to do things and let me work with them when I was just knee-high to a grasshopper, and it got to be that there wasn't much I didn't know about motors. This didn't qualify me, technically, to teach. They'd rather have somebody with half my knowhow, but with education courses and certificates. But this teacher had some serious health breakdown and had to take a year off. School was about to open, and they took me on because they were in such a fix. Any old port in a storm.

It was only a one-year job, but I thought it might lead to something for me. The Army got me right after my time was up at the school, and I didn't have a job to come back to. I didn't have anything else to take hold of, and I was flapping in the wind. Sure as God made little green apples, I couldn't stay home indefinitely and wash windows and the conch shell Momma used for a doorstop. As a stop-gap thing, I tried being a volunteer fireman. I soon quit that because I was as disgusted with the firemen as I was with the Army. When I joined up, they had two new fire trucks. Good trucks. But they were Chevrolets, and the firemen were bitching because they had wanted Cadillacs. They just wanted to show off. The fatheads didn't even know that Cadillac never made fire trucks, didn't make a chassis that heavy. Maybe they still don't know. I wasn't going to be the one to tell them.

One night a bunch of firemen from Highfield came by to pick a fight. Some Marlowe fireman had been making out with a Highfield fireman's girl, and he brought his buddies over to do whatever damage they could. You might think just the one would have come. And called out the fellow his girl been two-timing him with, and snatched him baldheaded. But the whole kit and caboodle came. I think the girl was an excuse. They were spoiling for a fight.

I was surprised that they'd bring weapons. I didn't figure that the Marlowe fellows would have any to fight with either. The more fool me. Things had changed while I was away, more than I knew. They all had chains and knives and they went to fighting like big-city street gangs.

Somebody called the police and they came and stopped it, but they didn't arrest anybody. Soon as they left—and they left right away—both bunches of firemen moved over to Vance Park and took up right where they'd left off. That's how much good the police did. The firemen stopped fighting when they were damn well ready to stop, and each side carted off its wounded to the emergency room to get sewed up. I quit. I had seen enough fighting, and those sonsofbitches made me want to puke.

The vanilla extract lady had to take some time off because of sickness in her family, and I knew this Mrs.

Durward. We used to buy from her. Momma always said to the girls, "Economize on other things, not on vanilla or mayonnaise." I asked Mrs. Durward if I could take her place for the duration. She sold door to door. I did that 'til she could start again, and then I subbed for a man that went way out in the country selling washable Bibles. These Bibles had imitation leather bindings that would wash, and this was supposed to be a big selling point. This Mr. Fisher impressed this on me. He never mentioned that when they were damp they smelt like castor oil. I followed his route, and I'm here to tell you I didn't like it one little bit. Those people way out in the boondocks, scratching for food to put on the table, they didn't have money to be spending that way and I felt backward about asking them. Didn't ask but precious few. One day a woman was just twisting up her apron into knots, she was so upset. She'd been laying out to buy new oilcloth for the kitchen table, but the Bibles were right pretty and she wanted one so bad she could taste it. She was thinking about using the oilcloth money for a down payment. I told her she needed the oilcloth more than a washable Bible smelling like castor oil, and I turned in those Bibles that night and didn't go out again.

Poppa would have liked for me to work the farm, get it going again; I knew that. But I couldn't see my way clear. The soil was worn out. It only takes a few tobacco crops to do that, and that might be one of the reasons Poppa had such a bad time himself. I didn't have money for fertilizer and help, and I would have needed both. You really have to put out on fertilizer. Tobacco's not like cotton except in that way. Cotton, you work hard five or six months and then you rear back and enjoy life, act like a man of leisure, which you are. Tobacco keeps you humping. This would have been too much of an undertaking for me anyhow, the frame of mind I was in. I couldn't see any hope for the future and I was sour on the world.

One while there I had vague thoughts about going to school on a GI Bill of Rights deal. I couldn't see my way clear to that either though, because I really wanted to stay home and marry Althea. I more than half-way wanted to marry her before I went overseas. No fault of anybody's, but her family situation complicated things. Her mother was dead, and she had a little sister to raise and a semi-invalid father. She had to be the breadwinner and, more power to her, she was that. But it wasn't an easy life for any of them. I thought like we used to say in school: "Althea, you done noble." I sure was proud of how she handled it all, how she kept the family together, single-handed.

I'm not proud of myself, but, when I thought about all the responsibility I'd be taking on, and how little I had to offer, I backed away from marriage. Much as I wanted to marry Althea, I backed away. Insult to injury, I did it in the biggest tomfool way in the world. I told her something like sometimes I was afraid I'd got myself into something I couldn't get out of. She said all I had to do was to "walk from here to there" and she literally showed me the door. It was after this that I turned from a hard drinker into a sot.

The big head never has been one of my troubles, but I believe I could have done better if I'd had a chance. Now I think of it, none of us has had much of a chance. We're not bad raw material. We're nothing like bad raw material. But raw material doesn't get too far right by itself. The war had beat me down. I was real, real down. I had nothing left of what Boone at the high school used to call fighting spirit. I didn't even have a rag of get-up-and-go, and nobody to steer me in any direction. Everywhere I turned, seemed like, something sprang up and blocked me. I felt aimless, and I'd lost Althea, and I took to full time boozing.

I'd always liked it, but along about that time I really went to town. I'd tank up every night at one bar after another, and

I'd drink 'til I fell over or got arrested, whichever came first. Those bartenders had changed too. Used to be they'd get you a way home. They'd got to where they'd just as soon call the cops as look at you; so I got arrested right often. The first time it went down about as easy as a hard-boiled egg. Unpeeled. After a few more times, I didn't like it any better but I let it keep happening and then I commenced to think it was no big deal. Whenever there was any kind of ruckus among the customers, I always seemed to be one of those they hauled off and put under the jail.

One of those times I got hold of Robby on the phone. They still would let you make one call. He came right away and got me out. After that I called him other times, but I couldn't always catch him. He was doing a lot of running around, and you couldn't just reach out and put your hand on him. Later, I noticed that he was following me. I'd make my rounds, one joint to another, and sometimes I'd see him in the joint I was in and sometimes I'd see him following me on the street. In my alcoholic haze, I just said to myself, "Well, I be" and kept on going.

But it was creepy. He never came up even with me and he never spoke to me. But while I was lurching along, there he'd be, darting in and out of doorways. I don't know if he was trying not to be seen by me. If he was, he was no good at it. Drunk as a lord, I still couldn't help knowing he was following me. I didn't care. I was no way up to speaking to him. I just kept stumbling on to the next stopping place. If I got so drunk I was nearly 'bout passing out, he'd come to me and stick me in a cab and get me home.

One day I ran into his fancyfaluted friend Serafina Bello on the street. I had never met her, but I knew her by sight and some way she knew who I was. She stopped me and asked about Robby. Told me he had been following *her*. She said she wondered what was going on with him, but I couldn't help her. She said they hadn't seen each other for a long time, but that lately every time she turned around he was following her. Made no sense to her, she said. She said it got on her nerves.

None of the family knew much about Robby along about that time. They were saying he was spending a lot of time with a lot of people. All kinds of different people. He was very chummy with a hard-drinking set, mostly young married couples. I knew some of them—girls from the beauty shop and the filling station fellows, and they did keep busy with the wild times. Robby was busy as a damn beaver, because besides them he was with Edmonia and her la-di-da studio crowd a lot and the people in that writing club. And, according to the best informed neighborhood gossips, with a pack of pansies too. All this at night after all day at work. I don't see how he held down that good job at Convoy with all this going on every night. I wouldn't have figured it that way, but he must have been strong as a team of oxen.

I don't know whether he was taking anything or not. He was thick as hops with some jazz musicians, and I know they were doping. He'd go from town to town with them when they played for dances, and I guess the musicians stayed spaced out most of the time. Maybe Rob was doping along with them, but then again, maybe not. Could be he was too timid to get mixed up with anything like that. After a while he must have cut loose from them, because he was following me most of the time. Even on Saturdays, their big nights.

II
ELEVEN

Kirby Northrop was the first man I ever felt really and truly wanted to share things with me. He'd call me and say he'd just read a wonderful story, and I'd go over and he'd read it to me. This charmed me, and in some way I found it comforting. He simply ignored my picked-up education and the difference between my experiences and his. He always treated me as if I were all to the good just as I was.

Serafina Bello had given me warm companionship, and, all unknowing, she had helped me resist the voices. She certainly had upgraded my taste. She had been indescribably kind and helpful. She was genuinely fond of me, but she could never forget that I was a hick. Before she introduced me to people she considered a notch up, she'd brief me. Kirby would take me anywhere with never any of this. He seemed to think I did fine. It hurts me deeply to remember this, because I don't like to think what I really know is true.

It would be hard for me to describe what Kirby came to mean to me. He drew me out. He helped me develop and grow. I used to try to draw, and I'd been taught a little during that one year of college, and I'd worked some with Momma's cousin Edmonia. But I had the same shyness that kept me from trying to learn to shoot pool in front of other people. I couldn't let them see my inept efforts. But there was a good art school in Marlowe, and Kirby took me there. The smaller the class, the higher the fee. I went into a very large class at a fee I could afford. Kirby made me know he'd be right there beside me and that nobody would ridicule my drawing. That was the sort of thing he did for me.

He was an excellent amateur photographer, and he took stacks of pictures of me; and this flattered me, but more, it made me feel that maybe I at least looked all right. There was the drawing, and the reading, and the listening to plays on records, and later a painting class.

Kirby was no culture vulture. He had grown up with all this. His father had founded and operated a talent booking agency. Mr. Northrop had inherited money, but he ran the agency because he liked doing it and he ran it successfully for years. Kirby had been around this all his growing-up years, and after his father's death he ran it and in the course of the work he met all kinds of artists.

His mother had been a piano teacher, and she said that, as far as music appreciation was concerned, he far outstripped her. He not only liked symphony orchestras, he knew the music. He not only liked ballet, he knew about it. He was even something of a patron of the arts. He contributed to different funds. And this cultivated man treated me like I was perfectly all right just the way I was.

Once he had a party for the Ballet Russe de Monte Carlo people when they were dancing in Marlowe, and I was just as much a guest as anybody else. I met Leon Danellian, Frederick Franklin, Alexandra Danilova, and John Kriza, and Kirby never said the first word to me about doing this or not doing that. He had no apologies to make for me to these glittering, glamorous people. At one performance, I was in the wings when Danilova was. To save her strength, I suppose, I don't know why else, she leaned on me. Imagine that. There were others around, but she leaned on *me*. I felt ten feet tall.

From January through spring I was at Kirby's place often, and at the beginning of summer he asked me if I'd like to go to the beach. I felt in my bones that this would mean something more intimate, although he certainly hadn't said so. I made up my mind that I thought enough of him that— well, all right, this wouldn't be so bad.

In the hotel room, while we were unpacking, he said I wasn't to worry about expenses. He said he'd be inviting me on other little trips and, while I wasn't without funds, it would be easier for him. That way, he said, he'd feel freer about suggesting trips. He said, "It happens that I have the money, and it doesn't matter." All these things he said as delicately as possible, and I decided, well, OK. I certainly couldn't pay my way for some things he might like to suggest, and this seemed to make it all right.

That evening he took me to a plush yacht club, and there were people there who were friends of his. He not only seemed happy to be with me, but happy to be seen with me. Happy to introduce me. So the evening was very pleasant. Then we went back to the room and we went to bed together.

It was then I found out that this was no better. I mean that this couldn't amount to any more than the thing with Lurleen. It was the thing with Lurleen all over. It was almost—I can't say just how I felt, but—He was—And I couldn't—. Again, there had to be a kind of disentangling and moving apart when I realized it was just no use. Kirby was like Lurleen had been, at least for a moment or so. He was just as much astounded as she was, and he couldn't see right away that I had intended to go through with it but that I couldn't and that I had to get away.

He was different from Lurleen in that he didn't make any issue of it. He was quicker to see how it was with me. He let everything drop and he eased things back into a more ordinary situation. It didn't change one thing about the way he behaved toward me. As far as I was concerned, this week-end was the howling fiasco of all time, but he was as nice as any human being could be.

After that one dreadful time, everything was smooth as a looking glass. We did all the same things we'd done before, and he made no advances. He didn't try to press me in any way, shape, or form. No matter how things finally turned out, this can't be taken away from him: he was kind, and he was a man of real refinement.

He made absolutely no difference in the way he treated me. But there was a difference in me. I knew for sure now that I was inadequate all the way around. Even though I had earlier decided that I'd make this different from the time with Lurleen, there was a little corner in my mind where I wasn't completely surprised at my failure. After all, I'd decided I'd make a go of it with *her*. With her, it would have been a matter of proving something. But with Kirby it wasn't that, but just to do something for him. And even at that it hadn't worked. I was a dud. A zero.

Kirby had given me more in kindness than anybody I'd ever known, the sort of kindness I'd never before had: total acceptance. I told myself this, and how there had been never the slightest tinge of being ashamed of me in any way, in any company. So the rest of the weekend was an agony for me. I had failed Kirby. I was a terrible disappointment. Long before, I had realized that I was not going to belong to either sex. But now it had been doubly demonstrated that I couldn't even fake it. I should have known what would happen with Kirby. But I had tried my best, and I just couldn't make the grade. And what could I do?

Sunday night, back in my own room in Marlowe, I thought this through the best I could. I realized that Kirby must—or I felt that it must mean a great deal to him, this friendship we had, because he hadn't changed after the fiasco fell on us. I decided that there were no strings, that he liked to read to me or he wouldn't do it; that he liked to take me places or he wouldn't do it; that he liked to introduce me to the kind of people he was used to or he wouldn't do it. So I finally figured that the thing I could do for him was to be as much a companion to him right along, the kind I'd been before that appalling weekend. I figured that he must be as lonely as I was, and that I could take care of this loneliness for him, and for me too, by keeping on the way I had been.

There was one time I felt that I really did do something for him. And I did, if he cared to take advantage of it. I had met a boy, a handsome boy who was working at Myrtle Beach for the summer. He had great good looks and a lot of surface charm, and he was extremely promiscuous. He almost amounted to a prostitute. I wouldn't think that money necessarily changed hands after an encounter, but he had so many valuable things that came to him as gifts that what else could they be but pay? Pay or enticements, one. Be that as it may, I introduced him to Kirby and I thought, "Well, maybe this can make up for my failings." I know nothing about anything that took place. If anything ever did take place. But that possibility was my idea in bringing them together. I saw this boy as an opportunity for Kirby if he badly wanted somebody young and good-looking to show off.

We took several short trips together, but I never let Fina know. I spent a great deal of time with her, practically lived at her place; so I had to be very careful to keep her from knowing. I'd say I was going to spend the weekend with my mother. This was useful because that was something I always did by myself. I never introduced her to any of my family. I kept Fina and my family separated, completely and utterly. She was so hell-bent on elegance—by now I was often very tired of slogging through elegance up to my navel—and she was so hypercritical that I didn't feel sure of her where they were concerned. They were simple people and I didn't want to risk her making fun of them.

I told Kirby about this, and he said something I didn't appreciate. He said, "I'm not a member of Serafina's fan club. I'd *prefer* for her not to know about the trips." She never did. And when I'd see Kirby of an evening or some time like that, even then I always would do it when she was away or doing something on her own. That summer really was quite fine for me, and the way I'd figured things out seemed to be right.

Then we went on another trip. Liquor got involved here, and that in itself was unusual. I never did much drinking when I was with Kirby. There was always liquor, but I didn't feel the need. Then, for some reason, on this trip I got plastered. Just pie-eyed. I didn't even know where I was, practically. Kirby went out next morning before I woke up. I don't know why he did that, but I woke up and he was gone. Soon he came back and said to come on and get breakfast, and we went down. At the table he said—and I wondered, approvingly? reassuringly?—"Now, last night was more like it. Last night was all right."

I didn't have the remotest idea what he meant, but he very well meant something radically different. This upset me but I was afraid to ask, and he said no more. I didn't know and I didn't want to know. It upset me that much. The only thing I remembered was being in the shower.

Kirby was considerate and kind and very discerning. I think he knew something about me that I wasn't too conscious of (but something I thought of when the Myrtle Beach boy came to my attention). He was careful not to give me presents. This was wise of him, I thought later, because that would have made me feel trapped. Bought. Up to this point— except for our fizzle at the beach—I felt I was giving as much as I got, or nearly as much. I thought this because we got along so well. This gave me so much confidence in myself that when the voices would start in on me about him—"Look at the queers," and that sort of thing—I was able to say to myself, "Let 'em rave. They don't know, and what difference do They make anyhow?" That's how much Kirby did for me. It's very seldom I've ever been able to take that attitude toward the voices; and the few times I could, it was this long ago. I couldn't begin to do it now.

We went to the beach a lot that summer, and Kirby made rafts of color photographs of me. He had had a seamstress to make up some skimpy swim trunks for me. He had a great color sense, and these trunks were the living end for color. They weren't called bikinis then, but that's what they were. He didn't give them to me. He still never gave me anything. He kept them, and he'd get them out and hand them to me when we went to the beach. I wore the gorgeous bikinis and I figured, "He likes to be seen with me in these," and I considered this a part of my doing my share for the friendship. This sounds vain, but in those days I did look pretty good. I was a farm boy and lean and muscular. I was little-waisted and I had thick black hair, and under encouraging conditions I did realize that I was good to look at. So I thought I was doing right by Kirby. He clearly took pride in being seen with me, and I kept thinking, "This is a pleasure to him and it certainly doesn't hurt me, and I'm grateful to him and fond of him."

We met a lot of weird people once at the beach. Kirby hadn't planned that. He'd just meant to go and say hello to an old friend, and we ran into this mob scene. The man insisted that we stay a while. I wanted to stay after I saw his beautiful house; I wanted to see more of it.

This man was highly talented, but debauched and simply lost. He was an interior designer—nothing he hated more than to be called a decorator—and very successful. He'd built an absolute mansion at the beach, and all sorts of people swarmed in on him there. Some just wanted a place to spend the weekend. They used him and his fine things any old way they wanted. That afternoon the house was teeming—tattooed sailors and everything. They were all over the place, eating his food, drinking his whiskey, and using his house for a place of assignation, group assignation. And, I'm sure, obliging him; he was a lecherous old man. Individually they were a sight to behold, and collectively they were lurid. They were making such a spectacle of themselves that I just walked around and stared at them and didn't feel bad about doing it.

One was spread-eagled on a wide couch, three sheets to the wind, with his arms and palms turned up. There was a broken line tattooed straight across the inside of each wrist, and below each line the words

> *Cut*
> *along*
> *the*
> *dotted*
> *line*

One was lying on his back on the floor, crunching celery sticks he was dipping into his salt-filled navel. One came up to me with the fingers of one hand curved around nothing but air, carrying his hand as if something was dangling from it. He held out his hand to me and said "Would you hold these lemmings while I go take a leak?" I took the "lemmings" and he lurched off. One was rouging his nipples. One was smearing mucilage and sprinkling glitter stuff all over the great thick mat of hair on another one's chest. They were eating grapes and everything. I thought, "Well, this is what an orgy must be."

Kirby was utterly repelled. He didn't thread his way through them, staring, the way I had done. He stood and looked around for a moment or two and then he said, "Poor in spirit and common as hell." And we left.

They hadn't been too busy with their various activities to notice us. It was clear they all thought I was Kirby's, in a way that wasn't true, and I purposely did nothing to dispel the notion. One even said, "You're his." And I even answered, "Yes." I believed that in letting them think it, I was showing that I did care for Kirby that much.

So I thought things were satisfactory enough to us both. Until one evening at Kirby's home in Marlowe. I was in the kitchen doing something or other, and he and his friend Elmo Davis were in the living room. Kirby was potted, the only time I ever saw him drunk. Coming back from the kitchen, I heard what he was saying. He was saying, "If only I could get him weaned away from that wop," and he was all but sobbing, "I could bring him around." He was telling Elmo that we had been lovers but that I was half-hearted about it, but that he knew I would come and live with him and shape up if it weren't for Fina. My oldest friend, and he kept calling her "that wop."

This was a staggering blow. I had felt that what we had together was as precious to him as to me, and also I couldn't stand to hear him talk that way about Fina. I was shaken. I knew this was the end of Kirby and me. Worse, it hadn't ever been the splendid shining thing I had thought it. It hadn't been anything.

As soon as Elmo left, I told Kirby I'd heard a lot of what he had been saying, and I told him how I felt about it. I said, "I didn't realize that it was quite this way. I'm sorrier than you could know, but what you want isn't possible now any more than it was before." He was blazing furious. He was almost swollen with rage. He said a lot of terrible things, things that I've tried to forget, before I could get to the door and leave.

I didn't hear from him, and then toward the end of the

week a package came. It was the negatives of all those stacks of photographs he'd made of me. Wrapped in toilet paper. That night I cried more than ever before or since. I believe I could have stood the hurt of losing a strong and tender friendship. I somehow stood it when it happened with Fina. But to find out what Kirby had told me, in word and deed, that was more than I could bear. It hurts me to this day. It had all been a mirage. I had been going around with my eyes dazzled, thinking everything was beautiful, and then suddenly I had to look at it clearly—and there I was, alone, afraid, a failure and a fool. All my tinsel treasure gone.

◎ It's the creamiest joke of all. Every time I think about old arty Kirby's being taken in by a stripling with hay in his hair, I nearly crack my ribs laughing. I might feel kindlier toward Kirby if he hadn't had the graceless gall to set himself up as some sort of rival to me. This was for some murky reason all his own. He'd put on that Mona Lisa smirk and ooze the message that he had something I didn't have. Puerile. Who was competing? I didn't need to and he couldn't. I've always had my lads; let him have his. The difference was that mine were always quite personable, and his never were.

Only that one, the kid who threw him over in advance, so to speak. That one was almost presentable. He was right attractive in his gamin way, but, to speak plainly, he was common. Cute but common. He had looks enough. His hair was curly as a hyacinth, and he had a fine high color. Of course that color could have been nothing more than a hectic flush. But, no doubt about it, if old Kirby had succeeded with young Wilde, it would have been the triumph of his dusty career.

Had he not started putting on such airs with me, I could

feel sorry for him. Because the kid didn't miss making Kirby the biggest fool east of the Mississippi.

The urchin was a salamander, damn his eyes, and I despise his kind. Exactly like some cheap prick-tease of a girl. Have to hand it to the lad though; he showed rare acuity, unless it was only low animal cunning. Led Kirby on from early spring all the way through fall, being coy and demure and hard to get, while he was eating food so good he'd never heard of it before and pouring fine wines down his peasant throat, having trips to the beach, and good hotels, and dances at yacht clubs—AND NEVER DID COME ACROSS. Oh, my aching ribs!

I don't condone what the fellow did. Tried something like that with me, I'd have broken every bone in his body. But I can't fight down a certain measure of grudging admiration. I can admire finesse even if I find the game unsavory. Served Kirby right. So busy with all his elegance and glamour to parade before the boy—the ballet beauties, the painting classes, the theater folk, the concert musicians.

By George, the boy was clever. To my certain knowledge, he never had one gift from Kirby. Technically. Wads of money spent on him, but no presents, nothing to keep. Oh, no. It was only friendship that was meaningful! Ha! I bet he laughed himself to sleep in the most luxurious bedrooms he'll ever see. How many bumpkins from Bentley's Creek ever lie between hand-monogrammed linen sheets? I happen to know that Kirby breaks out the linen sheets when he wants an occasion to be special.

Kirby should have shown some judgment. It's no good going that far out of your milieu to get emotionally involved. Or obsessed, or whatever he was. Oh, my eye! The fellow's beautician pals, his grammatical lapses, his recently discarded impossible shoes and his chartreuse jacket! Granted, he's a dish. Well developed without being bunchy, eyes blue as periwinkles, and all the rest. He really would have been a catch for Kirby. I wouldn't have minded a little dalliance myself. I could have had all that was necessary and pleasing to me and let it go at that. But Kirby went in over his head. Swam out too far, we used to say when we were kids at the beach. My guess is that he was getting desperate. Dat old debbil middle-age panic.

Oh, I know the day could come. Time's wingèd chariot and all that. When I'm pushing fifty—and Kirby's trampling fifty, no matter what he says—I'll undoubtedly ride not nearly so high a horse as I do now. It's even conceivable that I may get diddled in this exact same way. But I don't think it very damn likely.

Kirby has completely lost his grip. Regaling Elmo with his lachrymose drunken confidences about the whole hilarious thing! Excruciating. If he'd had sense enough to come in out of the rain, he'd have kept in mind that the boy with the auburn hair would come scampering straight to me. With a tidbit that choice, Elmo could never be content just to roll it under his tongue like a caramel. He'd strain a tendon rushing somewhere to tell it. Elmo's everybody's friend and nobody's friend. That's common knowledge. Nobody who's known Elmo for a week, and we've all known Elmo for years, would tell him anything he wouldn't just as soon see in the morning paper. Well, I don't mind saying it, I'm indebted to Robby Wilde for the best boffola of this or any year.

And N.B.: The juiciest plum of all in this rich moist cake is that the bratling not only held out on Kirby but walked out on him because Kirby spoke slightingly of his dago lady friend!

12
TWELVE

During the time I was at Convoy, worsening right up to the time I moved away, I went through the most troubled period I had had that far.

When I was at home and could keep to myself, things were less hard to handle than otherwise. If I couldn't keep to myself, it was more upsetting. (Later on, I was all day in an office and in a group, in a big room full of people at desks and that aggravated everything.) Without people around me, at home at Bentley's Creek, I learnt to manage my inner disturbance in some measure. That is, until it got too rough. It was bad with me though, even that way, because I bitterly resented having to stay by myself in order to handle things.

By "inner disturbance" I don't mean voices. When I was alone I seldom heard voices—at this time. Especially not out in the country, at home, at Bentley's Creek. (At the Y, I did.) It's true that the very first voice I ever heard was in the country, at home, but it could have been a real voice. That was the way Momma explained it to me then, and the situation was such that it could have been somebody. This is what I thought about the voices for a long, long time.

Aside from the voices, this period in Marlowe would have been stressful for me anyhow. When Fina and I broke up, this was a painful great loss. Mr. Appleby, the head man at Convoy, was going to be forced into retirement, and this panicked me for his sake and for mine. I had by then left my room and was sharing a small apartment with a friend of Lamar's, John Green Bowman, and I was having trouble with him.

John Green would be furious if I wasn't right there when he had dinner ready. I came to feel a great deal of hostility, unexpressed of course, toward him. He'd give me down the country and call me ungrateful every time I wasn't there right on the dot. I got tired of this. I was not ungrateful. But I did get so resentful that I began deliberately staying downtown and not letting him know. Then I'd hear, "There are phones." John Green would say this. Later the voices would say it too. I didn't want a tense, disagreeable kind of atmosphere in the apartment, but I decided that I was not going to be like "dumb driven cattle." I couldn't bring myself to say this to him; I could only act the way I did.

I would walk the streets at night until I felt sure it was too late for him to be up, and then I'd go home. One night I saw Mr. Warwick. The Warwicks were friends of Fina's, and I had been in awe of them. This was because by the time of our breakup I had gone down so far in my own estimation that I no longer could meet her fine friends. I never had met the Warwicks.

I never have known why I did this, but when I saw Mr. Warwick that night having a drink, I walked up to him, a rank stranger, although I guess he had seen me around, and said, "Would you give me a ride home?" I was surprised when I heard these words coming out of my mouth, and Mr. Warwick looked startled too. He took me home though; so that night was better than some other nights.

Twice it happened that, walking the streets late at night, I was noticed by men on the prowl for men. They'd pull up to the curb, and I'd just get into the car. Not knowing who they were, not knowing what they might be like, not caring, not anything. This is how crazy I was. On neither occasion did the man make any move. All the same, I began to have an inkling that they were cruising. But on both occasions, before they'd driven very far, and long before I would have been able to think how to get out, they became aware that there was something very wrong with me. Instead of my trying to get away from them, it would be that they were wanting to get rid of *me*. They'd simply stop the car and say, "Out."

And I wouldn't know why. I wouldn't know what I might have done or said, or how I might have appeared to them. This is how crazy I was. I'd feel very downcast about whatever it was that made them practically throw me out of their cars.

This was a time when day and night, day and night, day and night, there was hell to pay with the voices. I really did not know what was to become of me, and sometimes I got so dead tired that I hardly cared. It was a time of deep despair. One day, not because of any new provocation but probably because I didn't know what to do with myself, I went to the apartment at lunch time, got my few little things, and fled to the Y.

The state I was in, *God,* nobody could imagine the way it was. I started to say I couldn't stand one minute of rest. Rest was out of the question. What I mean is that I couldn't stand one single minute of not having something that I just had to do. Any time I was loose from something-to-do, I was done for.

It never would have crossed my mind at the time, blown about by all that hurricane effect I was in; but looking back, I remind myself of Preacher Parker. Preacher was a poor retarded boy who lived near Momma at Bentley's Creek. I say "boy" because that's what he seemed like, for all his pre-occupation with religion. He must have been well over thirty when I found him fallen into the creek when I myself was a boy. I had been fooling around not far from the water when I heard him shouting and raced over to see what was wrong. In between calls for help, the poor soul was praying at the top of his voice, and I heard that as I got closer. "Oh, Lord," he was bawling, "Save me, Lord." He was right at the water's edge, thrashing around. Just as I reached the bank he managed to grab on to something I couldn't see. Right that instant he stopped praying. "Never mind, Lord," he hollered. "I've got holt of a root."

For me, a root, a lifesaver, was a situation urgently calling on me to do something. Of course, *my* roots got me out of my creeks only temporarily.

One time along in this stormy period, I asked the man at the lunch stand to give me a part-time job as cashier. He did, and when I'd get off work at Convoy, I'd go down there and cashier for a while. I was doing everything I could think of to keep from going back to the room at the Y. This is the same reason that, much earlier, I had followed my brother Theo. It's true that I did keep Theo out of jail this way, but my own need was the main reason I followed him. That was not good. It was not even a healthy thing. I was just struggling any way I could to hold myself together.

It seems impossible that I could talk about it rationally like this; but even now I can't begin to tell how completely gone I was. I either had to be very busy doing something that required my attention or I would panic and have to hide. At such a time my dearest hope would have been to become invisible. I would stumble into a dark narrow place between buildings, a space I could hardly squeeze myself into, and stand there, stock-still, for hours. Until daylight.

During all that long time, I was in a peculiar mental state. I couldn't judge passage of time at all. I only knew the night was gone when daylight came. Sometimes this would seem to take forever, sometimes not long at all. Or anyhow, not awfully long. My thoughts wouldn't take definite form. They would just be little pictures in my mind. Nothing was clear, nothing had continuity; there were just these horrid mental images coming and going, coming and going. I felt battered, pounded to a pulp, but I believe now that I must have not looked like a pulp. I believe now that I must have stood there transfixed, like I'd looked at a Gorgon and turned to stone.

It wasn't fear of the Y that kept me there, wedged between two buildings. It was fear of going anywhere, being anywhere, unconcealed. Out in the open, I couldn't take it. This was a thing of sheer terror. I was all alone. I was going to be wiped out, annihilated. It was physical fear and every other kind too. I feared death less than whatever I was fearing, whatever would come before death. My death would have meant nothing to anybody else, and it would have been a relief to me.

What I was having to face was every bit as much the unknown as death. I would jam myself in between those two buildings, and I'd be hidden. This was the only place I could stay, and I couldn't budge out of it. I felt somewhat safe in there because not a living soul knew where I was. Because nobody knew, and this gave me some degree of safety, the voices would stop.

I would always carefully pick the time to pop into this hiding place, a moment when there were no cars going by and nobody in sight. That way, nobody saw me go in. Nobody knew where I was. So the voices would stop. No matter how many cars and people went back and forth after I was packed in. But if I took one step out when there was traffic on the street, every car that passed would be full of people talking about me. Saying terrible things.

I did this hiding between buildings quite often. Some nights though, when I was scared spitless but not at the uppermost level of fear, I would walk to sections of town that were quiet. There'd be nobody around, there'd be long stretches where there were no houses or anything, and I'd just wander. If I saw a police car, I would hear voices. Not directly from the police to me, but there would be questions and comments. "Wonder what he thinks he's doing, walking way out here." Or, "*Look* at him. Way out here." The voices always said that a lot: "*Look* at him." But this didn't upset me too much then, because I figured that's only what anybody would say.

All this time, while I was hiding, walking, wandering, I would be thinking that everything I'd ever done, while not horrible in reality, could be made to look horrible. Like church. I'd been to church to try to find something, and I'd felt hypocritical. I didn't feel grief when Poppa died, and I was disturbed by that. Everything was rotten, especially me. I had long since come to the feeling that hounds me, the feeling of complete worthlessness. Everything I did was motivated by the same need, the same wanting to be accepted, to be a part of something, to belong somewhere. Yet everything this moved me to do could so easily be twisted into something else.

It's hard to believe, but all this time I was so frenzied and frightened and beside myself, and standing like a stone statue half the night without stirring—all this time, at work I looked as normal as anybody in the world. I could sit there and do my work. I could sit there and talk with Claudia when she took breaks from the switchboard. I could go to the jail even, a thing that would ordinarily scare me stiff, and get Theo. It was whenever I came loose from whatever was anchoring me—Claudia, my work, Theo—the whole wild terror would commence again. Solid terror. I was going to be wiped out.

I would be afraid of physical attack. I was sure that sooner or later somebody was going to attack me. I didn't have any particular person in mind, but somebody was going to give me a sandbag in the back of the neck or something equally or much more terrible. Generally it seemed to me that They were gathering around to drag me off somewhere. I don't know where. They were going to jump on me, right then and there. They were going to take me somewhere and get me out of the way. Do away with me, once and for all.

I didn't think in terms of a mob, but more than one. As a matter of fact, the single individual never did bother me much. The fear that most people have when they go into dark alleys or dangerous areas is the fear of being robbed and hurt, knocked down by a robber and probably badly beaten up and injured. The idea of assault by just one never scared me. Yet my behavior invited this, and I don't know why it didn't happen. I really don't.

But as I think back to it, maybe my behavior didn't invite it. Maybe my behavior did, in that I was doing this crazy thing, but maybe my demeanor didn't invite it. I believe maybe something about me frightened even any mugger that might have been around. My brazen boldness, something like that. On the rare occasion when I did meet somebody, I'd speak to him. This would be disarming to somebody all set to be the aggressor. Of course this isn't why I'd speak to him. I'd speak to keep him from hearing what I was hearing.

This is only my own idea; I couldn't know what any muggers might have been thinking. But they could have been thinking that here was not a person to jump on and rob. "He's much too bold and brassy," they might have thought. "I might get mugged myself." You might think I would have looked like an easy mark, scared and shook up as I was, but I don't believe I did. Not now, looking back at it. I never sauntered along or looked aimless. I'd step out right smartly and try to look as if I were on my way somewhere. If I'd see somebody coming, I'd pick up in my step. I would move confidently. Not fast and not with big long strides, but I'd move along and I'd be with him before he could be with me.

Facing somebody, I could see that they weren't saying anything. But I didn't want them to hear what I was hearing; so I'd talk to them. This doesn't mean that I would talk loudly. You always study people's facial expressions under these circumstances, and I could see by that that they weren't hearing what I was hearing; so I never needed to shout or anything like that. I just kept on talking. My need wasn't to drown out the voices, but to engage this person's attention and distract him from the voices. And I'd watch his face to see how well I was doing this. I think my very craziness probably was the thing that kept me from having a great deal of trouble with thugs.

It was strange, but even in this kind of time, in the very worst of times, I could be pulled right out of it by knowing that somebody needed me. (The hope and almost prayer of my life was that somebody would need me and want me.) One night I had managed to make myself go to the Y from work, but I hadn't been able to sleep for the noise of the voices. At 3:30 in the morning I was sitting there, with the parking lot outside just alive and clamorous with loud jeering and the hall outside my door just the same. It was maddening.

Then all of a sudden came this "Help! Help!" from the hall.

I went out my door, and this involves two things that I can't explain. First, I don't know how in the name of God I managed to go out the door. That was the very thing I was most afraid to do, to go out there in the hall where the voices were. I don't know how I could make myself go out the door because somebody called for help. But it was a very distressing cry, and I opened the door and went out into the hall.

What a sight! Practically every man up and down the hall had his door cracked and was peeking. Like you'd think I'd be doing. Ordinarily, I wouldn't open my door even a slit and peek out, because out there was where the voices were. Anyhow, I had got into the hall and I went to the room where the cry was still coming from. It was easy to tell which room, because of all the ones eliminated by heads sticking out. I went in. He was an older man, and there was blood all over the bed. The man at the desk in the lobby said later, "It must have looked that way to you, but there really wasn't all that much blood." It looked to me like the whole bed was bloody. Actually there was a certain amount of blood on the sheets. The man had had an operation and the incision had broken open.

Incredibly, while all those normal fellows were standing around like Lot's wife turned to a pillar of salt, I did everything. I got an ambulance, I went with the man to the emergency room, I stayed with him until they looked after him and got him comfortable. I stayed until he was all fixed up and in bed in a hospital room. While I was doing all this, every voice had gone silent.

I got back to the Y at daybreak, and I didn't feel the least bit different. I didn't have any lasting respite from the voices, and I didn't feel any gratification that I'd done a good thing either. It had been almost a relief to have had it to do. I never had one small thought that I'd done anything fit to mention until I got the letter from the director of the Y.

◎ Dear Mr. Wilde: On behalf of everyone employed at this branch of the YMCA, I am writing to express our gratitude for your coolness in an emergency and your great helpfulness to Mr. Thomas a few nights ago.

Our night clerk, who is highly competent in more usual circumstances, is old and far too frail to have managed alone in such a crisis. Mr. Carpenter has said that he will be

135

eternally thankful for your taking charge and doing all that needed to be done. I understand from the hospital that Mr. Thomas is mending well and will soon be able to return to us.

It has distressed me to reflect that, as Mr. Carpenter tells me, with ten or more men on the floor, only one responded to a call for help. I do not believe that people use the word "help" in that fashion except in urgent need. I am thankful for your compassion and your humanity, and your readiness to step forward solely on your own initiative and without encouragement or support from any other person.

Yours was a Christian act. You are a fine example of what the YMCA stands for.

With kindest personal regards, I am,

Sincerely
Noble Jones
Director, Marlowe YMCA

13
THIRTEEN

At Convoy Motor Freight, it was a highly out-of-the-ordinary attachment we had, my boss, his assistant, and I. I don't care how poor or thin in texture it may seem compared with some people's friendships, I know this one included a considerable degree of kindliness and genuine regard and affection, and for years it meant everything to me.

Long before my time, Mr. Appleby and Johnsie had begun an affair that went on regular as clockwork. He was married—to a real roughhewn kind of woman; Johnsie was single. They were very discreet. I was the only person they ever discussed this with, and that came about because of our mutual liking. It may have been that in the beginning Mr. Appleby thought I might be slightly disturbed and that therefore he could use me, in exchange for which he'd put up with some small irregularities. But I think the reason he remained lenient with me was more that he liked me and because I did do my job well. I was cashier.

He would let me go in at night by myself, and this I liked. Nobody else could be there at night. For everybody else, it was 8 to 5 and that was it. Many nights, in troubled times, I worked quite late. This was a boon to me, and, because of it, the work never suffered. Naturally I felt gratitude toward this kindly man. I came to like him very much. There came times when I could smooth certain ways for him and Johnsie, and I did it gladly. I don't know, maybe everybody in the company was on to them, but we thought nobody was and we always behaved as if nobody was. So did everybody else, so maybe they didn't know. I know Mrs. Appleby did hear something, somewhere, at least one time.

Aside from Mr. Appleby, and of course that meant Johnsie, I had next to nothing to do with the others at Convoy. I didn't dare. I was hearing voices all the time and of course I thought they were hearing the same things I was, and I couldn't go through all that elaborate cover-up that was my only defense. Not with that many people. Convoy was a pretty good-sized outfit, and they were too many for me. I would have exhausted myself in less than one day if I'd had to do all that nonstop chattering and smiling at each one in my effort to divert them from what the voices were saying about me. Besides, it had to be some of the Convoy workers who were the voices, and I would never have known from one encounter to the next who had been maligning me and was now pleasantly chatting with me. It would have been too much. It couldn't be dealt with. All I could do was to be very, very reserved. I don't think I was ever rude to anybody, but I did rather hold myself aloof, and I'm sure I looked stuffy and stuck up to them.

The special relationship I had with Mr. Appleby made it possible for me to keep my job there long after I couldn't have held it anywhere else on earth. After I'd been there a few years, real solid, steady as a die, I began having a lot of trouble with myself. It was during this period that there was the ghastly escapade with Lurleen.

After I'd been ramping around all weekend with the married couples, dancing and drinking all night and leading a fairly wild existence, I'd be late to work on Monday. Mr. Appleby would never say anything about it. Sometimes I'd be away from work a couple of days at a time without even calling in. Nine times out of ten, on these occasions I'd be cowering in my room at the Y, scared stiff, with the voices accusing me full tilt. I sanctioned an adulterous affair, they said, in a sense was party to it, just to hang on to my job.

This may have been partially true, who knows? But it certainly was entirely true that I liked Mr. Appleby. He was friendly, and he and I exchanged books. I liked Johnsie, too, and the three of us spent some time together, just talking. Johnsie was a nice, simple girl, out of what she lovingly called the red hills of South Carolina. She adored Mr. Appleby, and had kept on for many years with this back-street kind of situation that must have been sad for her.

I don't know how much her family knew about her and Mr. Appleby, but they were straitlaced folk, and, in her own mind, Johnsie was forever cut off from them. Cut off as she felt, she still kept such a sense of family that I would get sick with envy, and, in a way, almost resentful of her, but just momentarily. I used to like to hear her talk about them. She'd tell about going to the cemetery as a young girl, even as a child, with her mother. She'd tell how her mother would point out the different ones' graves. It was from a headstone that she found out that her Uncle Leon's name was Leonidas. And Uncle Lee's, Leander.

"There's your Uncle John, your father's oldest brother you're named for."

"But his grave is sideways to all the others."

"It was a matter of space in the lot. But it doesn't matter; poor John went sideways all his life."

Across the head of Earle's grave was a flat, narrow strip of granite with a Georgia marble whiskey bottle a yard high at each end. Johnsie said her mother headed off any sassy remark, the first time she saw this, by saying quietly but firmly, "It was his wish. It meant something to him." This uncle had owned a small interest in the Lost Cause Liquor Company that still produces and bottles a fair grade of straight bourbon. Johnsie said her teetotaling mother would have gone straight up in the air if anybody else had to do with a liquor company. Earle was her prime favorite though, and he could do no wrong. Johnsie used to wonder if, all the same, this liquor business and the outlandish headstone were a well-covered private grief to her mother.

When she was just a small child going to the cemetery with her mother, she liked looking at the different kinds of tombstones. She said she used to pet the stone lambs on the tiny graves of infants, not in any real sense aware of what had happened to the babies. She remembered the broken shaft that meant her mother's Aunt Arabella had died young. When she talked about her mother and her aunt pulling weeds and keeping their parents' and kinfolks' graves neat, and planting evergreens—ivy and holly were symbols of eternal life, her mother said—I felt sad for her. I almost grieved that she had strained or at best weakened ties with her immediate family. It may sound like greeting-card sentimentality, but Johnsie had sacrificed a lot to be with Mr. Appleby, and I admired her and wished she'd not got such a raw deal from life. I couldn't see that she and Mr. Appleby were hurting anybody. There was no scandal to embarrass his wife, and she and Mr. Appleby hadn't been congenial for ages and ages.

I'm sure Mr. Appleby was fond of me, but then too I was doing him a favor by sometimes covering for him. One Saturday afternoon he was at Johnsie's apartment, and he telephoned me in a great flap and said his wife had driven up and was sitting in the parking lot. I dashed straight to the apartment house, went in the back way, got his car keys, came out the front way, walked over to Mrs. Appleby and spoke to her. I said Johnsie was sick and I had brought her some groceries, and I got into Mr. Appleby's car and drove away. Later I came back and got him. There must have been some special reason for that afternoon; usually they wouldn't have been so careless as for him to go to her place in broad open daylight. Anyhow, there were these two possible reasons to explain his putting up with my erratic behavior: liking and indebtedness. I was at Convoy ten years before it all blew up in our faces.

There was one other thing. For all I had been so thankful when they took me on at Convoy, they should have been equally thankful to have me. I was in my early twenties but exempt from the military because of a double hernia and poor eyesight. This was during World War II, when young men at home were mighty scarce. That was when war plants and companies started talking about how they'd have to make do with "Negroes and cripples and women."

When Mr. Appleby was approaching retirement age, a new manager was sent to the office. This change was handled very crudely. Cruelly, really. No official announcement was made, not even to Mr. Appleby in private. It was quite obvious from the start, however, that this Walker Barfield was there to replace him. This was terribly upsetting for the three of us. It would spell ruin for us all.

Johnsie and Mr. Appleby were heartsick, because of course it meant the end for them. He'd be retired and at home, and he'd have to have excuses to be away from the house and there'd be no job to furnish excuses. They'd be broken up, and they were devastated at the prospect. They'd been together—in the office every day besides the other—for years, and they'd been faithful to each other.

I worried a great deal about myself, because the voices were after me about how I'd never be able to keep the job without Appleby to put up with me. Before that job, I hadn't had a good one. In 1939, jobs were pretty hard for inexperienced young fellows to find. That was the reason Roosevelt founded the National Youth Administration, and after I finished high school I worked for the NYA, getting experience. After that my folks scraped together money for me to go to the state college in Highfield, but after one year they couldn't keep it up. Then a family friend got me a job at a textile mill, but the mill was a horrible place. My job there—well, all I was doing was toting heavy loads and making nothing. I'd have been wretched at the mill even if I hadn't got a double hernia from the work. I was young and I had *some* ambition. I wanted to do something, and I was sure I was smart enough but I hadn't learnt any skill. I felt not really qualified for anything. I had had some commercial classes in Highfield and some work as stock clerk while I was with the NYA, but that was about all I had going for me. But—and I always felt it was only because so many men were going into the Army—I got a job as clerk at Convoy Motor Freight.

To me, at that time—those were hard times—the clerking job seemed quite a plum, and it seemed so to my family too. I remember how Willene prayed that I would get this spot. I thought that was sweet, because she really did believe. When I told her I had the job, she beamed all over and said, "Pure cashmere!"

This expression went way back. When I was little, one of our older relatives on Momma's side, my great aunt Myra, had a cashmere shawl. Outside of my grandfather's gold watch and chain and Momma's one cut-glass bowl, it was the only luxury item I remember in the family. When Aunt Myra would come to the house, she used to let me feel the shawl. I'd stroke it and pet it and all but swoon with delight, and she'd say, "Pure cashmere." I had no earthly idea what cashmere was, but I drew a connection. Her tone was a mixture of almost reverential awe and deep satisfaction. I picked up that "pure cashmere" meant "perfectly wonderful." I applied the term to anything I placed very high in my childhood value system—Georgia cane syrup, a bag of beautiful marbles, blooming dogwood tree, a brand-new box of Crayolas, anything. The others began to use it that way too. I'm sure if I'd grown up to be the one who first broke the sound barrier, Willene or somebody would have said, "Pure cashmere!"

So that's how it was when I got the beginning job at Convoy. Pure cashmere. I made a rapid rise, and soon I was cashier. Now, ten years later I thought I had done pretty well with that, but the world seemed to be coming to an end for me and Johnsie and Mr. Appleby. More than once we all three sat together in his office, crying. It was a terrible time.

I was very much afraid of this man Barfield. He was shaking my security. I knew for sure he was not going to be good for me, because I saw that he wasn't good to the older men and his whole demeanor was discouraging. Besides, Johnsie knew him, and she expected him to be ruthless. She'd been with Convoy nearly thirty years. It was the only place she'd ever worked, and she knew everybody. She said, "I didn't like Barfield when cotton was *high*. He's a cold fish. There's no kindness in him, and we're in for it." Then one day it was all over and Mr. Appleby was gone.

First thing Barfield did, he was determined not to have Johnsie as his assistant. (Ordinarily anybody who'd been there as long as she had wouldn't be replaced.) And he didn't bring anybody with him, either; he just flat wasn't going to have Johnsie. Right away he started interviewing women. More than that, it was plain that there was no place in the office for Johnsie to be transferred. He wouldn't have fired her after all those years, but I think his idea was to give her such a hard time that she'd eventually leave. But somebody had to leave right away if he was to have a new assistant. Even he couldn't very well just toss Johnsie out; she had to have a

143

job. So he gave her mine. I could feel my security melting and running away from me.

Claudia's vacation was late that year and she was going away; and, after Barfield made Johnsie cashier in my place, he put me on the switchboard as a relief operator. On the *switchboard,* after I'd been handling all the money in the place for ten years! And when there were women right in the office who already knew how to operate the switchboard and I didn't. This was the crowning blow.

The job as cashier had given me stature with my family and with myself, and now it was gone and I had sunk to relief switchboard operator. My grandmother's prediction had come true. When I first went to Convoy as a clerk, she was green with envy. She had two grandsons she was extremely fond of, and she'd rather one of them had got the job. So when I got it, she threw off on it. "Just answering the phone," she'd tell people. Belittling. She was the only really nasty one, but now I had no prestige anywhere—not at the company, not in the family, not in my own eyes, not anywhere at all. I went to pot. Right then. All at once.

I would get myself soused. Regularly. Incidentally, Barfield's way with dirty work was what we called talcum powder on top. He played this asinine thing that he was intimidated by these middle-aged snappish women and didn't dare ask them to do the switchboard. Intimidated! He'd have ground their bones to make his bread if he'd felt the slightest need. He let me know that I was to relieve on the switchboard until after vacations, and then I could be Johnsie's assistant—and her in my job!—if I wanted "to stick around."

So I would get soused and come to work that way. I'd be on the switchboard all right, but whenever I felt like it I'd cut people off. Sometimes I'd tell callers I was in no mood to fool with them. I'd say, "Don't bother me. Go work out your own schedule." It just didn't seem to matter to me. This didn't at all mean that I was any the less hurt or the less concerned that I was losing control of myself. I rapidly reached the place where I had no control whatever. I couldn't stay on that switchboard unless I was practically stumbling drunk. I couldn't *get* on it unless I was practically stumbling drunk.

After a couple of days of this, Mr. Barfield called me in. He didn't say a word about my fouling up the switchboard job; he just asked me if I'd like to go to the Asheville office. I didn't want to go anywhere, so I said no. Shortly after that I found myself saying around the place, in a spasm of defiance, that he needn't worry his head about me, I was planning to leave the company.

One day soon, Mr. Barfield called me in again and said, "I've heard that you're planning to leave, and I think this might be the best thing. You go on now, and I'll give you two weeks' salary and your Christmas bonus." So there I was. I had no choice. I said sure, I'd go, I already had plans to go to Columbus, Ohio.

It was sheer bravado. I just pulled Columbus out of thin air. But from the minute I made that swaggering remark, everywhere I went, every step I took, the voices were jabbering and squawking. "Look at him—Fired!—knew this would happen sooner or later—knew he'd get it—finally caught up with him—Now they know what he is—fired—never get a job anywhere now!—fired—"

So I did begin to think in terms of Columbus. I'd been there once to visit and I'd met a few people, and I wouldn't feel altogether lonesome and strange there. And I did have to have a job, and I felt disgraced in Marlowe. So I made plans. But this didn't stop any of the hullabaloo. Everywhere I went. "Fired!" Every step I took. "Fired!" Every breath I drew. "Fired!" There was no way I could turn to escape from the voices.

It was a sight for sore eyes, mine and those of the other girls who sometimes worked the switchboard, to see that highflighty Robby Wilde get what was coming to him. I ought to be ashamed to own it, but I was glad when Mr. Barfield fired him.

We all took to Rob when he first came in the early war years. He was a soft-spoken young fellow with a spring in his step, and good-looking. He seemed shy. Later, I guess being the Convoy cashier at his age went to his head. Then too, we couldn't help but notice that Mr. Appleby was partial to him. It never helps an office atmosphere when the boss shows partiality.

Some of the younger women were miffed because he didn't show any interest in them. I call most of us "girls" by courtesy. We were more than twice his age. So it wasn't a matter of his not paying any personal attention to us. It was more an air about him. The thing was, there was something about Rob that made us feel like country-come-to-town. Ridiculous. For all his smart clothes and his sort of formal manner, it was Rob had come in from the country. We had always been town people. All the same, he made us feel country-come-to-town, and dull and frumpy to boot. Not that Rob ever breathed a word of anything to suggest any such attitude. He was too well-mannered for that. But he *did* so different, and it was so noticeable, that he must have felt that way. Him and his white-on-white shirts, and cuff links at work, and "This is he" on the phone, and never ever putting his elbows on the table if he did condescend to go and have a glass of iced tea with some of us. Maybe he didn't know that we had known so well and for so long not to put our elbows on the table that we could do it if we felt like it. In other words, we thought his table manners were a little too dainty for the Convoy cafeteria, so maybe they were new to him. None of this would have made a jot or tittle of difference if he'd been a little nicer to us. What I mean is if he'd acted like we were nicer.

Rob didn't have any call to be biggity around us. I'll tell you who he is. His mother, Mamie Millington that was, is from a branch of a rather substantial family. Not high and mighty, just rather substantial. Druggists, county employees, country lawyers, people like that. Her uncle married a distant relative of my mother's. Robby's father was a good, honest fellow, but the Wildes were what you might think of as plain people. Nothing wrong with them, just plain people. As I say, Robby came from good enough stock, but the rest of us came from good stock too.

If it came to that, you could have found, right within that city block around Convoy, some of the bluest blood in North Carolina. Not all of it behind mahogany desks at the Farmers and Merchants Bank either. This may not cut much ice in some places, but it does here. Some of us have got family behind us even if we don't have much else. It doesn't matter what you *do*. Look at Randall Stockdale. His mother was a Vance, and he's spent his entire working life behind the General Delivery window at the Post Office.

Some of us at Convoy were mature women, and I guess we *were* kind of frumpy but in a nice way. We certainly weren't the glass of fashion. I know perfectly well that some of Robby's former cronies at the beauty shop used to laugh at us. They made fun of us for wearing Enna Jettick shoes and our grandmother's bar pins. If they'd ever heard us mention having something long enough to wear the new off, they wouldn't have known why we thought that desirable. They literally would not have known what we were talking about. Raw shiny new is all they put any stock in. And quantity, not quality. Naturally they thought we were antedeluvian and poked fun at us. I failed to see the humor, but there are times when you simply have to consider the source.

The way *they* dressed was a caution. Ankle bracelets, lots of rhinestones, and new dresses on Easter Sunday. None of us would have dreamt of wearing a new dress on Easter Sunday. Not even our young ones like Stella and Vanessa Livesey, who had been clothes crazy from the cradle, did that. (I can still hear Vanessa,when she was in the toddlers' class at Sunday school, warning another tot, "Don't step on my pretty new shoes.") Those girls were determined to have Easter dresses, and I guess their mother had them on her hands. But after they were getting to be grown young ladies, Corrie Livesey wouldn't have let them get out of the house on Easter Sunday in brand-new dresses.What those girls did— they really were a caution—they had Easter dresses, no matter how much they said they didn't. How they managed it, they got new dresses early and wore them first on Palm Sunday. Then on Easter they could claim they weren't new. That's the way their minds worked. One year, before Corrie knew what they were up to, they gave up movies for Lent— unless somebody took them.

It wasn't only the way those Beauty Spot girls dressed; it was the way they went about things. One of them, Darleen Martin I think, was married in Luray Caverns,Virginia. She was enraptured by the idea of the enormous stalactite formation that can be played like a pipe organ. Not to be outdone, Willie Pearl Williamson married Buck Henderson in a burning building. Buck was a fireman. This tumbledown building on the outskirts of Marlowe had been condemned and the Fire Department instructed to destroy it. Buck had said that the two most exciting things in his life were being a fireman and getting married; so Willie Pearl suggested that he combine the two, and he was thrilled to a nub. They took their matrimonial vows while the house was on fire. With Buck wearing full fire-fighting regalia. Willie Pearl, weighed down by mascara and heavy layers of green eyeshadow, clumped up the improvised "aisle" in rubber boots and a coat borrowed from the smallest fireman. She must have been a perfect sight. The preacher wore a helmet. As far as I know (I only read the newspaper account), nobody carried an axe.

That was their style. So it's easy to see why they thought of us older women at Convoy as sticks-in-the-mud.

As for Rob, to tell the truth, I can't say I ever knew him to do anything to get fired for. It just got next to us the way he was always hobnobbing with Mr. Appleby and Johnsie. Johnsie never put her nose in the air, but, with her job as special assistant to Mr. Appleby, she was about as high on the ladder as you could get and she had been for a coon's age. She could have run that place as well as Mr. Appleby, but women didn't have jobs like his. Rob was with them lunch time, coffee break, all the time. Too grand for the rest of us.

He could have been in frail health. He looked strong, but he got to where he'd be absent right often and he'd catch up with his work at night. I know he did, because he told me himself, and right there that meant he was mighty fair-haired boy with the boss. Nobody else could have got in after five o'clock. Far be it from me to begrudge a helping hand to somebody who's not well, but, at the same time, there's not a one of us couldn't have lain up in the bed many a morning if we'd had the chance to work at a more convenient time.

We couldn't hold it against Rob that he was a civilian while the rest of us had sons and brothers and nephews overseas. It was a known fact that he'd had an operation for double hernia simply so he would be eligible for the draft. We had to hand it to him. But they kept him in 4F anyhow because his eyes were so bad.

Speaking only for myself, I don't think it was gossip that hurt him at the company. I never batted an eye at the talk about him and Serafina Bello. Or Willise Grady either. If there was anything between him and Serafina, well, young men have their wild oats to sow and he wouldn't have been robbing the cradle and he'd have been doing well by himself. And, if the truth were told, I imagine Willise was no better than she should be, with her husband off driving that Trailways bus all over creation.

No, it was something else that worked against Rob with the new man. What, I never knew. I only know what turned me against him. It wasn't his manners; it was his manner. I know exactly and precisely what sort of thing stuck in my craw. One day Rob did me the great honor to invite me to have lunch with him in the coffee shop. He opened the door for me and he held the chair for me, but it was more like he was doing the proper thing than like I was somebody these things should be done for. That's the way he came to make me feel about him. And that's why, though I haven't got a mean bone in my body, I was glad to see him come down in the world.

PART THREE
1950-1961

14
FOURTEEN

Too late, I realized that I never should have shot my mouth off and offered to leave Convoy at once. I was trying to do something in my favor, trying to show Mr. Barfield I didn't care. And I didn't do it right. I didn't have a leg to stand on. I should have stayed as long as possible, attempted to hang on to *something* as long as I could.

I thought it would be all right to go out home and stay; but it turned out to be impossible. Everything got on my nerves. I didn't know then that it was nerves. I thought the family kept coming in purposely when I didn't want them bothering me. And neighbors would come. Mrs. Stone came often, and she'd bring little Ramona with her. Ramona had her family troubles too. The Stones had some nice pieces of old furniture that had come down in their families, and they were very particular about them. When Ramona was very young, they had warned her off them so much and so emphatically that until she was nearly three years old she thought her name was No-No. If you'd ask her what her name was, she'd say, "No-No Stone."

When Ramona got fidgety at the house—I think she felt surrounded by hostile adults—she'd take refuge in Momma's old upright piano. She'd sit there and thump out "Marche Facile" and "Spinning Song." Over and over. That didn't bother me except in the sense that everything bothered me at that time. But it bothered the others. She would sense their irritation and make a shaky start on "Polish Drinking Song." This only made a bad matter worse, because she didn't really know it by heart. Often when Momma and the others had reached the place where they couldn't stand Ramona any longer, I had reached the place where I couldn't stand them any longer. At that point, I'd take Ramona out in the back yard and we'd string four o'clocks. Some were still blooming. In the house with the pestiferous family and neighbors or in the back yard stringing four o'clocks, I was miserable. I couldn't be up and I couldn't lie down. I couldn't stay home and I couldn't go out. I wanted to be home and I didn't want to be home. I didn't know what I wanted. I couldn't sleep. When I couldn't sleep, this worried Momma and she worried me.

All my things were still in the room at the Y, and I went back there for the last two weeks I was in North Carolina. That last two weeks is almost a total blank in my life. I was ab-so-lute-ly in flight the whole time. In my head, I knew exactly how the job was terminated. But in my interpretation and in the interpretation of the voices, I had been fired. The Convoy people had finally found out what a no-good bum I was. This new man saw right through me, he had more sense than the old one, and he had got rid of me the first crack out of the box. It finally happened: "*Look* at him—You can see what he is— This new guy knows—That's why he got rid of him." On and on, with no letup.

In my room I'd take this as long as I could, and then I'd go out. On the street. I didn't want to see anybody, I didn't want anybody at all around, because they'd hear too, and I wasn't up to the effort of putting up a front and keeping them from hearing. It was no good on the street either. Nothing helped. I'd go back to the room and I would drink. It was incredible, the amount of liquor I could sit there and consume. Nobody would believe it. And this time the liquor didn't help either; just the opposite. The more I'd drink, the worse the voices would get. Not only that, I couldn't black out, try as I did. After a while this is what I was after, to pass out, to have a little time of unawareness.

At intervals I would rush back outdoors. I would walk up to perfect strangers on the street and say, "Please, would you come with me? I'll give you anything if you will." Some people were horrified, some weren't, some would laugh, some didn't know how to take it and just wondered what in the world was going on. Nobody went anywhere with me. Not that I remember. And I don't think, under the circumstances, anybody would have.

I do remember that one night in the room at the Y I was playing "La Boheme," an aria that Mimi sings, and I must have been playing it over and over; I've got the record now, and it's very easy to set the needle down right where she commences. Somebody knocked on the door, which of course scared me. I somehow managed to open it, and this boy said, "I heard the music." I yelled, "Go away! You're one of the people that's—you're talking—you're trying to find out something! If you come back, I'll throw you out the window!" He was astounded. I can remember the look of utter shock on his face.

That's the way I would act. That's the condition I was in. I wanted somebody; oh, I wanted somebody. And yet, anybody I saw, they were the talkers, the tormentors. So what could I do? It was maddening.

Well, I was supposed to leave on a Saturday, and, in this chaotic state, I never would have made it without Lamar. He came, and I was simply sitting and not turning a hand to get ready. I hadn't been able to buy a bag even, and I didn't own one. Lamar looked at his watch and then he tore out and came right back with a secondhand bag he'd bought from one of the porters. It was a please-don't-rain bag, nothing but slightly glorified pasteboard; but at the moment I didn't notice, let alone care. Lamar cared, but he said. "It'll have to do." I kept on sitting like a bump on a log.

Lamar still thought this sort of thing in me was a sign of undiscovered genius, artistic sensibility; so he fell to and did everything. I have never seen a bag packed so well. He had that sort of mind. His own efficiency apartment was just so, every little cubby hole organized. He said he knew where every grain of rice was, and I never doubted it. Not for a moment. And this is the way he packed. He had more stuff in that one bag, and so neatly arranged.

I don't recall that I asked Lamar to come and help me get away, but he belonged to Vashti's Pen Club and they all knew I was going. They thought it was wonderful. I never said this, but they figured that Ohio State University was there in Columbus and that I'd be going back to school and would then have more opportunity. This is how they figured, and I knew it and let it go at that.

I was in a bad way during the time I was most active in the Pen Club. More than once I would get up and leave in the middle of a reading of somebody's story. They thought I was leaving because I was so brimful of artistic temperament and the story was no good and I was disgusted. What it was, I walked out at the moment that I couldn't take the voices one second longer. I was *crazy,* and the crazy things seemed to them brilliant and far out. This is the way they were. They glamorized everything. One of them had told me about his girlfriend, and he said she had honey-colored hair. I met her, and her hair was tan. Lamar had all these half-baked notions about me, so he came and packed and carried me to the bus station. Like I was above all that mundane kind of thing.

Once on the bus, I went to the farthest back seat and huddled in it. I thought at any moment I would start screaming. I felt I was just going to let go and shriek as loud as I could. That was why I got on the very back seat. I thought if I could get completely out of everybody's sight, then they wouldn't talk and maybe I could hold this thing down and not make any outburst. I desperately hoped the bus would get going before everything broke loose with me.

The pillow girl came back there, and she was somebody I knew. She had worked at Convoy some time back. She said, "You're an employee," and she winked. "Here's a pillow." Free. I can't imagine why, but that little personal kindness calmed me. For the moment, the terror left me.

There weren't many passengers, and that worked against me. Because there were so few I could hear people up front talking. Soon they were saying things about me. They kept it up, and I thought they must be people who knew me. It was rough. I thought the only thing for me to do was to get off the bus at the first opportunity and get to Columbus some other way. I thought that when we got to the first stop—Greensboro, I suppose—I'd leave. The pillow girl had calmed me enough that I could stay on the bus without going to pieces at least until it left the terminal at Marlowe. But when we got to Greensboro, I couldn't make it to the door of the bus. I simply could not get up and walk to the front of the bus. If I had got off, I don't know what I would have done. Started hitchhiking, I guess, because I didn't have enought money to buy another ticket.

This was all taking place at night, and the dark made it harder for me. If it had been daylight, I think I would have fared better. When this unknown thing was all around me, this terrible danger I couldn't get at and try to deal with, generally during daytime somebody would be available and I'd start talking to whoever that was. So in the day I could handle things much better. I could generally manage if there were only one or two people near me. I would just run my tongue, trying to hold their attention, to distract them and maybe keep them from hearing the voices I was hearing. But I couldn't talk a blue streak to people at the other end of the bus any more than I could a whole big staff at Convoy. On this trip, it was really more the bus situation than the dark that gave me such a bad time.

It was daylight by the time we got to Charleston. I had to change busses there, and I thought, "I'll cash a check. I must have some money in the bank." Then I realized that I didn't know whether I did or not. I really did not know what my financial condition was. I decided I'd better not cash a check. I could have. In those days people would cash checks for you. I hadn't eaten for a long time, so I had some coffee and doughnuts in the terminal at Charleston and then transferred.

The instant I set foot on that bus, all the voices stopped. Abruptly. No tapering off, no changes in volume, they simply stopped, bang. Suddenly I felt peaceful and at ease. This was mad. This was the first time I had ever left my home town, and I hadn't realized until the moment we pulled out of Charleston that I was leaving it gladly, that I was so happy to be away from Marlowe, away from home, away from all the trouble. From Charleston on, it was a delightful trip.

◎ Yesterday round about first dark, I ran up on little Robby Wilde. I still call him that sometimes, even since he's six foot tall in his stocking feet and had that big job at the motor freight. He looked worse than peaked and puny; he looked like a nickel's worth of cat meat. He came up to me and hugged me, and, when I put my arms around him, he felt like a bag of bones. Robby never was what you'd call hefty, but, name o' God, he had done got thin as a lath. He told me he was going to move to Ohio.

He had trouble on his job, I heard tell. There are some of

those women at the motor freight been badmouthing him. They haven't flat scandalized his name, but they badmouthed him some. The heifers. They should mind out how they talk. Things come back to you, and God don't love ugly.

Robby was *so thin,* not much bigger around than a dirt dauber. Could be it was that job trouble. Worry can make weight just walk off you, and Robby always was worrisome. One while, way back there, his mother was taken real bad and I cooked for his family. They needed help. The oldest sister, Willene, was down in her back and couldn't do anything for Miss Mamie even, Virginia had just had a baby, and Zaida was in school all day. Robby was just a little shirttail boy. I got to know them all.

Even when she was home from school, Zaida wasn't much use to anybody. She was at that flighty age. She'd be in her room, laying up there in her slip reading trashy magazines or drying out her skin taking a hot bath, one.

Virginia had had a hard time birthing the baby. Some said it was because her legs were so short, but that was pure-dee foolishness. What the trouble was, the baby was big and it was a boy. When it comes time to be born, boy babies don't help none. They're lazy. Girls will wriggle and try to come out, but boys just lay there. Lazy.

Willene couldn't twist or turn or pick up anything that weighed more than a small sack of sugar. But she could wait on her mother some, hand her her medicine and keep her company. Somebody brought her over every so often, and she laid on the sofa in the big bedroom where Mrs. Wilde was. It was during that time that she made the pie.

Everybody raved about my apple pie, and couldn't anybody ever make one exactly like it. Willene thought that was because I wouldn't tell my receipt. I never had a receipt for anything. My old granny taught me to cook, and I don't think Big Momma knew what a receipt was. Whatever I cooked, I'd just put in what looked about right, and usually it turned out fine for me. I couldn't *tell* anybody how to make good pie crust. The reason I was always real good with pie crust, I have cool hands.

I tried to sidestep Willene about my special pie, but she kept on after me worse than that one old nanny goat in my church circle. Finally one day I sent Robby to tell her I was fixing to make a pie, and, did she want to, she could come and watch me do it. She hastened out to the kitchen, and she got herself set. She jugged herself way back in a straight chair and held herself real erect, like she had a ramrod up her back. That was because it was hurting and she didn't want to angry it up. Robby ran and got her his school pad and a pencil—that was freehearted, because he loved those things—and everything I did, she wrote down. I'd show her each thing I was going to put in and she'd say, "Wait, wait!" and she'd have me to measure it and then she'd write down. Later she said she made a pie and it did very well but it didn't taste quite as good as mine and she just couldn't understand. Well, I didn't know nothing about her pie. Unless maybe while she was taking time to write, I did some little thing and it slipped my mind to tell her. Could be I didn't mention that glug of vinegar.

Young as he was, Robby was worrisome even then. I believe to my soul he's always been scared some way. He always did make like everything was fine, but that don't amount to a hill of beans. I know I went to work one while when I was so low in spirit that all I felt like doing was to crawl down a hole and pull it in after me; but I made like everything was smooth as cream.

All this turned over in my mind when I saw Robby yesterday. I couldn't just map it all out, but that child was rocked in a hard cradle. When I was cooking at his house that time, he never was with the other Wilde children. He never even acted like he belonged to be with them. He was lonesome, seemed like, maybe because his momma was sick. And the others were all so much older. Anyhow, he'd come out to my kitchen a lot. I didn't mind. He was little and sometimes he did spill things, and I do purely hate to walk on sugar. But that's not the worst thing in the world.

It wasn't like when I was working for the Jacksons. General Jackson was about Robby's age. He wasn't a bad child, but I didn't want him in the kitchen. Now, I'm not like Aunt Dorcas. A sweeter women than my Aunt Dorcas never wore out shoe leather, but there was one thing about her: She didn't want anybody in her kitchen. She used to say to us, "You all just move along now. When I'm cooking, there ain't room in the kitchen for anybody but me and the devil." I didn't feel that way, but I didn't want General.

He hadn't had good hometraining and he was always picking boo-daddies out of his nose and I didn't want him in the kitchen. I couldn't tell his momma why, so for a while I was betwixt two minds about what to do. Then one day things boiled over, and I took it up with General. I gathered all the blame to myself. I said, "General, you do very well and I like you fine. But I've get the high blood and I don't feel too smart these days and I've got my hands full in here and half the time I find weasels in the flour and the corn meal and I get nervous if anybody's in the kitchen, so *please stay out.*"

It was different with Robby. I'd give him bread-butter-and-sugar to tide him over to the next meal, or I'd plug a watermelon and, was it ripe, I'd cut him a piece. He'd get barefoot and go around with that slice of watermelon running juice down his chin. Two things he said he had to remember, eating watermelon—not to swallow a seed, or a melon vine would grow out of his nose, and to save the rind for his sister. Somebody had done told Zaida that if you rubbed water-melon juice on your face it would fade off the freckles. Zaida wasn't frecklefaced, not so you'd notice it. But, Lord have mercy, those things *are* ugly. And I didn't fault her for fretting about having any at all.

Robby would come out there to the kitchen and show me his school stuff. He hated school, but he loved the school things. The pads of paper and the pencils and a notebook with a stout cover looked like black-and-white marble. He was in such a low grade he didn't have a thing to put in that notebook, but he'd tote it around. Miss Mamie used to order these things up from the grocery store, along with the food, and he'd want me to see them when he got new ones. He said an Oriole pad cost the most and took ink the best. It was a kindly thin pad with slick paper and a colored bird on the cover. It was right pretty. He was really too little to write with ink, and mostly he had Doubleworth. This was a big fat pad with more paper than any of the others. Unless it was a cat, nothing he loved more than paper or a notebook and a good sharp black-writing pencil. One time he got a lot of this stuff all at once, and at supper he was still so excited he kept dropping his piece of push bread.

And there was something else I remembered about Robby. He was the only white person at my brother's funeral.

Robby was the last person, excusing the hospital people, to see my brother alive. He phoned me one morning and asked could he do anything to help. I said no, but I wished somebody could slip by the hospital during that morning for a while. Jesse was unconscious, seemed like. Still and yet, we couldn't feel sure, and anyhow we liked for somebody to be there in case he roused up. I'd been going regular, but that day I had to get out and pay bills and tend to some other things I'd been laying out to do. Certain and sure, Robby stirred around right rapid, because way before noon he had taken off from work and made tracks to the hospital.

He held my brother's cold hand and talked to him. Robby told me hearing is the last thing to leave you. He said things like "Beulah loves you, and she'll be here later today." The nurses told me. When I got there it was way up in the evening, maybe as late as three o'clock, and they were taking Jesse to some special place in the hospital, but they couldn't save him.

Robby came to the funeral. What I mean, Robby was *at* the funeral. He sent flowers. He was at the church services and he viewed the body. He was at the graveside services. The people in the Consoling Choir told me later they had a hard time to sing. They like to cried, they said, they were so proud and joyful to see that white boy at my brother's funeral. Robby didn't know Jesse very well. He did all that for me. And I'll remember him in my heart—him and his little pads and pencils and his white cat named Tommy and my brother's funeral—as long as I can remember anything.

My grandbaby Odessa cleans at the motor freight, and she told me things had been heaving up over there. Most usually Odessa pays no mind. Does her work and doesn't get too common with anybody. But when the new boss came, she said couldn't anybody fail to see that every soul in the place was all tore up, especially in the old boss's office. Robby was in there.

Robby worked like a field hand, Odessa said, sometimes from can't-see to can't-see. She got to work soon in the morning, and some days he'd already be there. Other days he didn't hardly stop at noon. He'd just have his something-to-eat out of a paper bag. That part was all right. A Moon pie and a bottle of Nehi will see you through the day. But that new man didn't give Robby nothing but a hard way to go. She heard some of the women talking.

He favored his mother, and when he was little he was real pretty. Like a big fat doll. Older, when he longed out and shaped up, he was trim-built but well set up and noways poor. Yesterday he was nothing but skin and bone. And his face wasn't right either; eyes like two holes burnt in a blanket. His face looked like when he picked up a foot he didn't rightly know where it would go down. When he said good-bye and went on, I turned around and watched him out of sight. Used to be, he walked right lightfooted, but not yesterday. I *feel* for him. Something is twisted inside that boy and he hurts. The Bible says there's a time for all things, a time to plant and a time to pluck up, but I wonder about this thing. Could be he ought to stay in North Carolina where he's known. Where he's lived all his born days. What will he do in *Ohio?*

Whatever he does there, I pray that sweet Jesus will hold His hand over Robby's head and protect him.

15
FIFTEEN

In Columbus my prospects looked bright as a brass doorknob. I had gone there in a big flurry, but I checked in at the Y and set about doing things right away. I couldn't remember the day I'd felt so buoyed up. All the Convoy nightmare was behind me. I wasn't hearing voices. I had no fear of failing to find work; this seemed just the simplest thing in the world. And it was.

It was Christmas-shopping time, and all the department stores were taking on temporary help. I went to the Union and left an application, then to Lazarus where I went to work immediately. Then the Union called me, and I went there. Everybody wanted me. I was fine. It was like a weight had been lifted. I never felt so free in my life.

I didn't mind at all when Christmas and after-Christmas sales came and went and the job was over, because I had hated the work. I knew good and well that I wasn't cut out to be a salesperson, and it was no trauma to be out of work under those circumstances. Also, I had something like four hundred dollars of my Convoy earnings, my Christmas bonus plus salary, and I put this in the bank. That was a tidy little sum in those days.

It was such a relief to know I could go on a new job without a qualm. Everything had stopped. I no longer heard any voices at all. I met people easily. I was completely free of all that had been breaking me to bits. I was barefoot in clover. I got a job at Columbus Ball Bearing right after Christmas, and they were so pleased with me they were doing nipups. They said they'd never had anybody who did so well. I had a desk in Personnel, but I was on the plant payroll because of what I was doing. It was something new for me, but I understood what they wanted and I was sure I could figure out a way to do it.

For a long time they had wanted somebody to do some sort of time-motion study, and they put me on this. I was to study out how many motions and how much time it took to do each segment of each job. They'd never felt they could afford a time-motion specialist, and they'd never before had any regular office worker who could even attempt it. I could.

There were three of us in the personnel office—the personnel manager, the timekeeper, and me. The timekeeper was a lush, and he made just the kind of mess anybody might imagine a drunken timekeeper would make. This was astonishing to me. I don't know why, because I'd been practically doing the same thing on *my* job. At Convoy; on the switchboard. Anyhow, I did my work and his too until they got somebody to replace him.

I wasn't very quick to see into things in those days. One day I met this timekeeper wandering around with his arms full of people's time cards, spilling them all over everywhere. He'd come in on a Monday morning, for example, and not even know what day of the week it was. I couldn't understand him, and this shows how foolish I was then. *I could have been doing the same thing.* Yet he was astounding to me. It's amazing.

Management liked me so much that when the plant went on strike they wanted me to stay, even though the men were all out and I had nobody to time-study. They would have paid me my salary for doing nothing, they wanted that much to keep me. I knew I couldn't dare be idle. I'd be inviting trouble. I told them I didn't think I could take being without work, even on salary, and that I had a chance to go to work for the Gas Company, which was true. They said as long as no time cards were coming in and there simply wasn't work for me, they'd send me to IBM school, and that's what happened.

While I was in Personnel, doing time-motion study for nearly two years, I felt reasonably comfortable. But after IBM school, they moved me out of this office and into the main office. The owners of the company were there. The owners were three brothers, Henry and August Mecklenburg and a younger one, Karl. This is not to excuse myself for what came about, but these brothers were incessantly having at one another. One was the president, one was the vice-president, and one was the secretary-treasurer. Each one wanted to be president, and there was resentment all around. Employees got the fallout from this. Everybody felt the effects of it.

As soon as I went to the IBM section, things began slipping, First of all, I started feeling inadequate to this mammoth task. There were only two of us, myself and a girl key puncher. She was slow as molasses in January and inaccurate too. Sue would give me cards just full of errors. What she punched into the cards was what I had to work with, so her incompetence reflected very badly on me. Her inefficiency did not come from having too much to do. She had about four thousand cards to punch, and she had time to do it. She simply wasn't any good.

In most places there'd have been a verifier to check her cards before they'd get to me and go into my machine, but at Columbus Ball Bearing we didn't have such a person. Either I had to verify all Sue's work—and I didn't have time for that— or else I had to use the cards the way she gave them to me. Just one time I checked her cards on the verifying machine. This machine reads the holes; a light comes on when there's an error. That girl had given me four thousand cards with eighty two-errors. Which is terrible. The Lord only knows how many errors she handed me after that. I never had a chance to verify her work again, and I was always getting a bunch of wrong answers.

That happened all the time, and then I'd have to go back over everything and figure out what had been snarled up. The management thought I was the slow coach and couldn't get my work done. I knew this, but I couldn't talk to them about it. I felt no common ground to meet on, no confidence in their reaction. I couldn't bring myself to say, "This girl must go. She's fouling up the whole operation." In the end, what happened was partly my fault because I couldn't say a word.

Sue finally got into financial difficulties. She got into trouble with the federal government about income tax, and she had run up debts in town and bill collectors were phoning and even coming to the plant, and they fired her.

The next thing that went badly wrong was a new boy. He was already at the company, and they wanted me to teach him what I'd been taught at IBM school. I couldn't. They assumed that I didn't want anybody else and that I wasn't trying with him. It wasn't entirely their fault that they misunderstood me. I simply could not tell them. I knew what they were thinking, but I could not say, "Look, you're wrong. This boy is not teachable." I couldn't. I'm sure I walked around with a stoic face, and I'm sure that when one of the brothers would come in I'd freeze. I think I must have looked very arrogant to them. It doesn't help me, but later on, after I'd had my day there and was gone, they sent this boy to IBM school and they couldn't teach him either.

At that time they fired Sue and replaced her with a good operator, Donna. She was the only person in the whole outfit who understood my job. She worked with me for about two months, and was really good. I was very fond of her. And grateful to her. Her being the key punch operator would have cleared things up for me if it hadn't been for Mr.Muller.

He was an older man who had been in charge of the payroll, among other things, and he was terribly worried that now that they had a younger man and all those fancy machines he would be let out. I could see what was troubling him, and I felt for him. So, to try to make him feel better, I would go to him as if he were the boss and ask him questions, and then they let this become the actual situation. They appointed him to oversee the IBM operation.

He was terribly against these machines, and he would do everything in his power to make them look bad. If he made me look bad too, well, tough. He had nothing personal against me. It was just my hard luck.

They didn't give me an ADT number, so I was helpless when Mr. Muller would throw his monkeywrenches. It might have worked me to death, but if I'd had an ADT number I could have got in at night—by phoning the detective agency, identifying myself by number, and saying I was going into Columbus Ball Bearing—and made up the work. As it was though, with the new set-up of machines and all, I'd work from seven to five, two extra hours, and still I couldn't make it.

What would happen, Mr. Muller would turn off the motors. He did this constantly. If the machine had a report on it being run through, and if he turned the motor off, I'd lose the whole thing. Whatever I had going at five o'clock that hadn't run out yet, he'd make me turn the machine off and he'd close up. I couldn't stay, because I couldn't have opened the door later to leave. So my entire report that had been running would be undone, and the next day I'd be having to start at the beginning again.

But I could not go and tell the boss what was happening. Certainly I was aching all over for the boss to know, but I wanted him to know without my having to tell him. This is the same thing in me that goes back to my early childhood: "Don't open your mouth. Don't dare say a word." It was impossible for me to say a thing.

So I would scurry frantically, trying to get all this hopeless mess straightened out and work finished, and I worked myself up to a point of being very angry. First I thought, "They shouldn't have taken me off the time study and put me on this." Then I thought, "They should make it their business to know how things are going. I shouldn't *need* to tell something like this." I was in a desperate fix, trying to keep everything running and that an impossibility, and not being able to say one word while I was blazing furious. Then one Friday the plant had a holiday. Not the office, just the plant. I was still on the plant payroll, from the time-study job, and I took the holiday, well aware that I wasn't supposed to do this. I don't how I arrived at this conclusion, but I thought that this would show them. I thought, "Now they'll know what to do."

Monday morning when I went to work they had another fellow already there and Mr. Muller told me I was fired.

◎ When Rob Wilde soured, we lost the best worker Columbus Ball Bearing has had since I've been personnel manager. When he came, he had had a relatively short course of commercial training and excellent experience—ten years as cashier at Convoy Motor Freight in Marlowe, North Carolina. Talking with him, I got a feeling he might be just the one I'd been looking for.

For a long time I'd been wanting to get a time-motion study made, but the Mecklenburg brothers never could get together on putting it in the budget. Consulting industrial engineers don't work for peanuts, but, if they're good, the investment pays off. I couldn't get the Mecklenburgs to quit squabbling long enough to see it, though. I'd had it in the back of my mind to try to do something in the way of time-motion study with a non-specialist if a likely prospect ever showed up. Until Rob came along, nobody promising had showed.

Wilde had never done anything of this kind, but he was game for it and I've found it valuable to be able to look beyond formal credits on occasion. I did this with him, and I was a hundred percent right. That is, until he went bad. He came on strong and worked for two years like nobody before or since. Then, just when we had a good thing going for him, he turned into a lemon.

We'd had a rapid turnover in timekeepers before Rob came. Those employment agencies kept sending me one tosspot after another. I've been known to look the other way a time or two. Once in a while an otherwise good employee had come in half crocked or sneaked a drink on the premises but got his work done nevertheless and didn't flaunt or repeat his indiscretion. But these timekeepers were full-time lushes. Three in a row before it was over with. For at least his first two months here, Rob was acting timekeeper while he was figuring out a method for the time-motion study and beginning the study. Did a bang-up job of it all.

We ran into labor trouble. The men had been pushing for a thirty-six-hour work week and higher retirement benefits. The Mecklenburgs always took some time to agree among themselves on anything, and, after a certain amount of their shilly-shally, the union called a strike. We had to release most of the office workers, but I persuaded the brothers to let me hold on to Rob. I didn't have any specific plans for him, but he was too good to lose. The plant was shut down and there wasn't a lick of work for him to do. I offered to keep him on salary anyhow. He didn't take to this idea, and he was about to go with the Gas Company when I thought of IBM school and my pet project.

We were almost ready to convert to IBM recordkeeping anyway. We needed to expedite the processing of all our data, and this seemed to be the time to make a beginning. We offered to send Rob to IBM school for the duration of the strike or until he finished, and he went.

The school gave us rave reports on him. Besides being remarkably quick to pick up new skills, he worked fast and he was accurate, they said. I expected him to transfer from the plant to the main office without turning a hair. I got a nasty surprise.

Every report from Muller was bad. He was dissatisfied with Rob from the beginning. Presumably he was right, because Rob never made the first complaint about Muller and Muller did nothing but complain about Rob. Muller said Rob was incompetent, and the record backed him all the way. The condition of the company reports bore him out fully. No set of figures was ever ready on time—payroll, inventory, production control, nothing. Rob always seemed to be working, Muller said. That was the one good word he ever had for Rob. He did say Rob put in more than a full day every day. That only made Rob worse, because still the work didn't get done.

Muller had earlier been opposed to IBM recordkeeping, and at first I wondered if he might not be blaming the delays more on the machines—which didn't make sense. He kept screaming that if the machines were any good, Rob wasn't. And all our records were in a mess.

I thought of calling Rob in for a talk, but Muller stongly advised against this. It's my policy to give people responsibility and then let them handle it, so I acted on Muller's recommendation and kept out of it. Muller assured me it would only muddy the waters if I tried to talk with Rob. He said Rob had become silent as well as arrogant and morose.

Said Rob didn't have a word to throw a dog. It was Muller's opinion that the IBM people had done us all a disservice by praising Rob so highly. Muller said that from the day our machines were installed, Rob had such a swelled head nobody could get to him. Disappointing. Bothered me a little about myself too. Any more I'm not quite as confident as I always was about my ability to judge character.

But Muller must have been right. If anything had been lacking in the way of equipment, Rob had only to say so. I was all steamed up about the new IBM section. It was my baby, and I would have cooperated on every score. It was simply that Rob consistently failed to get the work done. I couldn't understand it. Not after the way he performed here in his first years and later in the IBM school. He had the assistant he needed, and he was a demon for work himself, so, whatever he was so P.O.'d about, it couldn't have been overwork. I know it wasn't overwork. He couldn't have got in and out of the plant at night without an ADT number, and he didn't have one. If he'd needed to work nights, he would have asked for one and he never did. I particularly questioned Muller about this.

If Rob had been allowed to continue on, letting the records slide the way he was doing, the plant would have become inoperative. It was just as well that he quit when he did. I wish he'd done this in a different way, however. To quit without notice after all this company did for him, that's lack of loyalty and base ingratitude.

Left a bad taste in my mouth. I hired him and I promoted him. I promoted him on faith, to do a job he didn't have any technical qualifications for. I was responsible for his going to IBM school at company expense, increasing his earning power. He had been pretty much my protégé, but naturally I made no move in his direction when he quit the way he did. Columbus Ball Bearing doesn't have to beg anybody to work here. He didn't even have the decency to say, "I quit." Just didn't show. When Muller told me that, I wrote him off. He did come around some time later on, Muller said, but Muller told him he'd been fired and replaced. I didn't blame Muller for a minute. You know what they say about dogs and people. You do a dog a kindness, he doesn't bite you for it.

16
SIXTEEN

When I finally openly cracked up, people were inclined to think maybe it was from overwork. The truth is just the opposite. Work actually delayed the crack-up. Religion may or may not be the opiate of the masses, but—I can't say it often enough—for me, work has always been the best opiate going. This is not to reinvent the wheel, but to say that with me it's not simply a concept but something proven over and over in my own experience.

I always feel so confirmed, so vindicated almost, when I learn of some healthy, stable individual who has some reaction the same as mine. Years and years after this period, way up in the beginning seventies, only a year or so ago, I tried to read *Leningrad Diary* and did read bits of it. This woman who had survived the siege of Leningrad said somewhat the same thing as I just did. She said, in effect, that work spared her from facing fully and head on every bit of the grim stuff going on all around her. She said this when she had already suffered through more than a year in the besieged city. She also wrote,

> While I work, a bullet won't get me,
> While I work, my heart will not sink.

Well, a bullet didn't get me right away, because I had a new job. I had applied to one place through an employment agency, and then one day I just walked into Reliant Insurance Company, applied, and was hired. I was put in Central Operations.

This place didn't put me under the usual new-job stress. It eased things somewhat for me. Here, I wasn't the whole deal. Everything wasn't on me. At Columbus Ball Bearing, that's how it was, because nobody else knew how to run the machines or do a thing with them. At Reliant I had Ken Rockwood to direct me, and the chief responsibility was on him. That was better.

It was only at the office that things were eased, that I was safe from harassment. Outside, the voices would start right up. They gradually moved closer and then They came after me even at work.

Along about this time an unfortunate thing happened, and of course it was bound to move the ruckus over into the work situation, into my new refuge. I got a letter from a Columbus lawyer. I knew when I left Convoy in Marlowe that there might be at least a small discrepancy. Well, I didn't know, really, what condition things were in. This letter was about a money shortage.

I went to see Iona Leaf, an accountant I'd met because she had an office not far from where I was living. Except for stenographic help sometimes, she had a one-person outfit. She did things like preparing people's income tax returns. I felt she'd understand any financial problem and would know what to do. I told her if there was a shortage, maybe it would be something like fifty dollars. I had had a hundred and fifty in a petty cash fund. She went and talked to the lawyer who had written me, and she came back puzzled. She said, "It's a matter of fifteen hundred dollars."

Here's how crazy I was even then, even as good as I felt at the time: This was a thing I should have contested, and that never even crossed my mind.

The shop at Convoy was a different setup from the office. The shop was where trucks were cleaned and repaired and kept in good running order. There was a parts department and everything. Hinkie Plowman and Goat McGowan were down there. They also handled what was called Miscellaneous Sales, and they'd bring up checks that I'd deposit. Their inventory didn't reconcile with my ledgers. Everything else in my books was right—which I marvel at, considering my condition—but the number of parts not in their inventory should have been reflected in my books as checks in payment for them. Checks received by me. Hinkie and Goat were supposed never to accept payment in cash. Only checks.

This was the way it worked. Even crazy, I should have known to contest this thing. I mean, after all, what could I do with checks? I don't know what I was thinking about or what anybody else was thinking about. There was no way for me to make off with Convoy's checks. But when they told me I owed Convoy fifteen hundred dollars, I didn't question it. I felt I didn't want anything more to do with all that Convoy mess down there; whatever they say, that's OK with me; just get it over with. So, without any protest at all, I made arrangements to pay the thing, fifty dollars a month, and I did that. Paid it all and never raised a single question.

Obviously, this was tantamount to admitting I had stolen the checks. That's why I shouldn't have paid it. But it wasn't that simple. I was well aware of the chaos I'd been in at Convoy, and I was on the spot; I didn't know what I'd done. I might have stolen money, for all I knew. Although it would have had to be cash if I had, and I couldn't have stolen more than a hundred and fifty. Convoy should have known, Iona should have known, all of them, that I couldn't have used stolen *checks*. I was feeling pretty good when this happened, but actually I was on very thin ice. I was upright and balanced, but the ice was fragile and could break under me at the slightest pressure. My condition was such that if I'd been accused of *killing* somebody during that late Convoy period, I would have believed it. I would have believed anything; I had been operating in a fog. Furthermore, I was bad, no-count, worthless—the voices had been drilling this into me for ages—and anything wrong anybody accused me of, I could believe I might have done it.

I just didn't know what I'd done down there toward the last. I had been pretty concerned, even at the time, because there were stretches when I'd forget everything. I wouldn't even remember that I'd have been absent and written the combination to the safe and sent it on an open unfolded piece of paper to one of the girls at the office so she could open the safe. This is a thing you absolutely never do. No responsible person ever writes down the combination to a safe. And I'd do it and have to be told later that I'd done it.

But no matter what, it was not at all possible for me to have made away with Convoy's checks.

A good bit later on, when I went down home, I found that Hinkie Plowman had been fired, and Goat McGowan too, for a shortage of something way up in the thousands. I found out that payment of those miscellaneous sales sometimes were made in cash, and this cash they never turned in to me. As they weren't supposed to make sales for cash, none of what they did was observable to me. I had paid fifteen hundred dollars that they had stolen. After I left, they had kept on with their stealing until they got caught. Hinkie and Goat had finally overdone it, had got greedy and overdone it. They'd been selling motors and stuff, dirt cheap.

I don't think it ever occurred to the Convoy people that the fifteen hundred dollars I "paid back" was part of their theft. As far as Convoy was concerned, I had left, there was the shortage, so it was mine, and Hinkie's thing had come up later.

Iona was very sympathetic during the time after I got the letter from that lawyer. I began to see her rather frequently. She used to race around a lot with two quite young men. She must have been fifteen or twenty years older than they were. She was deeply in love with one of them, but he was in love with the other fellow.

Iona really had a tough time with this Gene and Frank thing, and she had already had a rugged sort of existence. She had married young, and the boy had killed himself shortly after. She seemed to like me, and she drank a lot and I started drinking with her. She had a flat not too far from her office, and I'd go there and we'd sit and talk and get plastered. She'd often talk about her troubles. I didn't tell her about mine. One, I didn't tell anybody, and two, at the moment I thought I didn't have any pressing troubles; I was living on the surface and for the moment.

Iona began using me for an excuse. I don't know whether she felt her drinking so heavily was bringing on criticism from her friends or what, but she began saying things like, "Rob came up wanting a drink." So I started hearing people talk about *this*. "—goes up there with that old woman and they just sit and swill liquor."

Well, that was true, but it wasn't all that terrible. If Iona and I wanted to sit up there in her flat and "swill liquor," we weren't hurting anybody and it was nobody's business. That's one of the worst things about the voices. There's always some basis for what they say, even though the way They put things isn't the truth at all.

At that time, of course, I still thought the voices were real voices of real people. I couldn't tell exactly what was going on. At first it wasn't something that bothered me to any great degree. When all this racket is just beginning, it's not a big buzz. It's not all over the neighborhood. It's only occasional and it's a faint and not too distinct sound, a mumble even. So, in the early stages, it didn't distress me much. I'd hear, but I'd think, "Well, so this one knows Iona and I drink" or "That one claims I made off with all that stuff at Convoy."

Then as it built and built, the way it does, it began to intrude on my job at Reliant. As it develops, it gets to you. The sniping makes you mad, the mumbling gets on your nerves, and of course They finally stop mumbling and talk out loud. The constant irritation gets you wrought up. Before too long, I was hostile toward practically everybody. This, then, was another pain I had to try to endure and to cover. Anger now lived with me. I was never free of it. But I felt an urgent necessity to hide this anger. Soon I was getting erratic again.

Knowing things that would annoy people I worked with, I'd do them over and over. I used to do this with Fina in Marlowe. Knowing what a fanatical housekeeper she was, I would wash my hands after doing something that had really dirtied them, and I'd leave the soap with nasty little gray bubbles and streaks all over it. This would have her tearing her hair. Now, at Reliant, I would throw at a waste paper basket, with maybe a crumpled cigarette package, and miss it. Purposely or not, I'm not altogether sure, I did it a lot and I wouldn't pick things up for anything, wouldn't dream of picking anything up and putting it in the basket. One girl, a girl I rather liked, hated this. I knew that every time I did it it just flew all over her, but I kept right on. I can't explain it except maybe as part of the overall feeling of hostility.

I did like this girl, but, without knowing a fool thing about it, she and a young fellow there were giving me a hard time. They were already working together when I went in and was put to working with the two of them. She and Joe were both very young, and they had a lot to giggle about. That's all there was to it, and I'm sure this was how it was with them before I came. But at the time I thought they were laughing at *me.*

Even when I made friends with Joe, it wasn't because I was able to junk the notion that he'd been laughing at me. I still believed that, but I forgave him because he was so young and, as I came to see, kind and good far beyond the average and staunch in friendship.

At the beginning of this job at Reliant, in the IBM section of Central Operations, I picked as my friend the very worst person in the office I could have latched on to. She was hard and mean. This Agnes Bunn put on a big poor-little-me act; but, as soon as it suited her purpose, she'd dig her hooks into you. She would tread on anybody to get what she wanted. There was a strongness in her, and this is the way she used it. If you were working on a machine and she wanted it, she got it. It was this way all up and down the line. She also had a way of talking to the supervisor, Ken, of setting people against each other. Once she goaded me until she got me upset enough that I said something nasty about Ken, and then she told him.

I learnt later that he had indeed said this thing she'd told me, but with what a difference! He had looked at me one day and said, "That boy looks like he lives in a shadow." He had said it in the most sympathetic way imaginable, I realized later, and it showed a rather penetrating insight. It very well didn't sound sympathetic when Agnes repeated it to me. She didn't intend it to. So I said, "What do I care what that asinine frip thinks?" And then she told Ken that I'd called him an asinine frip.

In one way I still admire this girl. She was absolutely turned loose at the age of fourteen. Out on her own. Worked as a waitress in grubby little hash joints, and had her own room and everything, at that age. She hadn't been brought up at all; she was jerked up by the hair of the head, that's all, and I can't see blaming her too much for using people for her own ends. She had clawed her way and got whatever she wanted.

She did that for so long just to survive, and, when it was no longer necessary, she kept on doing it. It had become her way of dealing with whatever came up. By the time she was twenty-two, she owned a little house. A cracker box, as somebody cruelly described it, but her own house. At twenty-two. Before she was thirty, she owned a nice little house. Now, in 1973, money values and women's situations have begun to change, but for that day and time what she did was very impressive.

When we were in the same office, she threw a lot of fuel on the flames of my constant anger, and that's the only reason I mention her. She did me a lot more harm than she ever knew. She busied herself and succeeded in getting all three of us—Joe, me, Ken—stirred up against one another. That way she kept her skirts clear, stayed in good with everybody, while the rest of us were hissing and spitting like vipers. I don't know what good this did her, but I'm sure she had a purpose in mind. Maybe, just in case it would come in handy some day, she wanted us to have more against one another than we knew to have against her. I was in such a condition it was easy for her to do this to me, and Ken, I learnt later, was somewhat shaky himself. And Joe's youth and inexperience made him an easy mark. I think Agnes was good at spotting people's weaknesses and using them. In spite of her, I became quite fond of Ken.

Not too long after I began at Reliant, they took Ken out of Central Operations and made him supervisor of the Charleston, West Virginia, region. He'd stay in Columbus; just his responsibilities changed. He was entitled to take with him any three people he wanted. I had been going great guns in that IBM section, and I was the first one he chose. He picked Joe too.

Ken took me to lunch and said, "You're the one I want for supervisor of operators. You're my first choice." This sounded fine and firm to me, and I thought it was all set. But when the time came for the actual change to take place, it went entirely out of Ken's hands. I didn't know this until much later. Higher-ups decided. They overrode Ken in his choice of me because there was a fellow there with seniority and they thought he should have the spot as supervisor. I did get a promotion and so did Joe, but I felt I'd been done out of something I'd been offered. I thought Ken had turned totally against me, and I was deeply, deeply hurt. Joe, too, thought I'd been betrayed. He was much upset about it; so it wasn't only my interpretation.

I went to Ken and said, "Do you want to get rid of me?" He said, "Of course not! What makes you think so?" He should have known what made me think so. Why should I have to tell him? That's how I thought then. I wasn't able to answer at all, and I went on back to work. I didn't believe him though, so I applied for a transfer. So did Joe.

Doing what I've always done, I talked it around that I didn't want the job as supervisor anyhow, I wouldn't be a supervisor for anything. I got myself down to Personnel and applied for a job in the Methods Department. Personnel wanted to know my reason. (When they asked Joe for his reason, he flat told them that he couldn't stand Ken. Said he didn't think Ken was fair. I don't know how much further they went into that.)

To back up, Ken was interested in tropical fish. He had mentioned to me a couple of times that he'd like us to go into a little tropical fish business together. I didn't want to, and when this big disappointment came I thought Ken had done this awful thing to me because I wouldn't go into business with him.

When Joe and I had jumped up at the same time and asked to be transferred, Personnel thought something was badly wrong in Ken's office, and they kept at me for my reasons. None of this was anything I wanted to happen, but when they kept pressing me—and to get me to speak out they finally said, "Whatever you say will be treated as entirely confidential"—the tropical fish business was all that came to mind. I said I thought maybe Ken had turned on me because I hadn't gone into business with him. They should have told me right then about the fellow with seniority.

This Personnel man—I don't remember his name—lost no time in running and telling him what I'd said. Ken could have straightened the whole thing out in a minute. Except that he had one of the same troubles I had: He couldn't. He was hurt, but he couldn't make himself say anything at all.

As for me, I was wanting to go to Ken and say, "I do not want to leave you. I want to stay right here in this office. I come in every morning knowing what I'm going to do, and I do it well. I'm happy here. I want to stay." But not one word could I say. So things were rolling and I had no brakes. They gave me a little party and a brief case, and I went on to a job I didn't want and soon hated.

It was all a chain of errors and failures, mine, Personnel's, Ken's. I was not serious when I applied for a job in Methods. I only applied to get back at Ken. It was my way of saying to him, just telling him, that I wanted to leave him, not actually leaving. I no more wanted to go to that Methods job than the man in the moon, and I never thought I would get it. When they gave me the job, I was the most stunned and upset person imaginable. But I was on the conveyor belt. I went to Methods as a junior analyst, and I got a raise. It was the most miserable mistake I ever made in my life, and I had absolutely no control over it. That was when the whole thing fell apart for me.

It was not any real fault of the company's, except maybe for sloppy administration with the right hand not knowing what the left hand was doing. It was Reliant's fault though, in that the job gave me nothing sensible to put my mind on. In Methods, I had time to brood, to be hostile, to be angry at practically everything and everybody. Once again anger was my inseparable companion, like we were joined at the hip. I started seeing a psychiatrist.

I thought maybe seeing this Dr. Richards would somehow pour oil on the troubled waters. For one thing, I thought maybe They would see what I was doing and either change their attitude toward me or else quiet down some anyhow. The job continued as a constant aggravation to everything, salting every wound I had.

This Methods was a wretched place that fortunately is no longer in existence. The work was alien to me and I hated it. It wasn't *work*. I would have been more useful back at Bentley's Creek stringing four o'clocks for No-No Stone. Almost daily there would be conferences with the manager and his little group. There were about ten of us in the office, and all around us were managers managing.

Some managers had two workers, some had three, some worked on forms and that sort of thing. Mine worked on procedures, and he assigned me to handle employees' suggestions. Lord have mercy. I'd get things like this: "I suggest that the Queen of Hearts keep her crown permanently." This was about a contest held each year. Employees would choose a sort of Miss Reliant, and on Valentine's Day she'd be named Queen of Hearts.

I would go and investigate this great foolishness just as if I were doing a reasonable piece of work. To find out why they put this thing on her head and then took it back. One suggestion was that they take the crown back but give her a heart-shaped pendant to keep. Then there'd be the conference, and I'd have to go and discuss this. It was all so stupid and silly that I could hardly believe it. This is what I got a promotion to! This is what I got a raise for!

I would go and investigate each idiotic thing, then I would sit there and write my little piece and have nothing else to do until the conference. So I'd copy my report. It would be finished. I'd have written it up the best I could with what I had to work with, but I had not one other lick of work to do until we had the conference and they sent me on another stupid investigation and I'd write *that* one up over and over.

When it first began to get me down, sometimes I'd be on the street and hear people talking. "Look. There he is. Look. Got a promotion—junior analyst!—What does he think he is!—Scandal about money at Convoy—Suppose they knew what he's really like!—empty title—a nothing job—hateful thing—doesn't write his mother—" On and on. Later, this all followed me into the building.

For a short time I had a respite by way of Adlai Stevenson's 1956 campaign for president. I was trying to do some work for the Volunteers for Stevenson, and, when the talk got too bad, I'd put down my many-times-copied report and I'd go sell those little silver shoes like nobody's business. These were the campaign pins and lapel buttons shaped like a man's shoe and with a mark to show a broken place because of Stevenson's famous shoe with the hole in the sole. Reliant was overflowing with Republicans, and I was getting a lot of criticism. I was well aware of this, but I didn't care. There were Democrats here and there, and I'd range all over the building selling those pins and buttons during office hours.

This held me together until the campaign was over, and than I started slipping. I'd hear people talking all around me—at my desk, in the cafeteria, in the lobby, anywhere. "Not worth the powder to blow him up—What does he think he is!—goofing off and doing that political stuff on company time—dirty dishes in the sink—If Reliant only knew about him—queer—drunkard—good-for-nothing—illegitimate—"

And no mumbling. Shouting and clamoring, louder and

louder, clearer and clearer, closer and closer. No mistaking what They said, no getting out of earshot. No way to do that, ever. I began making excuses to go home from work. Then They hammered on me so hard I couldn't *go* to work. For a while I could phone the office and make some excuse. Then the thing completely overwhelmed me and I couldn't even phone. I couldn't make a call, I couldn't answer the phone, I couldn't answer the doorbell, I couldn't do anything but stay huddled up in bed trying to keep the voices from beating me to death. I did venture out to the mailbox one day, and I found a form letter saying Reliant had terminated me.

◎ Dear Robby,

Zaida came out to visit with me yesterday afternoon, and I asked for you. I shan't let "the thief of time" delay my writing to tell you how proud of you I am. But then I was proud of you all the years you were at Convoy. It will be a cold day in August when they get another cashier of your caliber. I did feel some regret when you went off to seek greener pastures. You'd seemed so settled at Convoy.

Zaida tells me that you now are in a responsible position at a big insurance company and that you are doing a splendid job. You have always done more than creditably at whatever you set your hand to, your job and all else. I well remember the praise heaped on you for triumphs in Little Theater productions. My only misgiving is that you might work too hard.

You know that I'm not knocking work. I myself fully intend to get out in my garden and "work 'til the last beam fadeth;" but it's possible to go too far with anything, and I have reluctantly made some concessions to age. You're young, but take a leaf out of my book. One of your virtues is industry; just don't let a virtue become a vice.

Yesterday Zaida mentioned that once when you wrote home, quite a while back, shortly after you went to Columbus, you were dismayed about "the sad state of affairs" between my oldest living relatives, Cousin Lucia and Cousin Jessie. You said you hoped their that in old age they could become reconciled. Do, child. There's no sad state of affairs. They just won't ride in the same car, that's all.

Sometimes there's some shifting about to be done if several of the family are going somewhere. It used to be awkward and strained, but not for a long time. It all happened so many years ago, you know, when Cousin Jessie got so put out with Cousin Lucia for what she considered poor driving that she lost her temper and said she'd never ride in the same car with her again. Because of failing eyesight, Cousin Lucia doesn't even drive any more, hasn't driven for a coon's age. But they're used to riding in different cars, and the others see to this from force of habit and nobody even seems to remember that there's no reason to do it any longer, or why they ever did it in the first place. Cousin Lucia and Cousin Jessie have always been this way. When they were young women—sisters, mind you—with small children, poor little Waddy and the others never knew for sure whether their mothers were speaking or not.

Don't fret. They're not estranged now. They are entirely comfortable in the rut they've worn. They're both reasonably well; but of course, as you age, you accumulate things. Cousin Lucia has fallen into flesh. Cousin Jessie though, looks like she always did—like the first strong breeze might blow her to Kingdom Come. But that tiny scrap of a woman will probably outlive all the rest of us. That's the way with those wiry people. I'll tell you one thing, she's just as headstrong and perverse as she ever was. Last month she cut down a healthy well-grown *magnolia* tree because, she said, it was messy. "All those leaves on the ground," she said.

Speaking of wanton destruction, you remember that hundred-year-old wild grapevine covering trees that went around a corner of Uncle Hoke's house? You remember how, when you looked down on it from the living room windows, it was solid leaves, like a huge green blanket? And this blanket of leaves rose and fell like music or small waves? It was almost part of the house. It was there before the house, you know. Well, it's gone too. All gone. After Uncle Hoke died, the new owner got some bad advice and tore it down. Now there are nasty little golden biotas and stiff-as-a-poker upright yews, because "something formal" is what was wanted. Barbarians.

I haven't seen your mother for a while, but Zaida said she's fairly well. I sent her a big bottle of my rhubarb-peppermint-and-soda. It's awfully good for the digestion, and I always keep some made up. I take a wine glass of it every night.

I hope those northern winters are not going to be too hard on you. The very thought of that long season of snow and ice gives me the willies. And even when that's over, no crape myrtle and wisteria. Dear, lovely, messy wisteria. Remember to cloak up when you go out.

> Your affectionate aunt,
> Mozelle Blunt

17
SEVENTEEN

A nurse took me in, and, when she turned around and locked the door in back of me, I went hysterical. The doctor hadn't told me it was that kind of hospital. In fact, he had plainly told me different. I had to hang on to everything I had in me to keep from screaming right while she turned the key. Shortly afterward, I did scream.

I blame Dr. Richards for not telling me about this part of the hospital and what he had in mind for me. I hadn't liked him as a therapist either. For one thing, he was excitable and this didn't accomplish anything. When I got into such deep trouble, however, I had gone to him again, and he had talked calmer and generally acted more in command of himself than before.

He told me that there was no question in his mind but what I was sick. I agreed, because I could tell that things had gone a little too far. He said he had been in touch with Reliant, that they understood, and that I'd be reinstated. He said I was to go "to the hospital for a rest" and then go back to Reliant in the IBM section, not back in that Methods thing I couldn't stand.

He maneuvered to get me in there on Christmas Eve. A holiday, especially Christmas, makes a ghastly time for disturbed people. They're always piling into hospitals at this time, but I didn't know this then. Dr. Richards told me later he was afraid of what might happen to me over Christmas. He thought I might take off for some place or do something real wild. But what he said to me was, "I want you to go out to University Hospital and get some rest." He definitely said that. "—over the holidays," he said, "and get some rest." He made it sound like a regular hospital, not a place where I'd be locked up.

So I went, on Christmas Eve, by myself, carrying not much more than some pajamas. I thought I'd go to bed. I signed some papers, not paying a particle of attention to what they were, and followed the nurse. I must not have paid any attention to her either; because she surely *un*locked the door to the men's wing when we went in, but I didn't notice that.

When I saw her locking me in, the whole thing was borne in on me and I felt shock stiffening me, body, mind, soul, and bone marrow. She kept prattling away and seeing me to a room, and I walked along beside her like somebody had wound me up and set me on the floor. I was screaming bloody murder inside, and, as soon as we got to the room, I screamed out loud. Just sat right down on the bed and let loose, and then flung myself across the bed and beat my fists on it and screamed enough to tear my throat apart. I was beside myself.

As soon as I could stop screaming and speak, I said to the doctor who had come in, "How do I get out of here?" He said, "By writing a request to the director of the Institute and waiting ten days." This set me off again. Ten days can be a lifetime. While I was screaming the place down, they sent for Dr. Richards.

He came, which was nice of him on Christmas Eve, but he didn't make me feel any better. At one point I said, "If I have to be in a hospital, I'll go back to North Carolina and be in a hospital there."

"You couldn't get *into* a hospital there," he said. "You're not a citizen of North Carolina. Any more, you're a citizen of

Ohio." Now, this was pretty rough on me. I felt insecure enough, Lord knows, and now here I was not even a citizen of North Carolina. I had wanted to handle myself pretty well, thinking that might help me get out, but I couldn't make it. I screamed at Dr. Richards and he screamed at me. I guess they saw they weren't going to be able to do anything with me, the state I was in, so they handed me something and I drank it and it knocked me out.

Next day I woke up very late. I was still shaken, but I got up for a try at joining some others. This required a lot of me, and the very first thing I saw stopped me in my tracks. It was a visitor. But, in a line-up of patients and visitors, you'd pick her for a patient every time.

At lunch time I went to the cafeteria, and I saw my friend Janet Franklin. I had met her working with the Volunteers for Stevenson, and she was just the nicest young woman. She told me that she had a new baby and that shortly after it was born she had gone into a bad depression. I've heard this isn't so uncommon. She had been a patient for a few days before I went in. I described the woman I'd seen, and she was somebody Janet knew. She said there couldn't be two people in the world who fit that description.

It had startled me for this apparition to be the very first person I bumped into on my first day in the hospital. Her face was dead white—Janet said that she used white powder—and her hair, so black it was slightly purplish, was swept up in a great pile. Her eyes were black too. Her cheeks were a little bit thin, but she was rather pretty in an odd way. It was only all that shiny blackness and dead whiteness that gave me such an eerie feeling. And it wasn't just me. One of the patients was Haitian, and Ambroise took one big-eyed look at her and said, "Bee-zarre!"

Indeed she was bizarre. I'll tell you exactly what she looked like. She looked like Charles Addams drew her. If the woman in his cartoons were good looking, she'd be just like Janet's friend. She had on very nice clothes, but she was wearing white cotton gloves. This in the middle of an Ohio winter. Janet said she had dozens of pairs of such gloves and that they were hanging up, drying, all over her house all the time. She had a thing about germs.

She had gone to see Janet when her first baby was very young, and Janet said she stood around for a while and then sat on the edge of a cane-bottomed chair, wiping it off first. Marzetti's was the only restaurant in Columbus where she'd eat. Even there she took her own silver and napkin. How she managed other details of daily life, neither Janet nor I could ever figure out. She stood the whole time she was visiting on the ward. Of course all this I learnt later. When I saw her, it was her physical appearance that rocked me back on my heels.

After lunch, I went on and, as I said, tried to join some others. It didn't do my morale any good to see who I was in there with. One man was catatonic, standing stiff as a poker with people moving past him and all around him. A cleaning man mopped the floor around him. Bumped him once with the mop, and I could not make myself believe he couldn't feel that.

One had a great flowing beard, and at that time you didn't see many beards. One was busily poking at the keyhole in the locked door. A day or so later I learnt about him and his speciality. That was when I saw one of the doctors come in and deliberately upset a nurse by handing her the key he'd let himself in with and saying "Mrs. Foster, would you please hold this shitty key for me?"

Others, of course, looked as ordinary as anybody in the world. I saw some patients laughing and playing cards, and I sort of sidled up to them. They let me play euchre with them. I tried to calm myself as much as I could, and in a couple of days I was started on medicine.

There weren't too many patients. As many as were

better, they had let go home for Christmas. The hospital had tried to make things pretty for the holidays. There were soapy Santa Clauses on the windows, and a tree and coffee and cookies in the day room. The tree was all right once you got used to an aluminum Christmas tree, but the cookies were revolting. At home there's a special kind of cookie that people make at Christmastime. It's plain. They don't gook it all up with colored sprinkles; it's just The Christmas Cookie. Those at the Institute may have been luscious, but I never knew. I'm used to cookies looking like what they are, and I can't go a cookie with green on it.

At the same time they started me on medicine, I began talking with a therapist. I was as unfair with him as anything in the world. I couldn't help it. Even when I was trying, I could not hand myself over—helpless, revealed for whatever I was—to somebody else. So I made up a whole rigamarole so I'd be talking to him. This was about the equivalent of whatever went on with me in high school. That time I didn't go to the prom, I let them think I went to a night club instead. That's the sort of character I showed this Dr. Gamble. I know I presented myself to him as somebody who couldn't care less about anything. I couldn't help myself. I tried; I did try; but I I couldn't break through the barricade that isolates me.

I wouldn't like to call the barricade a mistake, because that sounds like I consciously and deliberately set it up. It did go up in my childhood because I didn't want to hear, but it's just not possible that I could have purposely done it. The mistake was the way I saw the barricade; I'd perceived it as a protection, but it overprotected me. It closed me in, cut me off. So, no matter how much I wanted to talk to Dr. Gamble, I couldn't. I couldn't even say I couldn't.

Then the strangest thing happened. Little by little, during that ten days, I stopped hearing voices. I didn't hear any at all. The whole world was quiet. It was true what the doctors and nurses had said to me: I wasn't locked in; the world was locked out. For a while I was limp with relief. Nothing was getting at me. It was heaven. The *quiet*. Oh Lordy, it was so beautiful. I even *slept*. Without medication.

But that note I wrote in hysteria that first night was effective. All patients at the Institute were there by voluntary commitment. On the tenth day, Dr. Gamble said I could go. I was afraid to go. I didn't know what would happen to the quiet, what it would be like when I left, and I was afraid to go. But I wouldn't—no, I couldn't—say this. If only somebody had said just one word: stay. I simply could not say, "I'm sick. I don't want to go." I was dying for somebody to say, "Stay." But nobody did. I had applied to go, and they said I could go, and go I did.

The very minute I got back to my room, the whole clatter started up again. "Reliant may take him back, but who would want him if they knew the whole story?" Through Dr. Richards, Reliant had found out that I had broken down and they sent me a letter of reinstatement. This didn't faze the voices. "No-good drunk—sold those silver shoes—rotten scurvy thing—illegitimate—pervert—started when he was a *baby*—" The same old hassle. I knew things couldn't go on like this.

At the Psych Institute, I had made the remark that I was going to Olentangy Manor. I said this was why I wanted to get out. So I got myself into a cab and I went out to this fantastically expensive private place. Reliant had written that I could do this if I wanted to, and I had to do something. I was only "out," between hospitals, over the weekend, and all during that time the voices were at me constantly. Whooping and hollering all over the place. Just exactly the way They were immediately before I went to the Institute. They talked incessantly. There was absolutely no letup. I can't say this too strongly. They never shut up.

195

They kept right on at Olentangy. Nothing stopped. This hospital had not the slightest effect on anything. I didn't feel the security I'd felt at the Institute. The people were different. They had religion, and they imposed it on everybody. They say they don't, but they do. Any time I can't take a shower one whole day because it would be against some attendant's religion to work, to go with me, they certainly do. Any time I have to go by their dietary laws, they certainly do. On top of all that gratuitous irritation, I wasn't even getting protection from the voices. They were at me in a regular torrent of vilification. Abuse, accusations, I got so worn out with it. I was far worse off than before I went to the Institute.

I phoned Dr. Richards, and he made arrangements with the Institute and I went right back. It wasn't the same. The first week or so there was frightful. The voices were still with me, all kinds of voices, dragging up all that old stuff, and all at full volume. It was horrible. There wasn't one minute I wasn't ready to scream.

In addition, I had all this banked-up anger. I carried it with me all the time, like an old man of the sea on my back. Then too, I was furiously disappointed and desperate because that peaceful interlude when the voices stopped was gone. *Gone*. Irretrievable. I was beside myself. I'd get so worked up that I'd blaze out at nurses for nothing at all. Once I threw an egg on a nurse. In general, I carried on something awful.

In a peculiar and inadvertent way, Olentangy had helped me. This Institute hospitalization did me some good which it could not have done if I hadn't gone kiting off the way I had. Olentangy let me be angry; it let me show it. Always before I'd had the ever-present corrosive anger eating on me like rust on metal, but never dared to make a peep. I could never fight back at anything—not at the taunting voices, which were really and truly a provocation, and not at people who were actually doing things against me. A man *hit* me once in

Marlowe, and I never lifted a finger. I was every bit as big as he was and I was furious, and I think I could have given at least as good as I got; but this sickening fear slammed the brakes on everything. To be that furious and that scared is brutal. It's a curious mixture, great fear and great anger. It's murder to have to keep every bit of it covered up and be cheerful—bright and breezy, everything peachy-creamy, and tennis anyone.

When I first entered the Institute, I maintained this coverup. The same coverup I'd used since childhood. Often, people on the floor used to say, "Why, you're just fine! I believe you're here for a vacation!" Oh Lordy, if they'd only known! As for the psychiatrist, I don't know. You never are sure how much a psychiatrist knows. Sometimes you find out something you're surprised he knows, and sometimes you're surprised at something you find out he has no idea of. Anyhow, these psychiatrists must have realized that I was off good and proper, because they did give me a sleeping pill every other night.

Those alternate nights were really something for me to handle. There was one attendant who was nice to me, and we'd talk in my wakeful nights. Even so, those nights were grim. There actually were people in the hall—patients who couldn't sleep could get up if they wanted to, and a lot of them did—and I just simply heard them all night long. Not that I could recognize which ones were talking when, but I was positive they were all sitting out there talking about me.

I didn't tell my therapist this. Of course I didn't tell him this. I was so convinced that the voices were the voices of those patients in the hall that I wouldn't have had him know it for anything. I'd be afraid he'd join them and talk about me too. So I kept everything they talked about as well hidden as possible and concocted whatever I could to deal with them.

Occasionally, I'd hear one voice say, "Well you know,

he's not fair with the doctor." And then I'd be less fair. I'd yell at a night nurse, right then, right that minute, and say, "I want me somebody with an M.D." I said this because I had been told that they were sensitive if they didn't have medical degrees, and mine didn't. Dr. Gamble was a psychologist. I'd say, "They put him in a white coat, but he's nothing but a ward boy. I want somebody with an M.D."

What made me do this, I do not know. Maybe it was trying to fight back at the voices, but I don't think so. I just don't know. It's something I used to do outside too. I'd make true or part true cracks about things I knew people were touchy about. I'd do it knowing it would make them angry. Once in a while I'd overdo it, and that got me knocked stemwinding one time. I never found out why I did this.

One thing about this hospitalization I'll be eternally thankful for is the habit Janet had of sharing her visitors. That's how I met Mrs. Ritter.

Mr. Ritter was one of what Joe called the high muckety-mucks at Reliant. I had been deeply hurt that I hadn't heard from even one person at Reliant; but I didn't know Mr. Ritter then and I wouldn't have expected him to come, let alone her. After seeing Janet, she came across the hall to find me, and before our visit was over I had invested full trust in her. I could feel that she wanted nothing out of me, and this had been excessively rare in my life. I can see her right now, walking into that ward, getting somebody to point me out, and coming toward me. I was flabbergasted that somebody I didn't know had come to see me, and just her coming did something for me. I don't know if I can make this clear; but I appreciated that, while she didn't make any foolish pretense that nothing was wrong, she treated me like a person, not a patient. And her being there had nothing to do with Reliant; it was purely personal. I thought she was wonderful. I even thought she was beautiful, which I'm sure she wasn't. A therapist said later that, fine as she might be, I had gone overboard about her, that no human being was perfect, and that I insisted on thinking she was superperfect. I guess he was right, but I don't care. I know what she has meant to me, and to me she'll always be in a class by herself.

When they'd done whatever they thought they could do for me at the Institute, and Lord knows I was no help to them, I was supposed to leave. I was supposed to get back to work and see how things would go. When I got back to Reliant, I thought—. Well, the whole time I was in the Institute, I thought that another change might cure it all. The way it did when I came to Columbus from North Carolina. After all, no therapy was in the picture that time. No therapy, no drugs. Nothing but the change from one place to another. So, even though the voices wouldn't stay stopped in the Institute, I thought maybe another change—. I thought, "I've let Them know that I'm aware I went a little bit off, and people will stop talking."

But They didn't. They didn't even slow up, not one bit. Of course it would have been better if I'd told somebody at the hospital that all this talking and jabbering and dogging at me was going on. But at that time I thought it wouldn't be safe to tell.

Back at work it was miserable. Dr. Gamble was at fault. He should have shown some judgment. He should have made it perfectly clear what he wanted Reliant people to do. He told the personnel people to give me no special consideration, and they passed this along to my office. Well, the people there took "special consideration" to mean saying, "Good morning." So back at work, already in fear and trembling, I found myself severely ostracized. Nobody would so much as give me the time of day. It was like we were all Amish and I was being shunned. And I didn't know why. Not until much later. To come back to work from the hospital and be treated this way was a shock, and it was profoundly hurtful.

Here's what it amounted to: I was crazy and they were what Aunt Mozelle called "dull of comprehension." This combination made a terribly destructive situation for me.

When I was college age, I worked on the men's ward in the University Hospital's Psych Institute. "Male attendants" they called us. We didn't get personal about the patients, neither we nor the medical staff. Didn't take them too much to heart. But I took notice of Mr. Wilde, and we talked, and I've always remembered him.

I was on duty the night he came in. It's true he did scream like a painter; but when I heard what happened, I didn't blame him. They had fastened him up in there without warning him, and then they had told him he wasn't a citizen of North Carolina, his home state. With all that, it made sense to me for him to scream or whatever else he did. I'm from North Carolina myself. Momma and I have been in Columbus from the time I began high school, but North Carolina is home.

I did some odd jobs daytimes then, and Momma did day work. I worked a night shift at the Psych Institute. Momma was studying up for her high school equivalency so she could get a job as teacher's aide. It wouldn't pay any more than what she was making, but she said she'd have a better feeling of herself. When I came across Rob Wilde, I had finished one year of college. I had dropped out to work and save up to go back, what my adviser called falling back to make a better jump. I had a daytime job and I moonlighted at the hospital. It was rough. Momma and I couldn't put by much, but we were mighty close with our money and we saved all we could. I had a scholarship lined up, but I had to have *some* money.

By the time Rob came, I had been at the Institute long enough to know that he wasn't the only one to go to pieces when that door was shut and locked right before their eyes. Lots of patients do. Even some who knew it would happen. I've studied over it, and it must be a terrible hard thing to take, watching somebody pen you in. After I worked there, I hated zoos. It does awful things to man and beast, to be caged up.

Rob felt railroaded, and I think he was. I don't mean he wasn't sick; I couldn't say about that. I mean they should have told him he'd be locked in. They should at least have told him when he got there. That would have been next to no notice, but maybe better than none at all.

I reckon he must have been mixed up some way, but I never heard him make an uncanny remark. I used to sneak peeks at him, and a couple of times he looked like he was ready to bolt but trying hard to hold still. Most usually he looked cool and collected. I had learnt at the Institute that some sick people look out of kilter and some don't. Rob didn't. He looked like anybody else except for that timid, scared look you could catch on him sometimes.

He got to talking to me one night. He was like a lot of them—couldn't sleep much. And he didn't get a pill every night. On his off nights he was restless and nervous and he couldn't settle down, neither out in the corridor nor back in his bed. In my lay-out times, we talked. He knew people in the Columbus NAACP, because he had been a member. This said something about him, in Columbus and at that time. I got along smooth in Columbus, but I liked North Carolina better. In North Carolina, as a black, you knew where you stood. You might not like it, but still you knew. In Columbus, you couldn't tell from one person to the next, and that kept you sort of off balance. Times were changing then, but not fast and not everybody, and not all those who did change did it at the same time. At bottom, I don't think most of them thought one bit better of us here than in North Carolina.

Maybe less. You could go to school, but don't move next door.

White and black, both, put on a show in Ohio, which they call Ohia. I wouldn't say he was a friend, but I knew a black fellow here, Raymond Field. This was his home town, and he really cut capers on the campus. Whites couldn't put any stock in a thing he said. He claimed he had a right to play dirty too. That's how he saw it. He got around, and it was something to do with the way he looked. For sure he was somebody you'd look at twice. He was more than six foot five, and he had a thick bushy head of hair that had never been conked. Looked like a basketball player, which he wasn't. He was a drama student. I saw him once when he was one of the witches in *Macbeth*. He always did a good job, and people took on over him.

He took a right low-down advantage of this. White girls paid a lot of attention to him, and he baited them along. It had got to where black and white could be seen together, around the campus anyhow, without causing any commotion. Nobody bothered you. But some people did stare and some remarks were passed. I think some of the white girls liked this part of it too. Anyhow, Raymond baited them. He'd go through the cafeteria, table hopping, seeing how many white girls' phone numbers he could collect at that one try. He said it was a lot. Every time. He said you wouldn't believe how easy it was. They were practically reciting their phone numbers before he could finish asking. "I'm a novelty!" he said. "They don't give a damn about me, any more than I do about them." He never called those girls.

He did have something going for one short while with a white girl, but he said he never cared a good God damn about her. "They're a novelty to me too," he said. "I'm curious, same as they are. I like to look at skin that's different from mine. I like to touch hair that's different from mine. That's all." I guess it was. I don't think he ever stayed with anybody long enough to count.

He talked a lot too about brothers, sometimes married men with their wives, who got invited to whites' houses. He said they'd drink the honkies' liquor and eat the honkies' party food and smile nicely and go off and fall out laughing at them. He thought that was cool. He said they had every right to fake out the whities. He said worse than honkies and whities, and he said worse than fake out. Sometimes he talked real rough.

I told Rob about Raymond, and he felt as uneasy about him as I did. In North Carolina—I'm talking about an earlier time—it wasn't like that. If a white person was friendly with you, you could feel sure right away that it was for true; because then it could be unhandy for that white person. But when I was going to school and working here in Ohio, you couldn't tell who your friends were, among the whites. Not until you'd known them a while. But with Rob, the time came soon when I felt more easy with him than I did with Raymond. I'm loyal to my people and I married my own color because I like my color, but color isn't everything in this life.

One thing especially hit me about Rob. It was about something that happened to another patient, across the hall in the women's ward. She was somebody Rob knew, and she was one of the ones that everybody said "looked all right." She looked so all right that the other patients took to coming to her with their troubles. She had her own troubles, and, after too many of them came, it got to her.

On top of all that, patients and aides were talking all night up and down the corridor, and patients weren't allowed to close their doors, so she just couldn't get away from the noise. One day she said to her doctor, "These patients are getting on my nerves." He couldn't have cared less, and he let that stick out all over him and it griped her. So she told him that he got to go home at night but that she had to listen to patients and attendants all day and night. He asked her if she'd like to be in a room by herself for a change. Of course she jumped at the chance. Next thing she knew she found herself in solitary.

The way it came about, I just heard tell. From Robby later, and from some of the nurses. But I knew of my own eyesight about that room they put her in. There was nothing in it but a mattress on the floor and a drain like that in the floor of a shower stall. What the drain was for, I hate to think. Anybody in there couldn't even go down the hall to the bathroom without getting an aide to come and take them, and lots of times they'd have to wait for an aide until the next meal was served. And the wall facing the hall was almost all glass. It looked more like a store display window than a room.

Rob didn't know about all this until a week later when she was back on her ward; but when she told him, he like to died. I never saw anybody all tore up like that and doing nothing. It's a wonder he didn't bust a blood vessel, holding all that in. He didn't cuss, he didn't cry, he didn't even talk about it. He just sat still as a rabbit in headlights, white as a sheet and looking sick. I felt for both of them, and I was right in there with them hating that doctor. Felt his importance and his power. Like a cop. It was stinking to set a trap for her, and no living creature should be put in a "room" like that.

After that I felt very kindly toward Rob, and that's when I dropped "Mr. Wilde" and called him Rob. Not the way those doctors, some of them, would walk up to women older than they were and call them by their first names. I called him Rob because he had already said he'd rather I would, and by then I felt like it. He wasn't one of your standard white Southerners the way they were then. There was one of them when I was in the regular part of the hospital for a while. No, truth to tell, that one wasn't standard either; he was a piece of rubbish. He was in a wheelchair. When he called and I'd be the one to show up to help him, he'd yell, "Get back to the kitchen where you belong, you black monkey!" I'd help him. It was my job and besides, he needed help. I knew it was true, like Rob said when I told him about it, that this fellow had had bad hometraining. I knew too that when people are sick, body or mind, they don't show up at their best. Just the same, and I may as well own up to it, I was glad to get through helping him and pass on to somebody else.

We had a few strange-looking individuals on the ward, but, as I was saying, somebody sick in the head doesn't need to look any different from anybody else. Some of the nurses didn't act like they knew this. They used to bother Rob, I was afraid. They used to say things to him like he didn't have anything wrong with him, he was just goofing off from work and having a holiday. Holiday? Fastened up in a psych ward? I was out of line, I reckon, but I mentioned it to two of the nurses. They both said the same thing. They talked that way to him to encourage him, make him think he wasn't so bad off. I thought more likely they made him feel made fun of. Rob may have been crazy; for sure he wasn't stupid.

A while after he came in, he did turn nasty. Not to me. To the doctors mainly and sometimes the nurses. That didn't seem crazy to me. It's hard to put a crazy or not-crazy tag on every little thing somebody does. I've seen doctors have the same trouble. I overheard some of them talking about Olentangy Manor, that sky-high private hospital where Rob went and then came right back to the Institute. The people who owned and ran Olentangy were vegetarians. I think it was for health reasons, not humane reasons. The thing about that was that they pushed soy bean "cutlets" and such on all their patients, no matter what they were used to eating. When you're already upset, a big change in food can go very hard with you.

One of our doctors was saying that an Olentangy doctor had told him that whenever their patients were out for an hour or two they made a bee line for the nearest hamburger joint. This one doctor said, "That shows their hostility." Another doctor said, "I think it shows they want hamburgers." I liked the sound of that second one, but one day as I passed the hall he was the one saying, "Well, you know, sometimes a candle is just a candle." They talked pretty strange themselves sometimes.

I took a short time off and when I came back, Rob had left. I felt bad that we hadn't said goodbye and good luck. Time went by and I finished college and have been selling insurance and doing right well. Momma is a teacher's aide and feeling better about herself just the way she said she would, and my wife teaches in elementary school. My days as a hospital attendant are far behind me, but I've never forgot Rob. There was something about him. He was somebody you remember. I've thought of him many times, and several times over the years I've looked for his name in the phone book. But I never found him.

18
EIGHTEEN

Reliant took me back then, but it didn't do me a fat lot of good to be on the job again. Not with those virulent voices at me every minute and not one real voice speaking to me during the whole day except when absolutely necessary in line of work.

So there I was. This time I had a terrible struggle at work. It got to be worse at work than at home, because the company had bungled my return so badly. At least they did keep me out of that hateful Methods job as they'd promised. But they put me back exactly where I had been, at the very same thing I'd originally been before the promotion to Methods. This demotion made it so that every time I'd see any of the people I had worked with in Methods, if they'd be talking to anybody, I'd be perfectly sure they were gloating over my fall.

To be met by a demotion and sent to Coventry was hardly designed to help me make a successful transition from hospital to work place. The period right in here became almost as bad as at Convoy. I couldn't be satisfied at work, I couldn't be satisfied away from work, and I simply didn't know what to do. I got to behaving so erratically at home— throwing things over the fire escape, leaving lights burning and water running, playing records at earsplitting volume— that one night the landlord came and packed my bag right before my eyes. He said I was to leave the next morning and that, if I had any sense at all left, I'd go back to my family in North Carolina. He was in such a temper that I was afraid of him, and I went and slept at somebody else's place. This friend was away, but I could get in. I stayed there 'til time to get the plane the next morning.

All the way to North Carolina I couldn't stand to think of getting there, because the whole family thought I was totally crazy. A whole flock of them met me at the airport, and, without even greeting them or letting anybody speak to me, I flat said, "I'm going with Zaida and Homer. I'm not going to Momma's." Zaida and her husband lived in a quiet section of Marlowe, and besides I'd always liked them more than any of the others.

They took me home with them, but before you could turn around it got so bad that I couldn't bear it. What causes a place to become unbearable, I don't know. I can't—It just seems—And then it builds up and builds up and it gets so that I am just obliged to get out of there. Much later, a psychiatrist told me something about this. He's the same one who made it clear to me that I was hallucinating, not hearing real people talk. This is getting ahead of myself somewhat, but the way this momentous thing happened was incredibly simple. I'm still astonished at that.

It was in Columbus. I was with a therapist who truly cared about his clients and let them know it. I'm convinced that this is why he was the one who made the breakthrough. In his office one day, I wasn't agitated but quite distracted. I lost concentration so much that, in spite of all my experience in concealment, he noticed. He said, "You're sitting here talking with all the aplomb in the world, but your mind's not on it. You're preoccupied." I said, "Hm?" That's how preoccupied I was. "Hm?" He said, "Your mind's not on this, and I'm wondering—are you hearing something I'm not?'' That's all it took. This secret, that I'd been so desperately guarding nearly my whole life, slid right out. I said, "I thought you heard too. It's the same old thing. They're always talking."

He explained to me that the voices weren't real voices and—because of his obvious concern, I think—I believed him. You might think that this would have cured me, just like that. But that's not the way paranoia works. To begin with, the voices are accusing and condemning and threatening. And mine had been dinning all this garbage into my ears since childhood.

Knowing that They weren't real did relieve me of the terrible strain of thinking that other people heard them. It also made me able to pay less attention to Them a good deal of the time (when I was busy enough). But it never made me stop hearing Them, and it certainly didn't make me voice-proof when They came at me in a full-scale attack. It might seem—to those who don't know—that when They all came at me, I could just pay Them no mind because I knew They weren't real. But this has got to be people who have never heard voices. And I would like to see *them* pay it no mind when They blare out like the Mormon Tabernacle Choir. It's overwhelming. During an attack, sometimes They slow up or get a little less obstreperous before They get back to the high-decibel tumult. In those moments I have said to myself, "They're not real. Not real at all." But it helps precious little or not one bit.

It was this same psychiatrist who got it straight in my head that if I ever really went running and running, I'd never stop. It helped me get this straight that I could remember how nearly I did that, the running thing, at Zaida's and Homer's.

It quickly got so bad at their house that I moved to a cheap hotel down town. Somehow a hotel always seems to be a place where I can be objective and maybe ease away from things. This time, nothing hushed. It was just as bad in the hotel as it was at Zaida's, so the hotel was just as intolerable. Soon though, I was afraid to go out. I got the porter to go to the liquor store and bring me a bottle. As always, this was the only chance at relief. I could almost expect that eventually it would put me in a frame of mind that I didn't care so much about the voices. Then I would fall asleep. This time it didn't work. There was almost a full week that if I slept a wink before I had liquor, I don't know about it. I must have. Nobody could stay awake that long. But I don't remember closing my eyes except after drinking.

I didn't dare step outside the hotel or even my room, and I'd get meals sent in. This cost me a lot. I had some money when I went there, and I thought maybe I had a check coming; but at the rate I was going, I nearly went broke before a check could come. If a check was due. The manager slipped a note under my door saying that I'd have to leave. I knew a boy whose mother worked part time on the desk, and I called her and told her I was expecting a check. She believed me because she didn't know I was off. She talked with the manager and got an extension for me. But then, as it always happened, it got to where even the liquor didn't relieve my anguish.

To make matters worse, although I didn't know it until I was in such shreds and tatters that I was about ready to scream and run, my room was on the floor where the prostitutes were. So there actually was something going on all night long, and this added to my uproar. When my money had nearly run out, I stopped drinking. It was too much of a production to get the liquor. I had gotten afraid even to arrange for meals. The way I'd been getting them, I'd call and I would stand at the door until somebody came, then I'd crack the door and pay right quick. Then I got to where I couldn't put up with that two-trip thing. The boy would have to come and get the money and then go and then come back with the liquor or the food. I couldn't stand that much close contact and all that knocking on the door. So I wasn't drinking at all even before I was quite stone broke, and without liquor I couldn't stand the place any longer. Not in the state I was in.

I called Homer and asked him to come and bring me something to eat. I knew I had to do something. Some way, somehow, I had to get out of there. So I called Homer; I was able to do that much. He came and brought some sandwiches; and when he left, I left with him. I sat in his car and he went back and paid the bill and got my things. I guess it was just as well that they all thought I was a lunatic, because he did all this for me. I asked him to take me to Bentley's Creek, to Momma's, and he did.

Things got a tiny bit better there. Because there was nobody around I could imagine to be talking so much. Not like at the hotel, where there were a lot of people who really were talking. But Momma got on my nerves, the way she always did in this kind of situation. She mother-henned me. She'd almost bring my meals to me on a tray. It was exactly like saying to me, "You can't do one single thing for yourself." Anyhow, it was quieter there and I had the distraction of television and I had my books to read. At that time I still could read.

I didn't sleep much though. The family doctor said he could give me something to help me sleep if I'd come in to Marlowe for an examination, but I wasn't up to that. Different members of the family would be coming in to see Momma though, and first one and then another would have something, some kind of sleeping pill, and I did rest some. After I got a little bit revived, I began to get some better.

Then, unaccountably, I got a whole lot better. And that was when I knew I had to do something. Like quick before it melts. I knew I had to get out of there while I felt able to get out. If I stayed too long and got worse again, I'd be sunk without trace. This is a thing that amazes me, that in such a condition I could figure that out.

And this is true: I figured that the day I'd be down there, the day I found I'd stayed too long, when Momma and all the rest of it had swarmed all over me like kudzu, when I'd disappeared the way anything disappears when it's been swarmed over by a kudzu vine, when I had become a vine-covered lump, the day I couldn't move, heave myself up and get out, that would be the day I would die. That would be the day I'd be ultimately, irreversibly done for. After that day, the body would "live" but the spirit would be destroyed entirely. Somehow, even at my craziest, I've most often been able to fight off going back home, because "going home to North Carolina" was synonymous with "suicide." God knows there were countless times when I'd rather have been dead than going through what I was going though, but I still kept up some shred of hope that maybe I could get *something* out of life.

What I did, I sold nearly all my books and I worked in tobacco and got together enough money to get me back to Columbus. My cherished books didn't bring enough to do anything with. Since it was a distress sale, I had to accept the paltry sum I was paid for them. I think I got like fifteen dollars for quite a lot of books in good condition. Working in tobacco wasn't too hard to do. I worked for the man next to Momma, so I was working almost within sight of her house. I knew I had to use my better time to get a toehold, and I had every intention of getting back to Columbus to talk to Dr. Richards as I'd never talked to anybody before. This time, I said to myself, I'd do it right.

I earned the money, I went to Columbus, I went to my job, and I went to Dr. Richards. And when I got to Dr.

Richards, I clammed up. I didn't actually clam up. I uttered, but I went through the same empty-talking routine all over again. I don't know why I couldn't talk to him. I wanted to talk to him. I was dying to talk to him. Although there is one thing. I have a hideous fear of somebody finding out things about me, even things that maybe they already know for all I could tell. It doesn't make any sense not to have talked to him. One of my main reasons for going back was to talk to him. Further, I thought everybody else on earth was talking about me; it might as well have been him too, if he wanted to. If I'd only just said to him one time, "Everybody's talking." *Two words* might well have started something going for me. Exactly the same as when I was in the Psych Institute. Not much more got it started when it did happen, later. But I never said the two words to Richards, any more than I said them at the Psych Institute, so he couldn't do anything much for me.

It probably didn't have a thing in the world to do with the whole witch's broth—I'm sure I would have clammed up at that point, no matter what—but the Personnel man and my supervisor called me in to talk when I went back to work. They talked about my coming back after I'd blasted off to North Carolina as if I'd been shot out of a cannon. They said, and I could understand their viewpoint, "You know, this can't go on any longer. We're perfectly willing to help you all we can, but this has got to stop." They were telling me that if I flipped again I'd lost my job. They'd help me, on condition that I'd get well.

This was only fair, as far as their interests were concerned. It was fair to tell me, but it didn't help me one bit. They did the only thing to do, they thought. They didn't want to some day fire me without warning. But when they told me, it threw me into a real raucous time. All in the blink of an eye.

I only remember that it was like that, instantaneous

terrible tumult with everything beating on me. I don't remember in any detail or with much clarity and I don't remember things in sequence. I went to *Lancaster* one day. I know I got on the bus and went to Lancaster, thirty miles away, and I had no reason on the face of the globe to go to that town. I kind of know why I had to go somewhere. I was in my room, in bed, and wasn't able to go out. (That's when I've just got to get out.) Here was another unendurable place, and I couldn't get out to save my life. If I poked my nose out even, there was a steady stream of vituperation. Every car, every pedestrian, was pouring it on. I think I figured if I got in a town where nobody knew me, there'd be nobody to talk. That's how I usually thought. But how I picked Lancaster is anybody's guess.

I checked into a hotel when I got there. I could go outside, so I figured I could come back in, even though I was still hearing voices. Even in this strange place. I was hearing things, but it wasn't as bad as it had been in my room in Columbus. So I did go out and walk around some. I was pretty much covering downtown on foot. Before I'd been in Lancaster two hours, I bumped into a boy I used to know at Columbus Ball Bearing. He said his family lived in Lancaster, and he was there to see them. We chatted a few minutes, and I went on walking around.

I'm sure I left Columbus in order to go to a strange place where nobody knew me. Because when I met that fellow, I was thrown right straight back to the beginning of that awful pattern that always forms. The mess built up the way it always did. I don't know the circumstance that brought on this next development, but somehow I got back into that hotel room and couldn't get out again.

Some way, that very evening, I did get out. This part is a blur; I'm not sure just how. When I did get out, I left my things in the room and found I couldn't go back to get them. I found a public phone in a drug store and called the bus station. It was going to be a long time before the bus for Columbus, and I had got out of the room and couldn't get back, and I couldn't stand walking around Lancaster any more, and I couldn't wait for the bus. The whole thing is cloudy, but, of all things, I went from Lancaster to Columbus in a *taxi*.

I found a form letter in my mailbox saying that Reliant had terminated me.

◎ At coffee break one morning I heard some of the men talking about tales they'd heard about Rob Wilde. This was during a time when Rob was badly upset and had gone home to Marlowe for a while. These men were just back from a meeting at the Reliant office in North Carolina. They were gossiping like they say only women do, and raising their eyebrows and lowering their eyelids, and they really looked ridiculous. They were being very insinuating. The gist of what they were saying was that people in the Marlowe office had seen Rob in the company of "a notoriously queer bunch."

I doubted this. I don't think anybody in the Methods office ever understood Rob. Not that I understood him so well, but better than they did. And I know there was a lot of quality stuff in him. Later I realized that what they meant was not queer bunch but bunch of queers.

I always felt Rob didn't belong in Methods. Nor did I. I was dying on the vine there. I only took a new lease on work life when Jim Kupka offered me a job in the office I'm in now. The whole Methods setup seemed flimsy and pointless to me and Rob. Many's the time we both felt as bad as Charlie Chaplin in "Modern Times," spending all day every day tightening that one bolt on each assembly as it rolled past him. I think we felt worse than that, because at least somebody needed those bolts tightened.

215

It was destructive to me to keep typing those inane letters that didn't make any difference to anybody. My husband kept telling me to quit. Before my rescue though, I had hit on a way to survive in there. I used to take personal papers to the office, and, when I was out of "work," I'd work. I'd write my radio scripts for the Urban League program I was helping with. Rob wasn't able to resign himself this way and then look for such an out, or he was too conscientious or something. Maybe the empty nature of his job got him down so that he couldn't even think of something of his own to do during his idle office hours. Whatever his trouble was, I'm sure this job aggravated it. Any more, that whole office is abolished, and good riddance.

In spite of his frustration, Rob was amiable, nice to have at the next desk. He'd notice if you had a new hair-do or wore something becoming. If he'd seen a movie or a play he'd have something to say that was fit to listen to, and we'd talk about his cat in North Carolina and my dog, and he was generous about race and religion. I say "generous" because I believe he felt very chilly toward my own religion, although neither of us ever brought it up.

He had a way of making small pleasantries that I found agreeable. One day another woman and he and I had a brisk little exchange because the woman was getting huffy about Negroes getting office jobs at the company. Rob spoke more softly than I did, but I knew it went against his grain to dispute anybody at all. And he did put his oar in and said a say for our side. Then he went to get coffee, and he asked me how I took mine. He knew how I took mine, but he gave me this chance, and I said loudly, "Black." The woman didn't raise her eyes from whatever she had found to do, just jiggled her beads and pursed up her mouth. I'm afraid Rob and I giggled. It was silly and it was hardly high-grade humor, but it relieved our tension a little and gave us a nice little feeling about each other.

Rob was sensitive and very quiet and gentle. I don't remember ever seeing him out of temper or hearing him say anything mean. I think he had only the kindest feelings toward most people. I never once heard him use profanity or tell a dirty joke, which is more than I can say for the men I heard spreading stories about him. They're hidebound Republicans, and probably they've still got it in for him that he worked so hard with the Volunteers for Stevenson. I was doing that along with him, and no telling what they were saying about me too. I admit that Rob should never have sold those little silver-shoe campaign pins on company time. Any more than I never should have written my scripts on company time. But then the company didn't seem concerned about wasting our time and us ourselves when it dreamed up those "jobs" we had. If it didn't even give us leaf-raking work, why shouldn't we save ourselves with silver shoes and radio scripts? I don't feel bad about it.

The tittle-tattle from those men irked me. It's a pity they didn't have something better to do than to jaw like that about somebody so recently in a hospital. But what they said about Rob didn't influence me. I'd heard their conversations before, and neither their mental agility nor their notion of masculinity impressed me. They were all beer and television. They called their little sons names like Butch, and thought Robert Ruark was the greatest. They couldn't be expected to have much understanding of Rob.

He wasn't coarse enough to fit in with them, so they had to smirk and say he was "an odd one." I didn't believe what this broadly implied, and I also didn't believe that Rob would throw away his time with dubious characters. I knew some of his friends. They knew him far better than I did, and they thought a lot of him.

19
NINETEEN

After one rockbottom time in Columbus, a friend did what a landlord did once. Simply packed a bag, put me on a plane, and sent me home to Bentley's Creek. There was nothing else he could do. I realized that. But I hadn't been in Momma's house ten minutes before I knew he'd saved me from Scylla and thrown me to Charybdis.

She wouldn't let me alone for a minute. She was always there, hovering. If she saw me start across the room for something, she'd spring up and dash ahead of me and get it for me. She'd fuss about and tell me to rest myself and restore my soul. If I tried to be quiet and put myself together, she'd be right at me, chirping. "Mustn't brood, darling! Have to try to brighten the corner. Get out and see people!" It would have been unnerving at best, and I was already in bits and pieces when I arrived.

After a while I got my head up enough to try to get some kind of job, anything to start with, but I couldn't. Momma had been thorough with her talk of her son the mental patient, and nobody I knew would hire me to do anything. When I'd go a bit farther afield, where they *didn't* know me, I couldn't put "Went home to North Carolina" on applications to cover the dates of hospitalization. I was *in* North Carolina.

I went to a man who was a former boss of mine, and I foolishly let him know how desperate I was for work. I truly was desperate. I had a nasty little job as short-order cook in a greasy spoon kind of place. It did practically no business and I got practically no pay. One virtue this job had, it left me alone in the kitchen. I scoured those pots and pans until you could see yourself in any one of them. That seemed to help me some. The owner had a nephew who was just before losing his job though, and I knew that my days were numbered.

When I went to my former boss, he took me on at his factory. He made small parts that the Marlowe mills used. He made me a general handyman at a dollar an hour. This was early in 1959, and a dollar an hour was starvation wages, practically peonage. By the time all payroll deductions were made, I had thirty-two dollars a week take-home pay. The boss wasn't so forgetful of my experience that he didn't use some of it for his convenience. In my spare time, when I wasn't moving brake drums that weighed a ton, I typed his letters and set up inventory controls. But my hours (forty-nine a week) and pay were those of "helper."

Another spare-time project the boss dreamed up for me was working on the roof of his building. It was a mammoth thing that spread over nearly half a block. The job wasn't re-roofing, but putting on an eighth of an inch of black liquid with a brush. I lugged this fluid up to the roof in five-gallon cans. A giant step down from IBM specialist, anyone would agree. And that fabulous wage of a dollar an hour. No one would easily believe a man could exploit another one in this way. I stuck like a leech though. I knew if I gave up that job I'd never find another one, and even thirty-two dollars take-home pay a week was thirty-two dollars a week more than if I hadn't been working.

After a few months, this went down to something like thirty dollars a week. This was in June, and a fellow had a major heart attack and had to plan on being out until October. In lieu of carrying insurance for that kind of absence, the boss *required* that after a person was out for two weeks the rest of us had to give a dollar and something a week until he returned. Among other things, this sure got workers back on the job before being quite able.

One lucky thing. I ran into somebody I used to know, Duane Cross, and he was working the swing shift at Duke Power. For very little, he let me share his room. This worked better than I'd thought it would, and meant I didn't have to live in a hovel or with my family any longer. I was alone a great deal. With Duane working at night, I was by myself until three every morning, a thing I could never have done in Ohio without being set upon by the mob of voices. I was thankful for this and for having him to be with some of the time.

I seldom went to Bentley's Creek. Whenever I did, something always happened and I'd get so depressed that the voices would come back and take over. My family was a never-fail source of trouble to me, and I avoided them all as much as possible. I didn't go near them except when absolutely necessary. I'm sure they took umbrage. I'd started this handyman job at the factory early in March, and through the summer I made real progress. Not with the job; with myself. I seldom heard voices except when I'd had a bout with some member of the family.

It became clear to me that I wouldn't be able to stay in Marlowe. I was so utterly and completely disgusted with the town. I was thoroughly fed up with its narrow outlook and its backward ways. The only thing I wanted from Marlowe was a job paying enough so I could accumulate enough to leave. I think my job probably had a great deal to do with my feeling about the town, but the feeling was there and nothing I could do about it. I don't take up much room in the world, and it didn't seem to me that I asked for much. By that time, my expectations and hopes had come down. All I wanted was a simple life with a little diversion to lighten it.

There was one thing I did get out of that factory job. That was the knowledge that I was able to work even under the most awful conditions, and that I needed to have no fear of working at a more normal job. All the time I was at the factory, I didn't miss a single day. A truly wonderful lady at the local employment security board was working at finding something for me, and this helped me endure the job I had. My oldest brother, Wibby, even came around somewhat. He said he'd try to use his connections in my behalf. He had been with the State Highway Department for thirty-five years and knew a great many people.

Nothing ever came from Wibby, but this fine woman found me a job cashiering at a small, inexpensive eating place. It paid little enough, but I got two meals a day thrown in and that took up some of the slack.

Then I met an Irish family that had moved to Marlowe since I'd been in Ohio, and I thought to my soul this would change my whole life. I thought they were just the loveliest people on the face of the earth. I still do, and they actually are.

There was a mother and father well along in middle age, and they had come to this country from Northern Ireland when they were in their early twenties. The father was a Methodist minister. There were two sons around my age and a daughter, younger. The whole family took me in, so to speak, and loved me. Except for one of the sons.

They were all teetotalers—except Wesley, who only drank once in a while and then so sparingly you could hardly call it drinking—and they didn't smoke, but they didn't push any of this at me. They had their religion and their principles, but they didn't go on at me about them.

Mr. O'Neill was very advanced for that day and area in his ideas on race and labor. I loved this in him, but it gave him some trouble with his fellow clerics from time to time. Not so much with his congregation, although of course most of them were light years behind him. Only a few ever outright complained, and they didn't get far. This was because the rest sort of uneasily put up with Mr. O'Neill because they loved him. Also they may have, deep down, known he was right. Complainers wouldn't have got far anyhow. Gentle and good as he was, Mr. O'Neill wasn't one to back down for anybody.

One of the boys, Hugh, was like him, and so was the daughter. Hugh worked in a law office in Highfield and Mary was away at college. But the second boy, Wesley, was plain on the other side of the fence from them. He didn't think like them. He didn't talk like them. He didn't talk like anybody; he talked like a business letter. He was all buzz and business, and he stayed out at that textile mill and bucked for promotions and fought the union and that was what it was all about. This brought on an occasional argument in the family. They all said their say, and this Wesley had a tongue that could cut the grass, but there was no breaking up. Somehow they were still devoted to one another.

It seemed to me that I couldn't do better in life than to be something like the O'Neills, and I tried every way I knew to be as much like them as possible. They would be my real kin, I felt. I thought the way they thought, and I would do the way they did. In a degree I was Protestant Irish too, and I felt this would make another bond. My dream was that no matter where I might be in years to come, I'd always have with me this feeling of union, of solidarity, of having my little niche. And my little niche is all I've ever wanted from life.

They were "frightfully wholesome," as my old friends at the Little Theater would have said. Not "zany" at all. They were all good sailors and swimmers, and they'd go in the summer to Lake Cherokee where they kept a boat, and it was wonderful. As a group, they had their own looks and their own definite flavor. They had black hair and dark-dark blue eyes, the darkest eyes to be blue that I ever saw. My eyes were much lighter blue, but in general I had the same coloring and that meant something tremendous to me. What impressed me the most was that they knew who they were and what they were and they didn't have to give it a thought.

They had their own tastes and ways of doing things. There were lots of little things, of no importance in themselves. With all their meals they drank tea, strong enough to walk out of the room. They called oatmeal "porridge" and they ate soda bread Mrs. O'Neill baked. They poured milk from luster "jugs," and the boys were dashing in their báinín jackets sent them by relatives in Ireland. On Sundays they were likely to have trifle for dessert.

All this soon came to mean to me the only way to dress and eat and be. My admiration and affection for them roused in me an interest in my Irish origins. I remember, when I was small, being told by my father that I should never let anybody call him an Irishman. He was an Ulsterman, he said. I said this to a man named Kelly once, in my childish ignorance, and he looked at me crossly and said, "Then he's no better than English." This confused and intimidated me, but of course I didn't say a word to him or ask my father about it. I just avoided the whole matter of my Irish ancestry until I became so enchanted with the O'Neills.

There came a time when the voices dragged up this old subject, and there'd always be one to say, "And that goes for your preacher friend too—not real Irish—he'd be a Catholic—Scotch-Irish—planters—." When this began to bother me too much, I rather hesitantly asked Mr. O'Neill about it. He said, "I don't need my Irishness authenticated by anybody, and doubtless neither do you. So, now!"

Well. Here was this thing that had gnawed at me off and on for years and, when it was applied to him, just dried up and blew away. Mr. O'Neill simply brushed it aside as if it were a fleck of lint on his coat—not evil but an unworthy thing, not belonging on his coat, insignificant and not to be concerned about. I was some impressed.

Not that I was ever the less impressed with him, but I learnt that he had good and sufficient reason for looking on what I'd considered a tempest and been unshaken. He didn't tell me right away, because I had beat around the bush so that he hadn't known what was on my mind. I kept on in my awkward roundabout way, and then it came out. He said, "My branch of the family was founded by a maverick. This was Daniel. In the seventeenth century he would have succeeded Owen Roe as The O'Neill only that he had turned Protestant." Again, I was some impressed.

The thicker I got with the O'Neills, the more Irish I became. When I got a somewhat better job, I sent off for a pair of cuff links made like the Tara Brooch. One of those museum reproductions. The first time I wore them at the O'Neills I felt some anxiety. I had remembered belatedly that the Tara Brooch had been found in Eire, not Northern Ireland. But this didn't come up.

Hugh gave me a top coat once when he got a new one. Even though it didn't quite fit, I loved wearing it. It was Connemara tweed and it had been his, it had belonged to one of the O'Neills. My friends. My family, sort of.

My happiness with the O'Neills and their glorious goodness to me nearly made up for the hateful little jobs I had. More than that, it held the voices at arm's length for a while. Mrs. O'Neill was the soul of kindness. When she spoke to me she always said, "Robby, dear," as if that were my name, Robby-dear. They gave me a key to their house. I could go there any time I wanted and be sure of being welcome. I feel certain that they saw my dire need. Being taken in to this extent had a remarkably steadying effect on me. It was heaven while it lasted, but then the same old thing started up. First the muttering, unintelligible and almost inaudible, then a gradual rise in volume and clarity until loud voices would be whirling and flying all around me and I felt as if physically assaulted.

Soon I was drinking again, the very cheapest rotgut stuff, which was all I could buy. It happened more than once that I let myself into the O'Neills' when I was in right foul shape. Mr. O'Neill would say soothingly the next day, "Well, you'd a drop taken, but you're all right now." He and Mrs. O'Neill held back any suggestions. I think they were afraid that that would have scared me off, and of course it would have. But I had trouble with Wes. He tended to make scenes when anything like this happened. Or anything else out of the way.

Sometimes I'd be late to a meal when I knew they were expecting me. Mrs. O'Neill would cook, and, if I wasn't right there, all hell would break loose with Wesley. The same situation I'd had with Fina. Wes would snarl and growl about ingratitude. Same thing I'd got from Fina. I was not ungrateful and this got next to me, the same as it had when Fina did it, coming on top of all the voices that were making me erratic in the first place. Finally I got so fed up with Wes and his stupid moralistic speeches that I started deliberately staying downtown and not letting them know I wouldn't be there. This should have warned me, because I'd been in just this situation before with other people. It was a pattern.

I'd hear from Wes about how there were phones and I knew how to use them. I grew more keenly resentful of his badgering. I simply was not going to be driven this way. Of course I couldn't bring myself to say this to him, but his constant hectoring made me behave worse and worse. And it was *not* my fault.

Then I started working on something to ease things. I had the idea to get Mrs. O'Neill and all the others presents for St. Patrick's Day. Since this wasn't a usual gift-giving time, I though it would be a nice surprise for them.

At the same time, I was having a tough battle with myself. I would walk the streets until nearly daylight, slogging along in the rain sometimes, aimlessly all the time, until I was exhausted. Even exhausted, I'd find it impossible to go home and get in bed. It's a wonder I didn't get knocked in the head. It was all just the same as it had been at other terrible times when I did such a lot of night walking. I didn't know what was to become of me. I got so deathly worn out with it all that I didn't much care. I was tired. *Lord,* I was tired.

Strangely enough, this turbulence didn't stop my planning and shopping for gifts. To get the money, I pawned the only pair of gold cuff links I ever had (never to be redeemed, of course). I even made a decoration. I went to the woods on the edge of town and searched out a nice broken-off limb. It was big and beautifully branching, perfect. I stripped it 'til it looked like a "dead" winter branch and tinted it pale green, with whitewash mixed with food coloring, and I nailed it to a wooden block. I went to a variety shop that carried things in season and out, and I got Christmas tree balls, all different sizes but all the same emerald green. I hung them from the branches and twigs with almost invisible white nylon thread. To me, it was charming. Panky Burgess at the Arts and Crafts Center saw it later and liked it so well that she put in on display. I heard that when Christmas came, the Center patterned their Christmas tree after it. They used a whole little bare tree. Spray-painted it pink and trimmed it with silver balls. I didn't see it. I was back in Ohio by then. Anyhow, for my St. Patrick's Day decoration, I cut big shamrocks out of green construction paper and scattered them all around its base.

I did all this, but still the tension kept mounting steadily in me. The voices got louder and nastier and there were more of them. "Theron Hearn says he needs to be analyzed—if anybody ever did, he does—what a queer—those O'Neills better watch him—have him in court—disgraced before the whole town—"

I don't know what anybody could have had me in court about, but while I'd be thinking this there'd be a voice saying, "It doesn't matter. They've got nothing on you, but that's no protection. What you are will show—guilty in the public eye—" In my own eye too, by then. By then, as always at such a stage, I could have been made to believe anything about myself. Everything was so confused and mixed up as far as I was concerned, they could have pinned any crime on me and made me believe it. I was so no-good that there was nothing so bad or so far fetched but what I could have believed it of myself. If They'd said I had killed Lizzie Borden's parents, I could have believed it. So there were all these wheels within wheels: the voices, my provocation of the O'Neills, Wes's anger, tramping the streets all night, the terrible voices, and my St. Patrick's Day plans.

The night before St. Patrick's Day, Wes and his parents were out and I decided to put out the green bough and the presents and have them ready and waiting when the O'Neills got home. Mary and Hugh were out of town, of course, but I had got presents for them too. I don't remember now what I had got for the others. It all got to be such a muddle that the memory is blurred. But I know it was a bottle of Irish whiskey I had for Wes. As little as he drank, he liked this.

I got out all the presents and began waiting for the O'Neills. I was longing for them to come and be happy with my gifts. I was wishing Mary and Hugh were there too, and I guess I got restless and impatient with the waiting while the voices banged on me. Anyhow, I began to think of all of them off somewhere having a good time while I sat alone. Then the horrid thought came to me that if the O'Neills took any special interest in any Irish day it would be the anniversary of the Battle of the Boyne, and the month would be August, and the color would be orange, and up King Billy, and all the rest. Oh, screw King Billy!, I thought, nearly weeping in my disappointment. Then things got disconnected and there was no logical sequence. I began to feel very sorry for myself, and the next thing I knew I was painting some of their furniture green. I think I meant well. I was trying to make things pretty for St. Patrick's Day, and I thought this would look grand. I got the green-tinted whitewash, and I painted two tables.

Then I put the bough in place, and I was arranging the presents on the coffee table for the hundredth time when Wes and Mrs. O'Neill came in. I don't know where Mr. O'Neill was, and I don't know where she got to. I heard her whisper, "Glory be to the Father!" and then she disappeared. From then on all I clearly remember is a lot of screaming—that was me, I guess—and shouting. I may have been crying; I don't know. I think it's understandable that Mrs. O'Neill was disconcerted. I must have looked pretty alarming by that time and the room was a mess, with the furniture green, but Wes's total anger was devastating. He said later I'd called his mother a dirty old Irish biddy, but I do not remember this and furthermore I don't believe it. I don't think I said one word to her. That doesn't signify, but I never in my wildest ever thought of her in such a way. I don't even remember her being in the room except at first, when they came in. Wes was bawling me out at the top of his voice, but the only thing I can remember is, "Get a cloth and a bucket." He stood over me, roaring and bellowing, while I did the best I could to wash the green off and dry the tables and put on lemon oil.

Somehow that got done, and I don't know how I got out of the house. Yes, I do. I went through the back door and down the steps, and I took the bottle of Irish whiskey I'd got for Wes. I don't know why I took it; I didn't drink it. I think maybe I thought, "This doesn't belong to you any more." How I made it to the bus station or why, I don't know. But I went there and put a quarter in a shower stall and went in and lay down on the floor. For the first time in weeks, everything stopped and there was quiet.

◎ Without wishing to indicate any lack of respect for my parents, the whole O'Neill family except me is soft on misfits. My brother and sister have stated they they observed things differently, but they were not often at home during the period our parents attempted to rehabilitate Robby Wilde. His presence continued a process of family disruption which began early in our contact with him.

I myself was impressed at first with Rob's enthusiasm and spirit. His behavior soon indicated, however, that this was only a technique for becoming entrenched in the family's regard. At the same time he continued in his disgracefully irresponsible way. It is true, as my parents reminded me pointedly, that he aggressively sought employment and took whatever jobs were available to him. It is also true that he was self-indulgent and undisciplined, and would fail to report to work whenever he felt blue. I can excuse physical illness, but I cannot tolerate a shirker.

I am human too, and there are days when I don't feel so cheerful, but I put down this weakness and go and discharge my obligations at the mill. That's all it takes. Moreover, I have people working under my supervision, and I have to set them an example as well as further my career. If Rob wants to be neurotic, well and good, but not about a job. Firmness is what's needed with people like Rob. Otherwise they lose incentive. My parents, and my brother and sister when they were home, coddled him, and in the end we all paid for it. In due course, he committed a number of acts of an unmistakably hostile character. Several times he caused me to lose my temper, and I hold this against him too.

Once he caused my father to speak very reprovingly to me. I have always felt that Dad was simply intent on defending Rob and did not have a legitimate grievance against me. I was completely out of patience with Rob's obsession with everything Irish, and I said to Dad that anybody would think Rob was more Irish than I.

Dad gave me what my sister calls his level look and said, "He'd be within his rights. Irishness isn't always a matter of Irish parents any more than it's a matter of two choruses of 'Mother Machree,' the same as a man may be an artist even though he never produces a work of art."

I was astounded. I didn't know what to make of this kind of talk. But Dad had just begun. He said, "We've been fortunate in this family. But it's very common, and well you know it, to find a strong streak of melancholy in anybody who's Irish. The Irish are a vulnerable people. Our long memories are our enemies, and our wounds don't heal well. This boy has a formidable collection of hurts. Confound it, I don't hear with my ears only and I don't see with my eyes only, and I know this about Rob. You don't believe this, I suspect, because I can't take a piece of graph paper and plot a curve, but I know. And this family is going to be a healing agent whether it strikes your fancy or not. We'd rather have you with us on this, but it isn't necessary, not one bit necessary."

I took this quietly, out of deference to Dad. He's a wise man except for those occasions when he's being gulled. But I did have a momentary queer feeling of being pushed aside in favor of a stranger. This feeling didn't persist, because, despite frequent crossness, none of us ever doubts the loyalty of the others.

Rob laid such emphasis on this, our "wonderful family life" he called it, that one night I tried to explain to him that while it was wonderful to have love and loyalty in one's family, not to have it wasn't any tragedy. If I hadn't always had it, I'd have simply done without it, that's all. I told him this. He looked embarrassed and uneasy and then he said, "Wes, let me give you my version of an old proverb. If the cap doesn't fit you, don't throw it on the floor and stomp it." This was so foolish, and I was so surprised that Rob had all this to say, that I made no further attempt to engage him in conversation.

The incident that caused our entire relationship with Rob to break down was brought on by his blatant lack of consideration for Mother. For a long time he hadn't had enough regard for her to be in the house to eat the meals she had cooked. He would come in late or not come. Sometimes he'd have inadequate excuses or none whatever, nothing but insolence. He was shrewd enough never to put his insolence into words; but his behavior showed it plainly. He and I had many quarrels about this.

The worst one came on the night before St. Patrick's Day. Because of the way this incident ended, I never understood how it began. But he had presents for us all, shamrock decorations, and a queer sort of "ornamental" tree-like object. A piece of *dead wood*. I had been working late at the office that night, and I went to pick up Mother and Dad at one of ther interracial meetings. This in itself put me on edge. I don't see why Dad had to get out in the open like that with his race and labor bias. It was incompatible with the times. Mother came with me, but Dad stayed on.

Mother and I came into the house to find Rob agitated and quarrelsome. Not drunk but very peculiar. The living room was in disarray and the furniture was green. One of the tables Rob had smeared with green paint was a family heirloom and very dear to Mother. My grandfather had made it, and Mother and Dad sat at it and ate their first meal as a married couple. She was perplexed and I was so angry that I led her from the room and insisted that she stay out. I think she would have taken no notice of me except that she was in a state of shock. I never before took it on myself to tell Mother what to do.

I yelled at Rob that he knew how my parents valued that table, and I made him wash off the paint and clean up the room. Most of what we both said isn't worth repeating. He kept snivelling that he had wanted to make things pretty for St. Patrick's Day.

He cleaned up and left, and things were never the same again. Rob knows when he's done wrong, but he can't take being corrected. The family doesn't harp on my part in this incident, but I know that they still consider I was too harsh with him. It has never been clear to me why they saw the trouble with Rob as any discredit to me. They know that I will help people who will help themselves, and have often seen me help people who are deserving. But I cannot tolerate refusal to make a sustained effort. Rob's drinking was a salient factor in his negative approach to life, and that negative approach was his real problem. He knew drinking would remedy nothing, and he knew Dad, his idol, preferred that he not drink, but he did it, regardless.

In all honesty I feel that I did my part to help Rob get on his feet. In the final analysis, everything we did failed because he was weak-willed. I hope it will be a long time before my parents undertake such a project again. My parents, to use Dad's old-fashioned expression, have hearts of corn. They will squander this strength and goodness on a self-pitying lay-about as quickly as on a deserving case. With all due respect, they can't tell the difference.

20
TWENTY

It still haunts and hurts me, the way I felt so excluded from the family all during my childhood. Even though I'd found out that I need not have felt that way, I *had* felt that way and I *had* lived in mortal fear and the damage was done.

Since then, an important part of the remaining hurt has been much eased, and in the most inadvertent way.

Even when I was very small I suspected that there was some difference between me and the others. Suspected. I didn't let myself really believe it. Nonetheless, the thought that kept coming to me was, "I'm not his son." Not the son of the man we all called Poppa. I don't know but what I thought this earlier than I knew, and had been closing it out. I didn't know definitely until one time when I went home from Columbus.

It happened that, during one of the worst of my holed-up raucous times, a time of deep trouble and violent turmoil, one of the voices told me this. That was when I first fully believed it, that Tom Ashcraft was my father. The voice was telling me this on a night when Joe came to see me. The voice was telling me this viciously. But it relieved me. If the voice hadn't told me, and if I hadn't believed it, I don't think I would have been strong enough to leave my hiding place with Joe the next day. That was the day Mrs. Ritter went with me to the hospital.

I remember phoning her, in a quiet moment in the very midst of the huge hullabaloo, and telling her that I wanted to see Joe. She called him and he came that night. The reason I had wanted to see Joe was that I thought he'd heard what this voice was saying, and I wanted to talk with him about it. At one point in the confusion, I thought Joe was part of some plot. The night before, he had taken off his coat and hung it up. I had looked at this coat hanging there, and the coat trembled and began to look like an old woman with her back bent, weeping. Now, I figured, I knew.

I knew about this "horrible" thing my mother had done, and she was sobbing. For a few seconds I really thought that Momma was in the room. At that particular moment, I wanted to tell her that I was glad, because this let me know about me and Tom Ashcraft. It let me know that for a while I really had had something with him, that the thing with him when I was so little was not what I'd been thinking it, but that he really must have loved me as his child. It was a jolt to know that I had had something fine back in that period when I had felt so totally out. He must have thought I was something special.

Even yet I don't understand why it took one of the voices to convince me of what I'd suspected for so many, many years. I don't know either how one of my voices could convince me without my having known it first. But during the time when I was wavering, trying to analyze the voices and figure if anything any of them said could be true, I went home. Then and there I definitely found out that this was true.

It was from Wilbur, my older brother. He was drunk, at home one night, and I said to him, "Well, you know, I'm Tom Ashcraft's son." He stared at me and started to cry, and he called his wife and said to her, "It's worse than we thought. He knows." I had taken something of a stab in the dark, really, but then Marruth told me that it was true. She said Wibby had told her long ago. Evidently he had known it for years and years, and, in the course of their being married, he had told her. But I never learnt how Wibby first knew it. There may have been some little stir when I was born. He would have been way up in his late teens and already working. He didn't tell me how he knew, and I didn't ask him. I was afraid he'd ask me how I knew, and I certainly wasn't going to tell him I heard a voice telling me. I'm sure he assumed I'd heard it in some ordinary way, and I let him think that. I had to. I didn't know whose voice it was I'd heard. I kept wondering how much Poppa knew about this, but of course I didn't bring it up.

I don't know whether this is why I felt so sure I didn't belong, that awful feeling I began having when I was so very young. The thing that still puzzles me is how I only suspected it for so long but then believed it when the voice told me. Because I was glad to know it, and the voice certainly didn't mean to give me anything to be glad about. No voice ever did, and this one was vicious. From all my long years of experience with the tormenting voices, I am absolutely certain that if They had known this would give comfort to me, no one of Them would have ever told me.

It was just the one voice, a man's voice. This man was repeating, over and over, as a bunch of people advanced into the room—Oh my God, that was a terrible time—repeating things They hoped would make me despise myself. I think too he was showing around pictures that that little man in blue had taken of me—doing what I don't know—and he was harking back to a time in the hospital. A fellow patient had worsened and was about to leave for the state hospital, a thing we all dreaded. This was Leroy Crowe, a Negro, and I felt so sorry for him, and I know I told him good-bye but I don't remember much about it. This voice kept saying, "Look at him. Got his arm around that nigger." Maybe that was the picture he was showing. "Going back on his raising. Blah blah blah." He was talking, talking, talking, and then suddenly he said a new thing. He said. "He thinks Tom Ashcraft was his father. Well, it's true. Tom Ashcraft *was* his father."

After that new thing, I could take that whole horrible time a little better. I realized with a certainty I'd never felt before that Tom Ashcraft had really cared about me. Holding me while I slept, he wasn't just being kind to a little neighbor boy who needed attention, and his holding me wasn't the homosexual thing I'd believed it was. He really cared about me. As my father. If my mother had been there—as I momentarily thought she was—I would have told her then. But later, when I was home, I never mentioned it. I thought about it, and I tried to think of a way to say, "Momma, I don't think this is as bad as maybe you do." I wanted to tell her I was glad she had had something with Tom Ashcraft, and glad that I had had something with him. But how do you tell your mother you know she was an adulteress and you're her bastard? I never could broach the subject. I never could think of a way to approach it. And now she's dead and I can never tell her.

When she died, it was sudden and there was no chance for me to see her before. I left my work and flew down to Marlowe. I had just gone on a new job and could only take off the least possible time. So I had an excuse to offer, and I was able to run in and run right back out without any arguing about my staying. I was not in good condition, not solid or steady at all, and it took everything I could muster to go and attend that funeral and be with the family. I was bad off enough without all their funeral talk.

It rained when we were on the way to the cemetery and during the short service there. I thought it was better that way. A beautiful bright day would have been all the more distressing. All her life Momma loved a fine day. She used to talk about being out in "God's blessed sunshine" and I remembered her quoting "Blessed is the bride the sun shines on, Blessed is the dead the rain rains on." So rainy was better and the funeral itself wasn't so bad. But I nearly climbed the wall at the wake. The things those people said! They'd spout what I suppose they guessed would comfort them, with absolutely no thought to what might or might not comfort me. Mostly I think they simply mouthed clichés, paying no attention at all to even the words they were saying.

Actually, I didn't want them saying anything. Not to me. I had long had mixed emotions about Momma, and when she died I felt like I'd been stirred with a stick. For one thing, I harbored a lot of resentment. For another thing, I could never say anything to her again. She was dead and I hadn't been strong enough to tell her something that would have been terribly important to her, and she could never know that I knew and how I felt about it. I didn't want to say this to any of them, and I didn't want them saying anything at all to me. But they did. Oh, they did. They just flooded me with their babble and their gabble, and I—silently, of course—took violent exception to nearly every single thing they said or implied. Momma wasn't feeling pain any more, it was true. But that was only because she wasn't feeling anything. She wasn't "at peace." She wasn't awake with the blest in the mansions of rest. She wasn't "smiling down" on me.

They might as well have told me she'd gone where the woodbine twineth, or emigrated to another star. They did tell me to "think about where she is now." I thought about where she was, and it wasn't just beyond the shining river in that far-off sweet forever. What was left of her was six feet under the ground in Magnolia Cemetery.

Even without these people and their stock phrases, I would have been hard pressed not to cry my eyes out. Right there in front of everybody. I didn't believe that I'd see Momma again. They did, or said they did. That would be on that bright and cloudless morning when the saved of earth have gathered over on the other shore. I never could believe it, and I couldn't suddenly believe it because it would have been a convenience and a comfort. There was no comfort. I just had to grit my teeth and bear it and trust that it would ease up as time passed. But oh! how I wished I'd been able to tell her that I knew who my father was. And that I'd always feel better that I knew.

I still wonder how the voices could have made such a mistake as to tell me something that made me feel better.

◎ I'm an old lady. I'm a very old lady. I don't expect what was considered fitting in my time. Regardless, I never thought I'd live to see the day when there'd be such flagrant exhibitions of poor taste at a time of death. I hadn't been getting out much, but I went to the wake for Mamie Wilde, and the funeral too. She was my double first cousin, and naturally I made the effort.

The church sevice was simple and dignified. It went smoothly except for Winona Hightower's sobbing out loud to the embarrassment of all. The funeral was held at Bethel Methodist Church where Mamie still had her letter, although she was an inactive member for many years. But this was only after a sharp contention with Willene. She surged up before her mother's body was cold and astounded the family by demanding that the funeral be held at her church. Her church is some strange offshoot of the Baptists. It has a long name I never can remember. Baptists are known to all as joy-killers, but this sect of Willene's makes regular hardshell Baptists look lighthearted and frivolous. Mercifully, the other children voted her down right handily. She was very persistent, and not quite pleasant, I understand, but they wouldn't hear of it. Mamie was taken to Bethel as a small child. She had her lifelong membership there. She was married there. Her children were all christened there. And Mamie always felt a powerful bond with Bethel, even though she hadn't been able to attend for years. Basically, as they say nowadays, Willene's a nice girl. But she's a fanatic, and that is not nice. She's offensive in the way she has thrust that religion of hers at the rest of the family. Imagine trying to have Mamie's funeral anywhere but Bethel! In my day, nobody ever questioned that the wishes or inclinations of the departed were what guided plans for services and keepsakes.

I was of two minds about the wake. There were a couple of baskets of flowers, to be taken to the church and the cemetery for the funeral. Nothing gaudy or splashy, just a few flowers. And none of those sickeningly sweet tube roses that nobody can stand at any other time because of funerals. Friends had sent eatables in nice amounts, not skimpy and not overabundant. Eulalie Morris sent her specialty, a splendid seven-layer jam cake. I lent my mother's silver service and six cups and saucers of my good china. At a time like that, you can't overdo coffee and coffee pots. Dolly Robertson sent a tray of ham and biscuits and a big platter of her famous pulled mints.

I never saw candy at a wake before, but let that pass. Come right down to it, candy's no more festive than jam cake. Anyhow, people are going to enjoy themselves at a wake, with or without encouragement. At Mamie's, there were more than a few who knotted up into jolly little groups and held reunions. With the open coffin in the next room and the door wide open.

Ah, well, it's always been that way. I complained once, countless years ago, about the hilarity at a wake. I was told that you couldn't expect people to go around all evening with

239

long faces. This got me. I said that when "mourners," supposedly paying their last respects, were no longer able to keep decently long faces, they should leave the wake. Well. I nearly got asked to leave that one myself. I never have mentioned the subject again. I just look at them and think my thoughts about them and keep my own counsel. Even with all that, I was glad Mamie was laid out at home and not downtown at Altenburg's. Those undertakers would have had her lying in a regular bed in one of those arrangements they call slumber rooms.

Zaida had set out the collation on the dining table with one of Mamie's good tablecloths, and it looked right pretty. Just before people began to arrive, she went to give things a last-minute check. And God's blessing that she did. She found Cousin Rufus's business cards placed all up and down the table. There's no accounting for what people will do these days, even in a house of death. There's no sense of the fitness of things.

I'm not Victorian about mourning clothes, and it has been a long time since these old eyes have seen anybody go into black, then violet for second mourning. Or even wear black to funerals. Of course, when people did wear mourning clothes, this was only members of the immediate family; but even now I always have one black hat in case of a funeral. Nowadays I think people wear whatever they have and feel like wearing, and in general that seems sensible. But it would have been nice if Jackie Turnbull had worn something other than a bright red hat.

No matter how careful you try to be, a funeral can stir up dissension and rancor in all kinds of quarters. My nephew, Cashel Moore, got into a little set-to at the cemetery. Cash is the family infidel. Fair is fair though, and I have to say that none of the rest of them can hold a candle to him for what they would call Christian ethics. Naturally, this causes strained feelings from time to time. I have to say this for him too: He never has intruded his unbelief on others the way Willene intrudes her belief. All in all, I've never felt called on to hold Cash's ideas against him. He had this run-in with a preacher from upstate who undoubtedly thinks he's going to sit on the front row in heaven. He's not kinfolks; he's a cousin-by-courtesy. I can't think of his name at the moment. To tell the truth, it was the preacher who behaved badly. In the car on the way to the cemetery, he chose that time to jab at Cash. He said, by way of a transparent "story," that when Cash died there wouldn't be anybody to perform services for him. No preacher would know him well enough to know anything to say about him, he said. Cash said, oh, well, maybe somebody from the ACLU or the Defenders of Wildlife would say a few words in his favor and that would be a nice enough send-off. Then Robby, *Robby,* who never in his life said boo to a goose, chimed in. He said, in that soft little voice of his, "Cash, you won't even need them. None of us really needs a send-off, because we aren't going anywhere."

The preacher was livid. Cash told me all this later. The truth is that the preacher himself didn't think Cash would be going anywhere, not even in the event of deathbed conversion, because everybody knew that Cash planned to be cremated. I don't understand the objection. We all claim we believe in resurrection of the body, and I'm sure the Almighty could do this as well from a small heap of ashes as from a large heap of bones. But Robby's comment had thrown the preacher into a state of barely contained explosiveness. I saw him arriving at the graveside, and he looked absolutely apoplectic. I really feared for him. I may stop going to funerals, no matter who dies. I am too old for this kind of thing.

Still, I was pleased to know that Robby spoke up the way he did. They all act as if he's going to have nervous prostration at any minute, or turn brown if anybody touches him, but he was steady as a die. Poor boy, he did look pale and drawn, but this was only natural. He and his mother had been very close, from the time of his troubled childhood and youth, and I can see why the family expected him to be the one to break down. Maybe he'd done a lot of postponed growing up. He'd never been away from home until he went to Ohio, and being up there on his own could have matured him. At any rate, he was calm and in his own hands at all times. And there amongst the business cards and the red hat and the howl Winona let out, he looked like wheat among tares. He said he had left his job at a critical time, and he just flew in and flew out. But while he was there, he never put a foot wrong.

I don't know, though. Even while I was thinking he was a model of deportment, I had a little nagging feeling that something was off color. Stopping to think, maybe he should have broken down at some point, in some discreet way. At least had his composure cracked. I know how stony-faced we all can look when we're deeply affected and fighting not to make a display. But Rob didn't even look stony-faced. He didn't look like anything at all. At the time I thought he was behaving beautifully, but he wasn't. Oh, he did everything that was correct, but he looked like nothing had happened. Now I think of it, it makes me wonder. He may have grown away from his mother. I heard several talking about how he never wrote to her. And I saw for myself that he went through her wake and her funeral and never showed one bit of feeling.

PART FOUR
1961-1973

21
TWENTY-ONE

In one of my hiding-out times I wrote on a hotel register, "Tom Foster." Nobody would find me. Not with this name. Not in this fleabag. I had a bottle in my hand when I went in, and I'm sure I must have been behaving oddly. Anyhow, the bellboy thought I was drunk.

He was overly solicitous, asking again and again if he could get me anything, He came by the room several times. Once he came late at night when I was in bed and all I wanted was to sleep, but of course I wasn't sleeping. At that moment I wasn't hearing anything, but I was agonizing over what I'd been hearing. I told him to buzz off and let me alone. He said he knew what I needed, and he walked out.

He hadn't been gone a minute when a girl came in. I looked at her and I noticed she was pretty in a tiny way, with dark brown hair and fair skin. She wasn't heavily made up, like I might have expected. She looked like she was in the wrong business, really. She was obviously a prostitute the bellboy had sent, because she came in undoing the top of her dress.

Then she looked at me and said, "oh." After that neither of us said a word, which was all right by me because I was in no shape to talk to anybody. I was just *writhing* on the bed when she came in. She walked over to the bed, sat down, and started rubbing my head and the back of my neck. She sat there until day started breaking, just rubbing my head and sometimes holding my hand. She had never said another word. She made me feel some better. I even dozed off from time to time. She left while I was asleep and she took ten dollars, which I assume was her fee for her usual service. What she had done for me was worth every penny of it. I don't imagine I would have slept a wink that whole long night except for her.

Next day things started at me again, getting worse and worse as the day wore on. I remember I got hungry, and I phoned the bellhop on duty and I had him bring me a hamburger. I just put my hand out the door and took it from him. None of the bellhops I saw that day were like the one the night before, overly familiar. I could just crack the door and get my sandwich and they didn't pay any more attention to me.

But that evening the same chummy bellhop came back on duty. He used his pass key and came right in my room with his loose-lipped smile and his oily brown eyes, talking about how he'd fixed me up. I'm not real sure why I told him what I did. He had got awfully buddy-buddy and I knew what for. He wanted to get money for sending that girl in. I thought if I told him this thing it would protect me, keep him from sending anybody else. I said, "You might as well know right now. I'm a morphodyte."

Next thing I knew there was such a gabble and squawk breaking loose all around me as I'd never heard before. Such a tumult I could hardly hold myself together. It was something like having a hard chill, when your body is jerking and jerking and you can't make it stop, only this was worse than physical. They were jabbering away at high speed. "Well, he's no such thing—putting this on the way he does everything else—just saying it for his own purposes—no regard for the truth— calling himself a morphodyte!—what he is is a nut—drunken worthless bum and a nut—"

246

All these voices yipping and yelping. And people started coming and knocking on the door, just in no time at all. Wanting to see me. Wanting to look at the freak. And they meant *look*. I didn't close my eyes in sleep all night long, what with the voices dinning in my ears and real people knocking on the door. I presume they were residents. I don't know who else would have been there. All kinds of people, some older men and women, some young ones, all came knocking and saying things like, "Could we *see* you? We never have seen a morphodyte. Would you let us look at you?" I'd say, "Certainly not," and close the door in their faces and they'd go away. Then another one or another batch would come. Often they offered to pay for a look. If I didn't answer their knocks, they'd crack the door and stick their heads in. Looking back, I suppose that cruddy bellboy had left the door unlocked. At the time, I was so distraught it never entered my head that I could just lock the door and leave them knocking out there.

Before it was over with, fifteen or twenty must have come. One man kept saying, "Then let me just feel you, please!" He was the worst one. All the others would take me at my word, and when I closed the door on them they'd go away. This one was persistent. He'd go away, but he kept coming back. I don't know how many times I sent him away. Then another man brushed right past me when I answered the door, and came straight on into the room. He started pulling his clothes off, and he said, "I'm going to let you do anything you want to, and then I'm going to do anything I want to." This startled me so that I momentarily forgot my lifelong immobilizing fears and I shoved him out of the room.

I was almost in tears. If what I'd said had been true, it would have been such a pitiful thing. And nobody was sorry. They all believed it, but nobody was sorry at all. They were only all a-twitter with morbid curiosity. At the same time I was ready to cry, I was mad. After they started coming, I looked for one decent human being. If one person had said he realized that this must give me great distress and he was sorry for me, I'd have let him or her in. I needed somebody to get me out of that place. But there was not even one.

Next morning, I had to manage without the help I really needed when I have to get out of a place. I somehow dragged downstairs and phoned a friend. The line was busy and I was in such turmoil I couldn't wait, so I told the operator I was making an urgent call. At that time you could get an operator to break in this way. You had to give the operator your name though, before she'd interrupt a conversation. The girl at the desk was listening, and she noticed that I gave a different name. She came out into the lobby and, when I finished and started upstairs, she called after me. She said, "You're registered under an assumed name, and we can get you for this."

She didn't bother me. Actually, what she did helped me get dressed and checked out. This girl was something real. She provided me with a definite person making a frontal attack on me, and I could handle that. Something outside, unseen, talking about me through the door, and I not knowing what on earth They were going to do—I couldn't handle that at all.

When I went down to check out, I spoke to her so as to get in the first lick. I said something like, "I knew the minute I saw you that you were no lady, standing with your feet so far apart. And you look very ordinary, with those long earrings dangling down this early in the day." She launched right into a tirade, taking up where she'd left off. Ending there too, because she finished by repeating. "And you're registered under an assumed name. I can get you into plenty of trouble for that. That's against the law." I said, "Oh, no, dear. Not for a morphodyte." And walked out.

◎ Buckeye Barbers is on the edge of the OSU campus. We give the cheapest good haircuts in town. There's just two of us cutting hair, and we keep busy. Any more we don't have a manicurist. We had had the idea that a manicure would be relaxing for people making day-long visits at the hospital. Have a time-killing value for them too. They could come over here for a manicure and a breathing spell. A few did, but we had to let Judy go. There just wasn't enough call for her.

I remember one customer she had. I remember him because he got my goat and because another one like him was in the shop yesterday. This first one was just out of the mental part of the hospital. He let that slip, but I'd have known anyway. He had that pale scared look. You'd think it would be the other way around, but they look scared when they come *out*. At least the ones I've seen; it's not that many. But they seem to need haircuts when they come out, and some come by here.

I thought this first fellow came in for a haircut. Even a trim might have made him look a little less seedy, but what he wanted was a manicure. Just a manicure. Thin as his jacket was, and scuffed up as his shoes were, he stepped in here and had himself a manicure while he waited for friends to come and get him. He looked to me like somebody on welfare. Yet here he was, throwing money around, having a manicure, giving Judy a nice tip. Not to run down my own business, a manicure isn't something you can't live without. Chiselers like him, they turn you against the whole welfare setup. We don't have many Democratic governors in Ohio, but we've got DiSalle now and I blame a lot of this kind of thing on him. He encourages it. He even has convicted murderers working in the governor's mansion. I don't hold with coddling. I had it tough; why shouldn't criminals and welfare chiselers?

Another patient was in here only yesterday. Not another

one just leaving the hospital, one that had been there sometime back. As many people as come in this shop, I never forgot a face. A friend had brought him here for a haircut when *he* came out. Now, I don't eavesdrop. But I was working on a glum, silent customer, and I heard this fellow and his friend talking. With practice, you can tell a lot from hearing a little.

Well, yesterday I cut this fellow's hair again—it could have used a little conditioner, but I didn't mention about it—and I rambled on, the way I always ask a few questions. Don't think I pry. But I do show an interest, try to strike up conversations with the customers. This one was in this general area job hunting, according to him. He must have come by here because it was familiar and low-priced.

What he said, you could have put it in your left eye and not felt a thing. But I can read between lines as well as anybody and better than most. Deep down, he was whining about needing a job. If he would have said it, the next thing would have been that nobody would hire a former mental patient. That's what they all claim. I continued on, and I didn't let him see how this gets to me.

There are employment agencies, for Pete's sake. They find jobs for people. There are organizations to help people like him, church groups and like that. Now I think of it, why shouldn't Mike DiSalle give him a job at the mansion? He has a murderer chauffeuring him around: Why not somebody from the loony bin?

The way I think, this fellow hasn't been trying. He wants a soft job handed to him with a cherry on top. I don't wrap myself in the flag, but I don't believe there's anybody in this country couldn't get a job if he was willing to get the lead out and find a job and then work.

22
TWENTY-TWO

To save my soul, I couldn't remember how many places I applied for work after I'd been in the Psych Institute. Jesus, the applications I made! As soon as they'd find out I'd been in the hospital, it was all over. I think it's better nowadays, but that was a long time ago and then it was dreadful.

What made it especially nerve-racking, many times you didn't get to the point of filling out an application form until they took a great deal of interest, had almost decided that they wanted you. Once when this happened, I was the only applicant and I know I was qualified and they'd seemed receptive. Still, I didn't get the job.

This man was like a lot of others. He read the application, which I was asked to fill out only after he'd expressed serious interest in me, and that was it. There was nothing pointblank, but he was radiating his change of feeling. I could feel his attitude change right while he was reading. Then he said he couldn't use me and didn't offer any reason. I didn't question him. I couldn't have questioned anybody about anything.

One man said flatly, "I can't take a chance on a thing like that!" This nearly struck me down, and I got out of his place as fast as my feet could carry me. Such terrible things those people said to me. It happened repeatedly. Once I got a piddling little office job, and it lasted two days. Toward the

end of the second day, the man came up to me and said, "I
thought I could handle this, but I can't. I'll have to let you go
now." I said, "But—" He said, "I know, I know. But I can't
sweat out waiting to see if you start acting like two people.
You're both fired."

At the same time I was trying to find work through the
State Unemployment Bureau, I was messing around in their
special counselors' office. That was the place where one
woman—oh, my! Her job was to assist handicapped people. I
was a former mental patient. That was my handicap. Well,
she hadn't counted on anything like that. I don't know what
she thought I might do, chew on the furniture or foam at the
mouth or what. But something of the sort, I gathered, because
this was the most upset woman I nearly ever saw. The minute
she'd lay eyes on me, she'd go all to pieces. She had lots of
nervous mannerisms, but the worst one was that she'd shake
her head sideways. She wouldn't be doing this until she'd
look over and see me, and then it would start right up. She
made me so nervous I'd be sitting there wagging my own
head before she was finished with me.

One day we had upset each other a lot. She had us both
doing little gestures and things, and she couldn't sit still a
minute. "If I get you a typing job," she said, wagging her
poor old head like mad, "do you think you could sit still and
type for an hour at a time?" She was terribly upset that day.
She was an old lady too, and I felt sorry for both of us.

Later, somebody told me that these elderly special
counselors were former secretaries and men who were retired
but wanted to work and could work. They were quite helpful
with some people. They did beautifully with people who were
hard of hearing, for example. Hard-of-hearing was something
they could handle. But they'd never before bumped into
somebody who had had a mental disturbance. Nobody else in
that fix had ever applied to them for counseling, as far as

anybody in there knew, and they weren't prepared for it and they couldn't deal with it.

One time I saw a Christian Scientist with her own employment agency, and she talked with me for an hour and a half or more. She was most kind and concerned about me, so much so that she kept other people waiting. She kept telling me to quit saying on applications that I'd been in an institution. She said, "That didn't happen to you. It happened to somebody else." But mostly she wanted me to read Mary Baker Eddy. She said, "I put it the way I did earlier because that's something you could feel even in your present frame of reference. Later, if you'll work with practitioners and learn the value of prayer and positive attitudes, you'll come to a better understanding. I know how real it seems to you, but sickness is illusory. You can't be sick if you reject the illusion."

She didn't have anything in my field, and I figured my crack-ups seemed real to me because they were real; but I was terrifically impressed and uplifted by her. She was like an oasis. I thought this was the most wonderful thing in the world, the way she treated my crack-up. She simply disregarded it, didn't "accept" it, she said.

On my own, I'd been wrestling with my wish not to tell about the hospitalization on applications, because it had made so much trouble for me every single time. It was marvelous to be talking to an employment-agency person who ignored the whole thing. This helped me a lot.

Then I got mixed up with Mrs. Elzie Bosch. She had her own agency too, and she was a ball of fire. Whatever she was doing, she just flew at it, POW! I thought this was grand when I met her, because what she was doing was finding a job for me. I didn't realize then that she must have had enough calls for IBM people that she could have placed every one in town. There weren't nearly enough good operators to go around, but I didn't know that until later.

It was when I went to see her that I acted on my decision as to the best policy: Don't tell it. So I filled out the application and I wrote "unemployed" for the period I was in the hospital and I didn't make one peep about it to her.

She was excited about my application, because of course she was needing IBM people. She asked me if I'd go to the State Board of Liquor Control, and naturally I said I would. She said she'd let me hear from her and that meantime she'd be checking my record. Reliant told her that I'd left them to go into a mental institution. I'm sure she phoned them and asked why I'd left, and I guess there was no way they could keep from telling her. (After her, I began putting, "Returned home to North Carolina" for the period I was hospitalized. I did this on all later applications.)

Oh, she was a scurvy, slimy creep. Really, she was the scum of the earth. She called the director of the Schizophrenia Research Institute, where I'd done some volunteer work, and early one morning Mr. La Roche called me. I remember clearly that he wasn't at all upset. "A little something's come up," he said, "but I don't think it'll amount to much." He said he had talked with her. Well, as one of his co-workers said, until Mr. La Roche gets hit in the face with human nature, all the hawks are doves. He did lock horns with her later, but at that time he thought she was fine. I don't wonder either, because she always put on a very good act until you came to the pinch. In the pinch she changed suddenly and frightfully. Anyhow, Mr. La Roche said to go right down and see her and get the thing cleared up.

I went straight to her and she said, "You didn't level with me." She had found out from Reliant. Before I got to her office though—this is the most astonishing thing that I found out later—she had already told the liquor control board that I'd been in a mental hospital and they'd said that was all right. I already *had* the job when I went down to see her that morning. But she was fixing things so that, whether I survived or perished, she'd come out the big end of the horn.

She would just ride roughshod over you, and she was accusatory. I didn't "level" with her. She kept saying that. I explained that I'd been leveling with people and it had done nothing but wreck my every chance. I even told her about the Christian Scientist who had disregarded the crack-up, and how I thought she might be right that it was best to leave this off applications. Mrs. Bosch said, in these exact words, "It'll take some doing, but maybe I can manage to land this job for you. If I do, can you pay me my whole fee in cash, in advance?" Her whole fee was three hundred and sixty dollars, for God's sake. In those days that was a bundle, and in any case this was not the customary procedure. I told her I couldn't possibly, and she went digging at me. First she wanted to know if I had any friend who would pay the whole fee for me right that red hot minute. She even said, "What about the Schizophrenia Institute? Would they advance it to you?" I said, "Certainly not. That's not what they're for." She pushed and pushed on this, but I wouldn't go to Mr. La Roche and ask him to do a ridiculous thing like that.

So she really began to give me the business. She kept trying to make me say I did have some money. She wanted to know how much I could rake up. She insisted on knowing exactly what I had on me right then. I was in such a defenseless position and she was such a Mack truck that I ended up turning my pockets inside and emptying my torn and worn-thin billfold on the desk before her. (The money came to about six dollars.) This is what I'll never forgive her for. I completely lost my dignity. She simply stripped it off me like peel off a tangerine.

That she-devil looked at my six dollars on her desk and said, "Well, unless you can get up the fee from somewhere, today, I'll be forced to tell them over at the liquor board that you've been hospitalized." My heart sank down in my shoes. I had been so hopeful, and now I could see my chance at this good job melting away. I stood up, and it was hard for me to speak because my lips were trembling and my mouth was dry. I barely managed to get out, "There's nothing I can do. If this is the way you're going to do it, I'll have to lose the job."

I began picking up my little things from her desk, and she said, "Oh, now, wait, wait, wait. Maybe they'll take you. They want somebody so badly. "(They wanted *me*. They had said so to her. They told me this later.) She went on, "They want somebody this afternoon. Since they're in such a hurry, I think maybe I can arrange it for you."

She got out some sort of paper for me to sign, and I realized later that I had signed a promise to give her something like the major portion of her fee out of my first pay check. This would have been a disaster, because those fees are figured on monthly pay. Of course it was more than I could possibly do; it was more than my whole first two-week pay check would be. But I was prostrate and wrung out, and, when she shoved the thing at me, I signed it without reading it. Then I put my pockets back where they belonged, picked up my billfold, and went out in the alley and vomited.

In a few minutes I pulled myself together enough to go over to the liquor control board. They took me into the tab room and introduced me to the supervisor and I liked him immediately and I went to work right then.

They were way behind. They were so behind that we were working all day and until way late at night, as late as we were willing to stay. You could have as much overtime as you wanted. This was a blessing for me, because I was stone broke. Besides that, it was steadying for me to have all this work to keep me busy. I'd work all day and then at night until I couldn't hold my head up. Mr. La Roche showed up in the tab room the day after I went to work, with an envelope for me with some money in it. Mrs. Ritter brought me big bags of groceries. So things began to move along for me.

But here came Mrs. Bosch, in her usual way of seeking whom she could devour. It was supposed to be two weeks before I'd get paid the first time, but it turned into a month. Mrs. Bosch was calling me, wanting money, before even the first two weeks were up. From then on she kept after me. She hounded me right up to the minute I finally was paid and could pay her.

I never was sure how much this extra stress harmed me. Sometimes an extra strain will make everything fall to pieces. Blows, when they come too close together, snowball. You get to where you simply can't stand up under one additional stroke of misfortune of any kind. It doesn't have to be much either, by itself. But you can't look at it by itself. When a snowball is building, it's not the last weightless flake that knocks you off your feet. When a river is already swollen, it's not the last little raindrop that makes a flood. They only precipitate disaster; it's the accumulation that does it. This is the way it works, and Mrs. Bosch could have destroyed me before I even got my first pay check. But this didn't happen. I went on with my job and, by the skin of my teeth, I survived her.

◎ I'm secretary to the director of the Schizophrenia Research Institute, and I'm finding it increasingly difficult to tell who's crazy and who's not. I can't tell the non-crazies without a program, and nobody shows me a program I like. Peter La Roche, our director, is in the same boat.

My husband and I have known Robby Wilde since the second Stevenson-Eisenhower campaign. The Stevenson group was small enough—after all, this is Ohio—that we all got acquainted in some degree. Besides, Robby was, as we are, not only Democratic but Southern, and we naturally took a second look at one another. Later Rob came to the office one day with Henry Ritter, a member of our board. After that, from time to time, Robby did a good bit of office work for us, free-will offering.

Even here he had trouble. One afternoon he was typing mailing labels, and in breezed Mrs. Saunders. She's the wife of a board member, but look what she did. She sailed over to Robby, her bracelets rattling and her hair still hot from the drier. She crooned at him in the gooiest voice imaginable, "I wish I could type like that." Robby said very quietly, "It isn't hard to learn," and kept on tapping away.

Then I knew she had to be the cause of his all but gnashing his teeth at innocent me one day on another occasion he worked here. It astonished me. He almost never said anything, certainly nothing the least bit resentful. But that day he had poked his head into my office, and said through clenched jaws, "It is *not* like having a broken arm," and went right on about his business. No preamble and no conclusion, but it served. Mrs. Saunders had been here that day too, and two and two isn't so hard to put together. I mentioned it to Mr. La Roche, but he sighed and said it was hard to work with volunteers.

Robby was terrific at office organization and planning. In time, he came to be something of a protégé of ours as well as a real help to us. He worked here several times, either to help get his nerve back after a bad episode or when we urgently needed another pair of hands. Mr. La Roche helped him in many a tight place before he decided Rob was a lost cause.

Lately, from home and from my desk at the Institute, I've been watching Rob struggle to get a job. I've seen him painfully picking his way across the mine field that society lays out for former mental patients. This depressing sight is one thing that sets me at odds with what seems to constitute mental health as the world presently defines it.

It isn't the legal term "sane" that's bothering me. Legal schmegal. It isn't what's legal that counts. What counts is what works. I know one wide-screen glorious technicolor *case* who, because she has an independent income and can manage it, is doing fine, thank you very much. I know she suffers sometimes, and sometimes I'm sorry for her. But I also know that she exploits and terrorizes five aged and either senile or disturbed women who are paying guests in her house. Two are slaveys and all are threatened and misused according to her whim and each one's degree of vulnerability.

She keeps the name of her first husband, dead for twenty years, listed in the phone book, and she has both her married names in full on her mailbox. She was pestilential to the relatives she'd persuaded to live next door to her for some years, in a house she owns. She's helplessly and hopelessly addicted to buying. "Shopping is my hobby," she'll tell you. She loaded that family down with a wide assortment of good and bad things. I remember stacks of sweaters, luggage, rotisserie, bicycle, acrilan blankets, ping pong table, dinnerware, mink stole, color TV, plastic plants, Persian rug, and orlon wig.

In between spells of oppressive giving, she'd take offense at something or other, and at those times she'd usually do something to their car. Once she painted the windshield black, three times she painted it battleship gray, and each time she scratched the hood with the fork of a carving set. They moved after she painted the headlights pink and poured glue between the windows and doors.

She flourishes. She's treated with respect by lawyers and other business people, and the state hospital farms out these poor old ladies to *her*.

The only things that seem to count toward being tolerated are (1) never to have been hospitalized and (2) to be solvent. The question the world puts to us is not, "How sane are you?" but "How well can you take care of yourself?" I'm resentful of this, both by inclination and by fondness for Robby. During the years we've known him he's precariously balanced at best. This means our friendship hasn't been easygoing or entirely uneventful, but he's been a friend worth having.

From what we know of his experience, I gather that even a definition such as "Crazy is as crazy does" wouldn't hold water. The way the world spins, it's crazy is as crazy fails. Certainly Robby has got his window up when he drops out for days and comes back looking like he's been pulled through a keyhole. But he's harmless. There are those around who might well be dangerous to others, but who haven't been stigmatized by being in a hospital. One psychiatrist I know says of a client, "Why should I try to get him shut up in a hospital because he well *might* harm somebody?"

I know of a pitifully embarrassed man who fetched up in the operating room for a footed bud vase to be removed from his colon, having put it there himself by way of his anus. He thought the vase would work better than the coke bottle that caused the other surgery. *He* isn't crazy; he just has his little ways. But Rob, Rob is crazy.

I have a friend who works in the Social Security office, and she tells me about a woman who comes in about once year to complain about the way her checks are handled. They're made out to her son, and she takes this as an affront. It is an affront, necessary though it be, but it's even more than ordinarily offensive to this woman. She's in such a condition that she periodically tries to get her name legally changed and her checks make out to Carmen, Queen of the Universe. I gather that she really is of a rather imposing appearance. Sometimes she's belligerent, but more often she's quiet.

She's as pleasant as any august personage could be when treated in this cavalier fashion. "How can you put a thirty-one-year-old man above the queen of the universe?" she demands. My friend pleads governmental vagaries and no personal responsibility. At the end of one interview, the woman picked up her pocketbook and smoothed down her skirt preparatory to leaving. Then she said softly and the tiniest bit reproachfully, "You know, I *am* the ruler of the universe." And went her way in peace when my friend said, "I've heard." My point is that Robby is at the tippy tippy top of sanity by comparison. But she's unlabeled. I'm thankful for her that she has her freedom and, apparently, some small comforts. But it's not because she's sane; it's because she's not bothering anybody too much.

I don't really care one red cent about trying to prove somebody else's craziness. I'm only saying that the one real test is the one of living in the world without inconveniencing or offending anybody who can hit back harder. And, or course, not being penniless.

For Rob it's more difficult than for most to live in the world. Every day he gets up and goes to work, when he has work to go to, he shows more courage than most of us are even called on to show during our entire lives. It would be nice if he could get a few points for this. Every one of his employers has said that he's a topnotch worker. No points for that either, now that he's a marked man.

Sometimes it does seem that employers are likely to find almost anything forgivable in some degree as long as you're a going concern. Rob was a going concern for years and years and years, even though that required a brutal exertion of will. There have been periods when he couldn't sustain this prodigious effort, and for those times he's forever labeled and passed over. Passed over because he's labeled and not always a reliable performer.

Untold numbers of the immaculately never-hospitalized aren't reliable performers, and many institutions are not reliable because of them. But they're comfortably unlabeled and they're considered employable. A department of the state government was screaming for a good IBM specialist at the time Rob was haunting the state employement office to no avail. He got that referral from a vampire of a private employment agent. Even Mr. La Roche, who, as Rob says, is generally as mild as a cup custard, had a spirited exchange with that one. On an earlier job, it didn't do Rob any good to be a reliable performer. It strained the brains of his smugly unhospitalized co-workers to distinguish between pampering him and being minimally civil. One temporary employer was hardly a heartening influence when he told Rob that if he were "going to have a, uh, spell or anything" to have it out in the hall so he wouldn't upset the other employees. And so on ad nauseam.

In the work-after-hospital situation, he's been kicked in the teeth with murderous regularity. Not all the kickers were outright villains like the employment agency woman. Some "didn't mean any harm," "didn't realize," and all the rest of it. But he's just as mutilated with his teeth down his throat whether he got kicked for reasons of greed, thick skin, thick head, or imbecilic and presumptuous volunteer therapy. Damn, hell, spit. If he hadn't already had paranoia, he'd have got it from being persecuted.

23
TWENTY-THREE

One of the most horrendous times I ever lived through was during my job at the liquor control board, when I had an apartment on Whittier Place. I was doing pretty well on the job, but the place I had lived became unbearable, the way places always did. It was just when I began to slide that I got this little unit. It was one of several apartments in a house behind a chiropractor's office. He owned the apartment building.

Mine was an efficiency, with a couch to sleep on. It had a little kitchen, and Mr. La Roche staked me to a phone, and I thought the new place would maybe keep things from closing in on me. Sometimes it worked that way. The place was fairly shabby, but the walls were fresh and clean and I put out the few books I still had and I hung up strings of bright-colored gourds and tried to make it as homelike as possible. It looked pleasant, and I was glad of the kitchenette. I felt I'd made a little spot of my own.

This horrifying time They pounced on me all at once. Ordinarily, this sort of thing starts at low volume and builds. But this time I had no forewarning. Nothing. I was just in bed one night more or less all right, and all at once They were talking away right outside. "There he is." Nobody could believe how this can send chills up and down the spine. "*There* he is." As soon as I heard that, I knew I was in for it.

There has always been this thing with me: If some wicked thing is done, even if some fiendish crime is committed, at a time when I'm in the least shaken, a time when I'm not real solid, I'll take on the guilt. "There he is," They were saying, right smack on the other side of my window, a lot of Them, hammer and tongs.

The papers that day had been full of a story about the sexual mutilation, or anyhow wounding, of a small boy. The child was recovering, physically anyhow, and he was going to be "all right," but it was a horrible thing. Something else was already troubling me. There was an alley in back of the house, and the police would drive slowly through it. Their car would creak, and this threw me. I did get so that I could make myself go and look out when I heard this creak-creak-creak, and when I'd see that there was a real car making the sound, it would help me some. But not much, because it was a police car.

The first morning after I'd heard this all night long, I phoned the liquor control board and told them I'd have to be absent that day. I sat all day long, afraid to look out the window, afraid not to look out the window. When I did look, because I'd be hearing that screek, there would be the police car. I'm sure they're still driving slowly through that alley every day and every night of the world. They've got to cruise somewhere; they're supposed to be on the go all the time. Naturally when they drove up that alley, they went slowly. They wouldn't come barging through such a narrow place. But these are all things I couldn't understand then, not in my condition, and I didn't know whether the police car pushed me on over the edge or what. But one night there I was, fairly sturdy, and by morning I was *gone*.

I took the *Journal,* and I can hear that until this day, the thud of the paper against the door. It was like a benediction. Every time I heard that thud, the paper had just been delivered. That was an inexpressible relief. Any time I could identify a sound with a reasonable cause for it, that was blessed relief. One morning I opened the door, got the paper, unfolded it, and there was a drawing. It was an artist's conception of what the criminal looked like, done from the child's description. It looked just like me.

I went to pieces. This was the end of the line. I was done for. I knew They were right about one thing: They did have me. I was exactly where They wanted me. With this picture in the paper, They had me. I was shattered. I couldn't go to work, of course. I couldn't even phone and say I wouldn't be there. I stayed in the room for two or three days. That's another thing. In this kind of state I would lose track of how much time passed, the same as when I was hiding between buildings in Marlowe. I stayed in the room, wrecked. Part of the time I'd be doubled up in a knot on the couch, and part of the time I'd be peeking out the window, and part of the time I'd be going in frenzied little dashes about the room and pounding my fist into my palm and never at any time more than one jump from beating my head on the wall.

All the time the voices were thundering. They sounded worse than I can tell it, because often They'd all be talking at once. "Even though you weren't anywhere around, you'll get the blame—You can be sure you'll be blamed, and you can't deny it—Oh, no, of course you didn't do it, but who'll believe you?—Why should anybody believe you?—no good—no background—illegitimate—thief—been in an institution—had your arm around that colored man in the hospital, going against your raising—drink—known as a drunkard—sat up in that woman's apartment and just swilled liquor—Oh, yeah, he'll catch it for this—We'll get him now—the authorities—take care of him—"

This is how the voices are. They have no sense of proportion. They revile me just as brutally for drinking as for an atrocity; the unimportant one I did; and the appalling one I did not do. They can't distinguish. They've always been that way. When I was in grade school, being carted around to do storytelling, it was the same with me as it became with the voices: no sense of proportion. The lying involved in passing off my own story as one I'd read and in keeping it all a secret from my family, that kind of lying was no big deal. But I was as hagridden by guilt as if I'd set the schoolhouse on fire while it was full of people.

Besides the voices having no sense of proportion, there's still another thing; there is some sort of possibility that I've overheard a real person talking. And there's always *some* kind of *reason* for what the voices say. It's often not significant but there'll be a reason; it's not just a mindless chatter. Like that time about the pin hooker.

Once in North Carolina, after a terrible period I went in the late afternoon to the American Hotel. It's on Commerce Street and it's the bottom of the barrel, as cheap as you could find. I got a room for something like a dollar and a half and I finished out that day and spent the night there, all the time hearing voices. All night long.

They were saying I was at this hotel for immoral purposes. "He's a queer. He's looking for another one." That sort of thing. And then one voice said, "Well, what could you expect? He's got a cousin that's a pin hooker." Actually, I did. And I wasn't proud of it.

A pin hooker goes to the tobacco market, comes along after the big tobacco company buyers. He finds farmers whose tobacco wasn't sold to these buyers. Sometimes he finds tobacco that he thinks isn't properly graded. Grading isn't easy, and it's not everybody who can do it, but a pin hooker knows all about tobacco. Because the farmers don't have money enough to hold on to their tobacco, the pin hooker can buy it for next to nothing. He regrades it, packs it, and sells it. He takes something of a chance, but generally he makes pretty good. Frequently he makes very good. All in the world he does is regrade the tobacco and pack it! He sells it for no telling what, and he makes more money in one day in the warehouse than many a poor farmer made toiling in his own tobacco field for weeks. I never thought this was an up-and-up way to make money, but it's done. It's done right out in the open. It's not illegal, but I never had much respect for a pin hooker.

And here came this voice. "What could you expect? He's got a cousin that's a pin hooker." And as I say, I did have a cousin that was a pin hooker. And this dump of a hotel was right in the market district, where somebody could have said that. Next morning I was down in the coffee shop, not feeling very well but drinking my coffee. I got to talking with a man who was there when I went in. It turned out he knew my cousin. He knew what he did and everything about him. And this man lived in the hotel on the floor my room was on. So it very well could have been that his was the voice I heard.

But I didn't know in advance about this man. When I heard that voice and what it said, I didn't know there existed such a man as this fellow. So why the voice? This always throws me, and even the best therapist I ever had, the one who let me know that I was hearing voices, never could straghten out this kind of thing either.

Those voices at Whittier Place didn't let up for a minute. I'd think, "If I could just get to doing something, They'll think I'm not listening to them and maybe They'll feel 'the hell with it' and quit." I'll do something, anything, like that time I worked a crossword puzzle in a bar. So I'd sit in my room and type furiously, not knowing, not caring. Not words even, sometimes. And "Now is the time for all good men to come to the aid of their party," and "Pack my bag with six dozen liquor jugs," over and over and over. I grabbed up a

New Yorker somebody had given me and I copied a whole story, but I can't remember who wrote it or one word of it. I was frantic to get away from the voices.

But the stream of vilification didn't even slacken. All the abuse was poorly grounded, hideously distorted, but sometimes there would be some grain of truth. Such little mites of truth, ridiculously doctored up to grow prodigiously into their deformed shapes, like poisoned weeds growing themselves to death. The voices give a wholly false picture. This false picture, however, was offered to nobody but me, the one person in the world who would believe it—for the time being.

Once in a while I'd go to the kitchenette and eat something, sometimes tuna or beans straight out of the can, or drink some beer. I lost track of time somewhat, but I know that the phone rang occasionally on more than one day. I remember answering once, and it was that she-devil employment agency woman, Mrs. Bosch. The instant I answered the phone, she said, "Don't you hang up on me!" So I don't know but what I may have been answering before and hanging up on her. After that, I could no more have answered the phone than I could have jumped over the Lincoln Leveque Tower. Every time it rang, my terror mounted; and I'd been in spasms of terror already.

After a couple of days or so, the voices began to die down, so gradually that at first I didn't notice any difference. Then suddenly I was aware that they were slacking up just the least little bit, then a little more, a little more, and then They got quiet enough that I wasn't afraid to fight back. I certainly don't know why I picked this way to fight back, or if that's why I did it, but I painted all over the wall. On paper on the wall. I had paints and a brush and I got out big sheets of brown wrapping paper that for some reason I'd hauled along with me, and I tacked them up on the wall until I had a great huge spread of pieced-together paper.

I haven't the haziest recollection of what I painted. All I remember is that I was working lickety-split, just sloshing the paint on. I raced ahead; I couldn't stop or even slow down. When I finished painting, I threw the brush on the floor and got out of there. I flew out of there with nothing but the clothes I stood in.

I learned he was an undesirable tenant in one hard lesson. After he disappeared, I found drawers full of beer bottles, unopened newspapers lying around, the phone under the couch with pillows stuffed in on top of it. He had cooked in anything that could be cooked in, and he hadn't washed a pot or a dish. There were empty cans all over the place, stale bread hard as a rock, and cans with some food left in them. He hadn't turned a hand. The place was like an overturned garbage can.

But it was his painting all over my wall that really burned me up. Most likely I was working on Mrs. Baker's stiff neck not thirty yards away from him at the same time he was out back making holes in the wallboard and slopping paint all over. Not even bothering to stay on the paper he'd stuck up. Lots of times he ran the brush over the edges of the paper and continued on, painting right on the freshly Kem-toned wall.

One huge splotch. At that, it was better than some of the paintings by those OSU professors that keep riling people at the state fair. Not to be funny, I don't know anything about art, but I know what scares the socks off me. If emotional response is a yardstick, that mess on my wall was art.

It was all done in red and black, a savage thing in itself. I never would have thought of it that way before I saw that Nazi flag during World War II. One day a patient brought in this flag her brother had captured and sent home. She said, "Even if it weren't for that crooked, crawling thing in the middle, it would still be horrible. Such a brutal color combination!" And, you know, she was right.

All Wilde's reds weren't blood red like the red in the flag, but they were plenty bad enough. Mostly they looked discolored, like bruised blood. There was black mingled and drizzled all through the painting, the way bits of burned matchstick will dribble black fuzzy-edged streaks through sealing wax. It was a painting, not a picture. Absolutely no discernible shapes in the whole thing. Every time I thought I could almost make out something, it would stop before taking form and continue on to something else, and that didn't quite take form either.

In a backhanded way, it made me think of a picture game from my childhood. There would be a line drawing of a landscape and a caption reading, "How many faces can you find in this picture?" At first you couldn't see anything but the obvious objects; but once you found the first face, you saw faces jumping out everywhere. What he'd painted on the wall worked in reverse. At first, all you could see was a hodge-podge of massive, lowering storm clouds; monstrously huge fists, and stamping heavy shod feet that would have crushed anything caught under them; bomb bursts; clubs. Rather, only the beginnings and suggestions of all these. Once I thought I saw a blunt snub-nosed thing that could have become a pistol. But, like all the others, it wavered away and didn't quite become anything. None of these things was in the painting, I'm trying to say. Just vague masses that hinted they were going to be these things. It was a wall-sized blob he did. There wasn't one identifiable object or person in that whole big smear. But it held more concentrated frenzy and fury than I ever want to see again.

If you could have seen him, you'd have thought he was the gentlest guy in Franklin County. Any more, I'm proof against being taken in by a neat appearance and a soft-spoken manner. I'm more careful about tenants since him. I get references, good references that stand up under checking, or they don't move in. I think maybe it was his being Southern that faked me out. It's hard to tell about Southerners if you're not used to them. They "sir" and "ma'am" everybody, but that's not to say they're meek. Any more I know that's only their brand of everyday politeness. It's being a little formal because they don't know you very well. Unless you're old. Then it means extra respect. It can mean just the opposite. Once I heard Wilde say "sir" to somebody who had offended him, and it sounded contemptuous. They open doors and carry packages for women and they have soft voices, even those that are what they call mean as snakes. By itself, this thing of soft voices doesn't mean a thing. And they don't necessarily mean to be putting anything over on you. It's just the way they sound and the way they talk.

It's like birds. A bird sits in a tree and people think, "Isn't that sweet, the way he sings" and they talk about "happy as a lark." He may not be happy; he may be hungry or thirsty. He may be serving notice on other birds that this is his tree or his yard or whatever, and for them to KEEP OUT. For sure, mourning doves aren't mourning. All those bubbly cooings that sound so sweet, so sad to some, are either meant to invite or drive away, depending on sex, whatever doves they're cooing at. These birds are all saying their say, and they're saying it in the sounds that come natural to them. If these sounds are pleasant to our ears, it doesn't always have to do with what they're saying.

Same way with that Wilde fellow. There was my wall to prove it. Vandalism. That's what he committed, vandalism. Criminal type. Anybody who'd paint a fire-and-smoke splotch like that, no telling how many heads he's bashed in, him and his soft voice and his yes, sir. Even if his friend did have the place cleaned up and the damage repaired, I should have called the cops.

24
TWENTY-FOUR

In full headlong flight I called a cab after dark and went to a liquor store. I didn't have much money, but I got two bottles of bust-head liquor, came right back out, got into the waiting cab, and went to a hotel on Spring Street.

I told the driver to take me to the Jackson. It was the only one I could think of the name of; but when we got there, I saw a place across the street marked "Hotel." This seemed more like it, and I went there. I was thinking that it would be harder for anybody to find me, any of Them, in a place named "Hotel" than in a place with a regular name. Anything to get hidden! What was in my head was, "This is the way to get away from it. Nobody and nothing on earth will know where I am. So I won't have to hear Them."

This place wasn't like a usual hotel. There wasn't a ground floor or a lobby for an entrance. You had to walk up *nar-row* little steep stairs to get to it. At the top of the stairs was a desk and a long bench for people to sit on. All it was was rooms over a lot of stores.

I checked in with my liquor. Liquor never stopped anything, but sometimes it would make me not care so much. It's a tremendous relief to feel, "So what?" when the voices are holding forth. Even to be able to say this for a very short while. So I started in on the liquor.

Later on I learnt that I was on a floor that only men could

stay on. There were some worse off than any I'd ever seen, even including that one time I was at the State Hospital. There was one poor old man who made me nearly scream everytime I'd see him. His head was all misshapen. And he just went from his room to the bathroom, to his room, to the bathroom. His head was probably shaped all right. There were great warty looking growths all over it, and this gave his head a misshapen appearance. Also, he couldn't move his head around. He was so old and pitiful. No knowing what ever became of him.

With a little guts in me—that is, with enough liquor in me—I'd go and sit in what passed for the lobby, on that long bench near the desk. Once I took an old indigent woman out and ate with her. This was wonderful for me, because it let me get out and back and have something to eat. This is only my own idea, but there's another reason I believe I do things like this with people like that. It's almost as if I hope my actions are saying, "Let me be good to this one. Let just this one know I'm not the rotten creature the voices say I am. Let this one person know, and then I'll have *some* proof that all these vile things are not true."

While I was drinking, I'd just throw open the door—I, *I* would throw open the door!—and call to people, "Come on in and have a drink." That was the opposite of what I usually did, and I can't explain it. But I'd be hearing all these voices and I wouldn't know where to turn, and I'd get brazen and do this. Courage of desperation. Once a lot of racket was going on. It reached the point that I was hearing voices right outside my door, that terrible stage of things when They're right outside the door.

I wrote a lot of notes and threw them out the window by the fistful. I'd write, "Come on up," and put down my name and room number. "Come on up and have a drink, anybody." And "Why don't you stop by?" And "Feeling lonesome?

Come on up." Any number of times there were people in the room, and I'd give them whiskey. Much of this is heavily clouded in my memory, and I don't know how much of the cloudiness is due to liquor or how much might be due to my old barrier of I-don't-want-to-hear. There's no telling what all might have gone on in that room that night. It's a wonder I wasn't killed. It wasn't exactly the cream of the cream coming in off the street.

I do know why I was calling people in. This was one of the times when I was dying for somebody real and alive, and with a body I could attach a voice to, to knock on the door. When I've stiff-armed the voices, I can often handle them. That's when They're talking at some little distance. Like I'm in the room and They're down the hall or They're on the street. When They're right on the other side of the door, that's the worst. That's when They're saying, "Now we've got him. As soon as he gets here, we'll have him." What They mean is that They're going to open the door in just a few minutes, just as soon as "he," somebody or something arrives. Sometimes it's a wagon that's going to take me away. Sometimes it's a person who's going to prove that what the voices say about me is true. They're only waiting for that person, and after he comes They'll get me. I'll be wiped out.

Now, of course, the very last thing in the world I'd ordinarily do is open the door. It's only when something, like what happened that night at the Y, pushes me to it that I can dare. Naturally. Ordinarily, opening the door would be suicidal. So my opening the door in this "hotel" was crazy. None of this makes any sense. When I'm right, when I'm rational, and think about it, I wonder, "What in God's name could I have been thinking?" Of course there were other times in this same place when I'd open the door and find nobody. That's always a severe shock, to hear voices right at the door and then to open the door and the whole hall is stark empty.

One other thing I remember definitely about this dreadful episode is that I got hungry, very hungry, in the night, at a time when nobody was in the room. I thought of going out to eat, but I simply couldn't leave the hotel. There was no place there to eat; you had to go out. I called a taxi around two or three in the morning, and had the driver go to the White Castle and get me a lot of those little flat hamburgers and bring them to the desk. While he was gone, I sat with the old man on the desk. He kept saying, "Why didn't you just go out and eat?" and I kept making excuses. When the driver came back, I took the bagful of White Castles to my room and ate ravenously. There wasn't a drop of liquor left, but I didn't want any.

During the day after that wild night, I was lying on the bed in that dump of a "hotel." The voices were still right outside my door, waiting for somebody to come and get me. They didn't budge away from the door, they just yammered away. At some point during the daylong hullabaloo, I decided I had to go back to the hospital. It has always been during this kind of time that I've had to go. Nothing special had happened to me. The anguished and stormy night was over. It was just that I had reached the point where I could not stand the voices at the door one more minute.

And They kept on, some of them as if I'd already gone. They began saying, "*Look* at him (They always said that). There he goes again. Back to the fit farm." Other times I went to the hospital, I felt pushed by somebody else. This time I pushed myself. This was the one time I made up my own mind that I needed to go back to the hospital. And I did it. I got up, put my few things together, opened the door, and went out. With the voices all going lickety-split. Down the stairs and out into the street, the voices were following me. Dogging my footsteps. "Back to the hospital—Out of his mind again—Sick in the head." That sort of thing for the most part.

I called Joe at work and asked him to go at lunch time with me to the place where I'd been staying, on Whittier Place. Just to it, not inside; just as far as the door to get my mail out of the box. There was a notice that my final check from the liquor control board would be at the Post Office on Whittier Street. As it happened, I could spend that night with Joe. His mother was out of town and not due home until the next afternoon. This was a mercy. I'd have been scared to go home with Joe of she'd been there, and I'm sure he'd have been scared to take me. I got through the night without any noticeable uproar, though, and the next day I went to the Post Office and got my check.

I went and bought a pair of shoes and got things ready for the hospital. That afternoon I re-entered. It had all been arranged; I'm no longer sure how. I guess I had called Mr. La Roche, or maybe I had even called the hospital myself. Anyhow, I went and they were expecting me, but I lost my nerve. I asked them couldn't I wait 'til the next morning. I said I'd rather go in in the morning than tough out a night of it right at the first, and they said that would be OK. I took my package and went to another fellow. This was somebody I'd met when I first came to Columbus. I didn't exactly go to this friend; I spent the night in a cramped little storage room he had. He lived in the ground floor apartment of a two-story house, and this place was sort of under the house and to one side. I still had the key to his apartment in my wallet, from some other time, and this opened the storage cubby hole and I slept on a pile of things with a rug on top. He never knew I was there.

Next morning early, I got on the bus and went back to the Institute alone and signed myself in. I can't remember what I was like that time, except that I still never mentioned the voices to a soul. Again, I had a chance to say at least,

"People talk about me," but I couldn't. I didn't tell them much of anything, I guess. I went back to the same old superficial thing. I couldn't help it. Part of it was fear, but part of it was the same barrier I've had since childhood. The same barrier flies up between me and other people even when I don't want it there. It's flying up now, this very minute, when I'm trying my best to get it all out. It flew up when I was trying to tell about the time I said I was a morphodyte and people crowded in. I think this barrier really was a protection to me when I was little, because it kept things out; but when I grew older and, from much therapy, learnt a good deal about my condition, I realized that it hobbled me. It kept me unable to be open, which would have relieved this agonizing isolation.

After I'd quieted down—the hospital is always unsettling at first, but it's not too hard to calm yourself if you've been in before—I went right back to my pat little story. I didn't mean it to be a pat little story, but that's what it was. I had a new psychiatrist, and we would just talk the same things over and over without ever touching on what I really should have been talking about.

I'd talk about my childhood, and there are always plenty of things to say. It's amazing how many things you can think up when you don't want to talk or can't talk about what's really troubling you. You can tell what you do, talk about this or that job. There are any number of things you can fill up a session with, and sometimes you can just sit there. And all the time you don't know you're doing this. You think you're doing what you ought to be doing. It's confusing.

I think there's a misconception about psychiatrists. Lots of people think they want to find out all about your childhood. Maybe it did all start in your childhood, and maybe they do want some idea; but to get with your trouble, you have to get with it as it is. My therapist didn't need to hear—right then, anyhow—about my rotten childhood in general. He needed to know I was hearing voices. The only reason he needed to hear about my childhood at that point was that I heard voices even then. I couldn't tell him. For one thing, I was afraid of him. I shouldn't say "afraid." He upset me. I don't know exactly what it was, but he had a manner that put me off. He was a skier, a sportsman, a real robust fellow, tall and big— and German. He had worked at ski lodges in Austria, and he—well, he upset me.

It also upset me and waked a lot of only lightly sleeping dogs when I got a package from my sister. The wrong brand of cigarettes and a box of chocolates. *Milk* chocolates. That's how much they knew about me.

Another thing, I was taking those little pills that the druggist on Maple Street would sell me. Miratan. This is a stimulant. I'd been sort of intermittently taking them since I first went to Reliant. This druggist would refill the prescription long after it was outdated. I was careful not to overdo, but still he shouldn't have kept on giving me refills.

This time when I went to the hospital, on the same day I bought my new shoes and got things prepared, I got some of these pills. I hadn't had any through this bad period just before I went back to the Institute. Maybe if I had, they'd have helped me. The only trouble with Miratan, it will keep you awake. When Dr. Richards first gave me the prescription, I was supposed to take a pill in the morning and no more through the day, and he gave me something to take at night so I could sleep. The morning pill would give me a sense of well-being, it really would.

At the druggist's, when I got the Miratan, I got a can of tooth powder. I half emptied it and put the pills in. First I put in cotton over the tooth powder, then pills, then cotton, then the rest of the powder, and I took this to the hospital with me. If they didn't give me any medicine, I'd have this. I didn't know what they were going to do, and this was just so I wouldn't be completely helpless. I wanted the pills in there with me as some measure of security.

They didn't start giving me medicine right away, and I would take these. This made me feel pretty good actually, during the day; but they would keep me awake, and I wanted to sleep at night. Anyhow, somebody found out I had them and I had to quit. I think in a weak moment I told some bigmouth, and so Dr. Meyer found out.

After that there were a few times when I would get to a point where they really did get a few bits of information from me. Once was when Janet Franklin left, going to the State Hospital. Patients dreaded that. To leave the psych ward in University Hospital to go to the state institution meant that you were going to take a long time to get well. If you got well.

Janet and all the other women were in a ward across the hall from where I was with the men, but I could see her every day. We nearly always ate together in the cafeteria. I think anybody there would have agreed that the food was quite good. Not that we were in any state to find solace in food, but because, when you have no choice but to take from among what's set before you or go hungry, you feel angry and humiliated if it's bad. You feel like they're really wiping their feet on you. So the cafeteria was a good thing for us.

Janet and I were both bloated out of shape from massive doses of Thorazine, and we felt miserable about this and we condoled with each other. Thorazine is a depressant—maybe they didn't know this back at that time—and the very last thing on earth Janet, with postpartum depression, should have been taking. It may have been more suitable for me, but, aside from all that, it does not lift anybody's spirits to look like a feather pillow tied in the middle. She put on a lot of weight, and I was monstrously swollen and awful looking. Seeing each other two or three times a day, I got to be very fond of her and I was beside myself the day she went to the State Hospital.

I'm digressing. I started to tell about the best sessions I had with my therapist, but I can't skip casually over the way Janet went to the State Hospital. No wonder I was beside myself. It happened just like that week she spent in solitary. The doctor was irritated with her, and took his revenge. He was openly angry with her because they weren't "getting anywhere" and even more because she wouldn't believe she was sick. One day he said (in the way I've heard parents say to children, "Do you want me to pop you a good one?"), "Do you want to go to the State Hospital?" By that time she was plenty angry with them too, and she said, "I'd go to hell to get out of this place." And bang, he set in motion a quick transfer to the State Hospital. She asked for this to be a voluntary commitment, but she was refused. No reason on earth for it not to be a voluntary commitment: I was *crazy,* and they let me commit myself. That doctor was plainly and simply spiteful and abusive. It was a contemptible thing for him to do, because, on top of the trauma of having somebody else commit you, being committed in that way means that you lose your driver's license and your voting rights. Not permanently, but you lose them.

They had something called a commitment hearing, but Janet wasn't heard at this meeting. She wasn't present. One of the testifying doctors didn't even go to see her. The other one showed up on the ward, breezy in sports clothes and brisk about getting it over with because, as he said, he was shortly due to meet friends on the golf course. He asked her the most ordinary questions, the same as you'd be asked in any doctor's office, never even touching on her emotional condition or the treatment she'd been getting. And she said she knew well that she didn't say or do anything irrational. I have grave doubts that what they did was even legal. Her husband never got to even talk with her doctor.

281

She was "escorted" to the State Hospital by two police-men in full uniform including prominently displayed pistols. And I don't want ever to hear anything out of anybody about how policemen in uniform always carry guns. On such an errand, it could easily be made standard procedure for them to leave off their guns. And to wear plain clothes. Or wear plain clothes and keep their guns out of sight. It's not as if they were delivering a dangerous criminal. It was just one more degradation exercise hospitals indulge in to brandish their power. Janet wasn't a long-term patient, as it turned out, and she never was dangerous, yet this is how her transfer was effected. I had known she was going and was upset about it, but later in the day all of these details—every one of which she confirmed later—flew all over the cafeteria. It so unnerved me that my involuntary guard didn't stay up, and that day I guess my doctor had the best session with me that we ever had.

Another time I had a good session was when I found out what had happened to Volvo. He had been in the hospital when I was there the first time, and the nurses had told some of us about him. He had been a truck driver, and he'd been in an accident where somebody was killed. He steadfastly claimed innocence of any driving error, and they didn't put him in prison or anything like that. But they did as bad or worse. They took away his driver's license. He couldn't earn a living and this preyed on his mind.

He was miserable, the nurses said, until he cracked up and began to think he was a car. From that time on, he never walked anywhere. Any time he was outdoors, he was in the middle of the street, where the cars were, running. He stopped for red lights and stop signs, made turn signals and all the rest of it. He called himself Volvo, and that was the only name he'd answer to. He was calm and cheerful when we saw him on the ward.

On the ward, of course, he wasn't doing any of that car stuff, and to look at him you'd think there wasn't one Lord's thing wrong. On the streets though, he was in danger of his life. He was also a traffic hazard, and he kept getting arrested for that. His sister had brought him in. Well, this time in the hospital, I asked about Volvo. They told me he had been running home one bad night, and in the dark and the rain a truck hit him and he died right there in the middle of the street.

For some reason, this threw me. I don't know, I didn't have anything like the same feeling for him that I had for Janet. I hardly knew him. But somehow, to hear of his dying like that, in the street, in the rain, unnerved me again. And again, the doctor and I had one of the rare good sessions.

But when my guard was up, I coasted right along. I had my foot between the floor and the stair, but I didn't see that. I was hearing no voices, and I noticed things in a detached sort of way. Detachment is not usually my way, but then I was somewhat detached and I coolly noted what some of the others were acting like. (What I might have been acting like, I don't know. I think all right, judging from what came later.)

There were several older men who would cry out in their sleep. They'd give long drawn-out quavering moans and cries. This got me. Every time it happened I'd go off down the hall some place else. If you couldn't sleep, you could sit in the hall. There were always patients all up and down the hall.

One man would buttonhole anybody he could, and complain about "the blacks." This term in itself was strange, because at that date the word was not "black" but "Negro." They all steal, this old man said, and they're lewd and noisy. But the worst thing, he said, was "that awful smell." He said, "even if they wash, it's just terrible." He said he lived in an apartment house where there were lots of "the blacks," and he said the building had granite walls and the odor shouldn't be able to but it seeped right through.

So long as my guard was up, just being in the hospital was the only protection I needed. As long as the guard stayed up and didn't let the doctors know, didn't let them get really at me, then the hospital was a wonderful protection. The voices would go away. Every one of them went away. This is one reason I came to think that the hospital wasn't so bad and that sometimes I'd prefer being in there to being out. With my guard up—I can't say it enough—the hospital was absolutely all the protection I needed.

I had no trouble with voices about what I did at Whittier Place. I know I left that apartment looking like what Beulah would call the hind wheel of destruction. Not only paint spattered all over, but those last days I wasn't able to clean up a thing. I didn't wash a dish, and I know it was like some dotty recluse had been in there for ages. The landlord must have been shocked and mad. But I breezed through every bit of this and never heard one voice talking about it, because I didn't tell the doctor and I felt protected by the hospital. Things rocked along, and I preferred not to see Meyer but didn't too much care whether I saw him or not.

Thanksgiving was approaching, It was snowing, I remember. I come to another confusion here, because this was when I started thinking people were taking photographs of me. A little man in blue was always lurking around, and he was somebody I'd seen on other turbulent occasions. I think there really was such a person. I'd hate to think I saw things as well as heard things, but I never knew who or what he was. It never occurred to me to mention this to anybody, so they thought I was doing pretty well. They said they'd release me the day before Thanksgiving. Why they picked that time, I'll never understand. They know about holidays.

I didn't want to go. This is the thing that sticks with me the most: I never have wanted so badly not to leave a place. It was like they were pushing me out. They were going to release me, ready or not. I wouldn't have told them all this for anything on earth. I played it the other way. Oh, boy, I wanted to get out. Why on earth I would do that, who knows? I can't remember at all what made me do it, but this is something I'll do any time. Any time anybody does anything at all—gives me a Bobbsey Twins book, doesn't let me play on the ball team, fires me off my job—it's A-OK with me. It suits me to a t.

Meyer had said, "We're going to release you soon. Won't be long now." So I was carrying on, practically plucking at his sleeve, about how I couldn't wait to get out. One day we were all getting ready to have lunch, already in the line, and Meyer came out of the office. I knew by then they were going to release me the next day, the eve of Thanksgiving. So when I saw Meyer, I called to him and said, "Hey, Doctor, can't I go today?" He said, "All right. I don't see why not. Right after lunch, if you like."

I have never been more terrified in my life. Everything came crashing down on me. Every voice. Right there in the hospital. Where I hadn't been hearing a single voice. Right there in the cafeteria line. The very instant he told me I could go after lunch. I don't think anybody knew this. Maybe because I always carried such a heavy load of guilt, and unearned guilt is just as heavy as earned, I long ago became very tightly controlled, and I believe I show very little of what I'm feeling.

What I was feeling then was terrible. I was so panic-stricken I had no idea even what I was doing. How I got my little stuff together is a mystery. But I put my things in a shopping bag and I left right after lunch.

I don't remember going down town, but I found myself on Fourth Street over by the market. I spotted a liquor store, and I bought a bottle of rum. For a while I was flinging about in a blind, aimless rush, and then I spied a place with a sign,

"Rooms." I had to go some place, *right then,* and certainly I had no place to return to, so I went in there. What I wanted was a room, but they didn't have any. There was just a big dormitory, a ward. It was a flophouse. A dollar a night and all you had to do was put down your first name.

I put down my first name, paid my dollar, and sat on the side of the bed and drank the rum with things coming at me right and left. The voices were in great choruses. "Out of there before he wanted to be. Out of there before he should be. LOOK at him. Nothing cured about that one. Just as sick as he always was. Sick. Sick. Sick." And a lot of old hashed over stuff They always brought up. I drank the rum, but They kept on coming. Louder, faster, louder, faster, closer, closer, and They absolutely would not quit. Everything fell in on me.

Dear brother,
    I am fully persuaded that with prayer and faith we could keep you out of that asylum in Columbus, if you would write me just one line. Just one line to say that you're ready to come back to your family.

Your trouble is a care that nearly weighs me down. But if we stoutly oppose the powers of evil, they cannot prevail. Now, don't misunderstand me. I'm not saying that sickness is the wages of sin. (Aunt Placidia would have said that. You never knew her; she's our great-aunt on Momma's side.) But you are surely caught up by an evil force, and Christ wasn't called The Great Physician for nothing. He did cast out devils, and you must put your faith in Him. I earnestly hope and pray that you will turn to Jesus for help rather than doctors who, plenty of them, probably don't even believe in God. If they did they would stick to ministering to the body and not meddle with weaknesses of the soul. I know you are trying, but you are on the wrong track.

If those doctors knew very much about what they're doing, they could tell in a minute that you don't belong in any institution. You wrote me that sensible letter, you knew the date, you recognized your friend who came to see you. There's nothing wrong with you. It's just nerves. But I'll tell you this much, you cannot live and do well without God in your life.

Please pay close attention to what I tell you about my hope for you, so you will know why I believe it and you must try to believe too. You don't know much about my church because it never could hold your interest. But you do know I'm a Two-Seed-in-the-Spirit Predestinarian Baptist. This means I am certain that there are two great divisions of people on earth—the offspring of God, who will be saved, and the offspring of the devil, who will be lost. I never forget to thank God daily that through His grace, which no man or woman deserves, I know myself to be among the saved. In light of this belief I have studied and studied over you, and I don't feel that you are hopelessly lost.

Robert, I have not searched the scriptures for an answer. I quit studying the scriptures when I found that this was undermining my faith. The devil himself can quote holy writ to his own ends, and in our church we don't even hold with schools for training ministers but set more store by God-led preachers. We believe that layman and preacher alike, it is the right and duty of every one of us to experience God in his own way. My way of wrestling with your trials has been through solitary prayer and meditation. I have gone into this alone with my God.

I am praying for a miracle.

In our church we believe in predestation and total depravity. You know that much. But, Robby, we also believe in irresistible grace. Robby, even if you are of the seed of the serpent and your immortal soul predestined to be eternally lost, there is still one thing that could save you, and that is irresistible grace. My poor child, I'm afraid you may not even know the meaning of what I'm saying, you've grown away from me and Orie so.

I am not criticizing you for deserting the faith of your fathers and taking up with Jews and Unitarians. As a Christian, I am charitable and I harbor no hatred for the Jews; but, Robert, they did kill our Lord. As for the Unitarians, I don't even know what they are besides pagans and I doubt if they do either. I've heard how they say they believe in "one God at most." I have given them over into the hands of the Lord, and do not put any thought on them. I doubt you've been having anything to do with papists, and anyhow I've heard they don't think well of psychiatry themselves. It's more likely Jews and Unitarians who have led you to misdirect your efforts. If you would just stay quietly in your room and pray, it would do you more good than all the hospitals in the world.

Robby, I was telling you about irresistible grace. Grace is the working of divine love. Its most exalting manifestation is in God's taking the first step toward reconciliation with man and in His forgiveness of the repentant sinner. By this I am not saying one word of blame, and I never will, for any of your past habits or companions. Each one of us is a miserable sinner in some way. I am only asking that you repent of your sins as we all should.

If you will do this, meekly and earnestly, and if we would all pray (you, me, Orie), pray without tiring, for the gift of grace, how do we know but what you would be the one for whom a miracle would be passed? Couldn't you at least try? Can't you try to believe? Don't worry because you're unworthy. Everybody is unworthy. No mortal man can earn grace. It only can come as a free gift of God. It could come to you as well as anyone.

I have not talked about this with anyone but Orie. I never breathed a word of this to Momma. It would have been too hurtful. She was brave and she never complained, but she was an old woman, Robert, and it was right pitiful for her to have to say her prayers at night and lay her head on her pillow not even knowing where you were sometimes. You were always her favorite child, and it's no wonder if she shed a tear or two when nobody was around to see. She never really let on, but I know she did. I never wanted you to worry about her; I just wanted you to write to her. Even if it was only a line to let her know that you were all right. It probably hurts me more than it does you, for me to tell you this now when she's no longer with us. But I tell you because I think you ought to know how the way you lived affected Momma, and now Orie and me.

If you would come down here, you would find real help. This has always been true. Momma told everybody, not just you, that if you would only come home she would be too glad to take care of you for the rest of her life. It's too late for that now, but Orie's and my home will always be open to you. You know that.

I am between two fires about a package I'm sending you, as the body certainly is the temple of the soul and we of my church frown on smoking as an unclean and wicked habit. But I know you wouldn't think this enough of a reason; you're too used to tobacco growers, even Poppa. And I want to do something that you can't help knowing is done because I love you. I am sending you some cigarettes and candy.

Orie and I would like to send you some money, but we can't. Anyhow, at an institution that's part of a state university, I suppose all your needs are met. I'm not crying poor mouth. We're not having to scrimp too closely, but we do have to put every dollar where it will count. Orie has had to have some dental work done, and Luke is going to begin training at the auto mechanics' school next month. Also, we tithe, you know. We don't find tithing a hardship, as we do it to the glory of God. Other people spend that much or more on personal adornment and cards and whiskey. But we just don't have the money to help you another time way up there when we can't feel sure the money would be used for your benefit. I hate to say it, but it would be sending good money after bad. I'm sure you will understand and not mind that I have to put it this way.

Come back to Marlowe and we will give you a home. If you can put your faith in God and in Him crucified, and cleave to your homefolks, you will find peace and rest. I can't tell from your doctor's name whether he's Jewish or only German. If he's a Jew, he may not think much of the power of Christian prayer, but they *are* strong family people; so maybe he will realize that if you come back to us you could be healed in the bosom of your family. Still, I think psychiatrists in general lack a sound view of religion. But no matter how he feels about it, you must be firm in your own conviction. Come home where we can help you. May God bless you in wisdom and in health.

Your loving sister,
Willene

P.S. Robby, everybody has trouble in this life. We all have to bear our crosses. You can't just give in to things the way you're doing. Hospitals are for sicknesses; home is for happiness.

25
TWENTY-FIVE

Another place, another mess. I had just moved yet another time. This time it was to a light-housekeeping and rooming house Mr. La Roche found for me on Smith Place. Once more it looked like maybe a new place would be a solution. There was a bed, refrigerator, and stove, all in just a tiny space. The room was less than twelve by twelve feet, the size of a *rug*. It was a horrid little room. The little bath was off to itself. Still, I thought, well, maybe this time moving will turn the trick.

I had a new job and it wasn't going well at all. I had started badly and got worse. It's quite an ordeal for me to go through each time anyhow. Each time I've ever had a blowup and I'm coming back from it, I've approached a new job with all the trepidation imaginable.

The morning I was due to report for work, I was ravenous. I hadn't had anything to eat for nearly two days, and this didn't help anything. I went downtown early to wait for Mr. La Roche to get to his office. I just couldn't lose this job before I even got it. It was my new chance at survival. I went to a café and ate. I took my ticket to the cashier and told her I had eaten because I was so hungry I had to have something, but that I didn't have any money. I told her I was going to see a friend and I thought he'd come later in the day and reimburse her, and she let me leave without making any fuss. I went to Mr. La Roche as soon as his office was open, and I told him I couldn't go to work. I said, "I'm not sick. Physically, I feel all right, but I just cannot make it." He said for me to phone the office, and I did. They said it would be all right for me to start the next day. Mr. La Roche let me stay at his office with him all that day. I made a good start on reorganizing his filing system. He told me later it worked like a charm. We went to that same café for lunch, and he paid for my breakfast too.

The next morning I did go to work, scared to death of everything. I was afraid of everything, everything I could think of, including the people working there. I didn't know at what moment one of them was going to be one of the people that did all this talking about me. I never could know about anybody. That day went smoothly enough though. They showed me where things were and what I'd be doing. The second day was all right too.

Those two days, when I went home at night, I felt pretty good. The new job looked OK. I didn't hear anything. I could sleep. I began to feel the world wasn't too bad.

The third day, one boy and I just sat there doing absolutely nothing. He said—I don't know for sure that this was true, but I never questioned it—he said we couldn't read or do anything like that when there wasn't work for us. He said that the big shot, the man who owned the whole kit and caboodle, came through occasionally, and that he was peculiar about seeing anybody sitting and reading. He'd know why they weren't working, but he couldn't stand to see them read. He'd rather they'd just sit quietly and do nothing or maybe walk around a little. That day we sat eight hours holding our hands. then we worked until two the next morning. We got paid overtime, but that didn't ease the effects of having had to sit there and twitch for eight hours.

This was the way the place was run, and actually it was

the way it had to be run. It was a highway planning outfit, and everything depended on the engineers. They'd work their eight hours, and whenever they were ready to have something done on the machines it had to be done that instant. Somebody had to be there to do it. It was nobody's fault, it was the nature of the work, but it was something I couldn't take.

Right at the time I started there, there were no jobs getting completed; so there was nothing to put on the machines. It was awful. Then we worked until two in the morning again. One more day that week we sat idle all day and then worked even later into the next morning. I struggled through one other day and, as it turned out, it was my last day. That weekend, things boiled up at the place where I was rooming.

At this house on Smith Place, I had met a couple. Roger and Rosie. I couldn't have been less interested in any two people in the world for friends, but there it was. I needed somebody so badly that I fooled myself into thinking this was just the way to live. Friends that had me in, that went out with me, all that. We were all cozied up there together. Rosie would cook, and they would drink, and we'd all eat, and they would fight and each would tell me his side of the story. And I thought, "I'm really getting over it. Now I'm living like people. I'm part of something."

One Saturday I started drinking with them. While he was under the influence, Roger cried and cried about his watch that he had had to pawn. At my insistence we went downtown to the pawn shop, went in a truck Roger had. This is insane, but I gave him money to redeem his watch. I thought I was doing some good. I felt wonderful. This was real living.

It was crazy. I know how crazy it was. My clothes were shabby, I owed money; I needed glasses. I was wearing

Woolworth glasses right that minute, and my vision is so bad that I'm always terrified of having something happen to my glasses. I couldn't work without them. (I couldn't do anything without them.) Without them I'm all but blind. They're right beside me when I go to bed at night, and I reach for them the first time I open my eyes. But I was so befooled. "This was real," I thought. I had friends. I had the very staunchest friends in the world. That was even more important than *glasses*.

But somehow, underneath all this, some undercurrent stirred and told me this was not so. It wasn't such a deep undercurrent, either. I knew it was not so. But I was so desperately reaching out that nothing could have stopped me. I actually knew, and yet I kept plowing right on with it.

Roger and Rosie were doing the best they knew how. She was cooking special things, baking homemade rolls and everything and inviting me in, but it wasn't honestly meaning a thing to me. This is an extremely hard thing for me to get reconciled in my own mind. I was saying to myself, "These are real friends. I'm right in it." And all that. And at the very same time I was saying to myself that I knew there was not a word of truth in it.

While I was in the thick of all this, the thought of knowing that this-is-not-it wasn't constant or even frequent. For a while the only thought was, "Here I am, like everybody else." For instance, when I was handing over the money to Roger outside the pawn shop. "I'm like everybody else now," I said to myself. "I'm helping out a friend. This is how other people live." It's only when a thing like this is finished that I realize I knew all the time it wasn't good and wasn't genuine and wasn't what I'm really after. The real thing has been so rare in my life and my need is so great, fool's gold can look like twenty-four karat for a time.

In the new place, in the beginning of this "friendship,"

everything stopped. All the voices stopped. I'd go up to my room and I'd be perfectly comfortable in my mind. Nobody was talking. Any time I got ready, I could go downstairs and knock on their door and Roger and Rosie would receive me with open arms. That's the way it was for a while. Maybe they did like me, I don't know. But they were in pretty sad circumstances and, like me or not, they did find me useful.

I wasn't buying all the food we ate together in their place, but I was paying for most of the drinks and for most of the other things we did together. We never sat down, the three of us, and had an ordinary conversation. We were always doing things—going to a bar, going to a movie, going bowling, And I was paying.

This fool's paradise went on for about a week and a half. Then, as I said, things boiled over. Roger and the caretaker were going into my room when I was away. I knew they were. Roger was good at picking locks, but he didn't have to pick this one because the caretaker let them both in. They took my bottle of liquor.

Then one evening, another thing. Roger and Rosie and I had been having some drinks, and I went up to my room about ten o'clock. Later, when I was asleep, somebody knocked and, when I opened the door, there was Roger. Drunk. He leered at me and said, "How about you and me having a little fun?" and there was no mistaking his meaning. I shoved him out in the hall and locked the door.

There was something about me that brought this on. I don't know what it was, but I have an idea it was something sort of fluttery. I came to think of it as my butterfly wings. No matter what, it was wrong signals. I have even been accused of inviting this kind of attention and then rejecting it, but this was not so.

I went to work the next morning, but it was awful. I no longer had Roger and Rosie. I no longer had a job that I could handle. It had all dissolved. That night I got drunk by myself, in the room. Next morning I didn't go to work.

During this bad period there seemed to be only one thing that I could cling to, one normal thing that I could get my hands on. The laundromat. I would go around the corner to the laundromat, and I washed everything I had twice, even a suit that shouldn't have been washed. An old man would come in about two-thirty in the morning to clean. He had a job some place and he was trying to retire, and he was running this laundry place. A couple of nights I helped him. I tidied up, put detergent packets and bleach in the vending machines, mopped the floor, things like that. This would take until almost four in the morning. I don't really know what I thought this washeteria was doing for me, but I clung to it.

I used to go across High Street from the laundromat into a bar called Mac's Grill. It was rather rundown, like that whole neighborhood was getting. There was usually a lot of distinctly tough looking people milling around in there. This is the joint where Queen Bee used to sit in the bar. I knew about Queen Bee because I'd been in Mac's Grill before, and besides, she had lived in the rooming house on Smith Place and Roger and Rosie knew her. Rosie didn't like her. The situation was very simple: Queen Bee worked this bar.

There was one fellow always with her. Supposedly he was her husband, but nobody ever knew whether he was or not. And most of the time she had, besides him, an entourage of muscle men surging about her. Roger said, and I have no reason to doubt this, that Queen Bee would pick up men in the bar and take them to a place almost across the street. If she picked up a married man, this would serve her purpose even better. She'd take him down the block a piece to where she lived and, when things had gone far enough, in would walk these muscle men and he was absolutely at their mercy and they would take all the money he had. This team must have done well, because certainly Queen Bee did wear fabulous clothes.

She and all her hulking bruiser types were young and she was wonderfully pretty. None of that cheaply pretty look. She wasn't flashy looking at all. She had a fine face and figure and carried herself well and wore terrifically expensive clothes, and the clothes weren't flashy either. I've thought about this quite often. Here she was, a professional tramp and blackmailer, working a dingy dive like Mac's Grill, and always got up in a way even Fina wouldn't find fault with and nothing coarse in her whole appearance.

It was like the time I saw the cat. Once, long before I ever left North Carolina, I went with the family on a short trip to see some relatives. The highway was torn up and we were most of the time on detours through back country roads. We got lost. In a desolate backwoods stretch, we passed one lone ramshackle house and next to it a store of some sort. The house and the store were both fixing to tumble down, and there wasn't a bit of paint to be seen anywhere. I especially remembered the steps leading up to the store. It wasn't that the paint was worn off; those steps had never known paint, I'm sure of it. There was all this gray welter of poverty and isolation and dust and decay and Godforsakenness, and, in the midst of it, on those never-painted broken down store steps, there sat—erect and vivid and regal—a raving beauty of a Siamese cat. This is something of the effect you got when you'd go into grungy gritty Mac's Grill, full of rough-toughs at best and lots of outright bums and hoods, and see Queen Bee sitting up at the bar.

The night I had my little brush with her, she had on a dress of Chinese silk so fine I could have held it in my hand like *this*. No telling what the price was. In comparison to the clothes she wore, the place where she was said to live was a squalid dump. But it was necessary for working that section.

It was easier to take men there from the Grill than to go a long way—she would soon go back to the Grill and get another fellow—and she would naturally live in whatever neighborhood she was working at the time. I think she moved around a lot. The night she came and sat by me, she said, "I very seldom come in here. Usually I go downtown to the Unicorn." Which I knew was a lie, because I knew about her from the people at the house. Later I wondered why she didn't really go to better places, where men would likely be carrying more money. But she looked like she was getting plenty and I guess she knew her business.

During this particular bad period, after Roger and Rosie had fizzled, I went in this bar a lot. I was deeply troubled, and the voices were just having at me; so I wanted to be where there were people. Not to have contact with them; I was studiously avoiding contact with all people, even the few real, true friends I had. I just wanted to be where there were people about, near but not at me, to give me a feeling of some connection with the real world. I'd be there by myself, of course. Queen Bee was sitting at the bar that night, I remember.

I sat at a table by the window and I was working a crossword puzzle. I'd do anything that I'd think of to keep attention from me, or rather, anything to make the voices think I was so busy I wasn't paying Them any mind. Actually, I guess somebody working a crossword puzzle in such a place might attract some slight notice; but—anything to concentrate on, anything to put my mind on, anything that might possibly fool Them.

All of a sudden, somebody gave me a beer. I had one. I hadn't ordered another one. But the man took mine away and put this one down. I said, "What's this?" The man said, "It's from the young lady." I didn't say anything. I looked and saw Queen Bee.

She sauntered over and sat down at my table. She looked at the puzzle and said, "If it calls for the same old three-letter word meaning morsel of leftover food, it's o-r-t," and she laughed. Even though she rather surprised me by that remark, I didn't get into any conversation with her. I didn't even thank her for the beer. I said nothing at all, and she drifted away.

I sat there drinking beer, and, for some unknown reason, I kept looking across the street. I saw Mr. La Roche. He went into the laundromat and came back out and stood on the corner right under a street light. Somebody must have told him I spent a lot of time at the laundry. It's too vague to describe, but somehow he seemed to me to look so lonely standing there, in that little pool of light with the dark all around it, and I knew I had let him down.

I burst into tears and cried hysterically. Not a soul in that bar paid one bit of attention. I had my head down on the crossword puzzle on the table, and I just let go. I was crying as hard as I've nearly ever cried in my life. Not one person said one word to me. People would walk right by me—I could hear their feet beside the table—walk by, and see me, I suppose, and go right on.

Finally I got myself under control, straightened up, got some more beer, and joined the people at the bar. Queen Bee's troops were around her. I don't know what anybody was doing or what the circumstances were, but something caused me to pass a remark. I wasn't myself, and I said something very ill considered. I said something like queen bees were the cleverest and most gifted of bees, the only ones who could sting more than once. What happened next, I remember even less clearly, but it happened quickly and it ended with somebody ripping my shirt half off me. I never knew just who did it. I think I left right after that; I'm not sure but what they threw me out. I can't keep it straight. There was a whole bunch of stuff going on, and it got confused and murky in my memory.

But this shows the kind of thing that would happen to me. I'd go snarl myself up with people like Roger and Rosie, and then fall apart when it went rotten. I did this for years, beginning way back there when I was a boy in Marlowe and before. Always when I was in deep trouble, I would almost buy rank strangers. Whatever they thought, I'd think, "Let 'em think it, let 'em think it—until I can get them alone, away from all these voices, and they'll see different. They'll see that I'm really nothing like what the voices are saying I am."

Each time it seemed that this would be the time when one somebody would see that all that talk was not true, that I'm pretty nice, and that this time this would be a person who would be my close friend, somebody whose regard I could count on. I've done it so much and been in so much difficulty because of it. I've quit doing it because it never works. Once in a while I'd fall in with somebody half decent, but mostly it was barroom bums, when all the time there were good people and good friends and they were the ones I'd stay away from.

Once I remember fouling up things even when the situation was good and I was pretty much myself, not at all like the time I took up with Roger and Rosie. I got off the track without being pushed. I wasn't even being pulled. I just slid along with circumstances.

I had just got my pay check and I was going to do everything. I paid for my room and I got my affairs all straightened out. That same evening I was walking out to get some supper and I met a boy I had known at the Y when I first came to Columbus. He was with a fellow I'd met in the Psychiatric Institute. This second one was still quite disturbed, and this is why I feel it's not too good for people who've been hospitalized together to spend much time together later on.

The boy from the Y was no more than a companion who went along. It was the old-friends, hard-times-shared camaraderie between me and the boy who had been at the Institute that started this. We had a lot to talk about and we were talking. We were drinking too, and this was fatal. One thing led to another, and I passively went along with the current. Before the evening was over I was blind, staggering drunk.

They came back to Smith Place with me, and I found a note there from Joe. I don't remember what caused Joe to write me a note and slip it under the door, and I don't remember what he wrote. But there was the note from Joe. And I let this, almost deliberately let this, throw me into a frenzy. Yet, when I say, "deliberately," I don't quite know what I mean. I'm not clear either why I used the word "frenzy."

It's similar to the way I described Roger and Rosie. All the time, somewhere in my mind, I knew that drinking and roaring and ramping around with those two fellows was not what I wanted, and I knew that Joe was a real friend, and yet I couldn't help myself. There was no way I could control this fooling away my time with cheap, superficial people that would never mean anything to me, people that, under different circumstances, I wouldn't want for friends. It tore me up, finding Joe's note right when I was with two people who didn't mean a paper of pins to me. We had been drinking and carrying on. I don't remember much beyond that.

I don't know. I can't say. But I think it was for the same reason I cried so hard in the bar when I saw Mr. La Roche. There was absolutely no hope. I was lost. I mean, why didn't I get up and get out of that bar and go across the street to Mr. La Roche? I couldn't. Why didn't I go downstairs and pick up the phone and call Joe? I couldn't. Why didn't I get in touch with one or two real friends? I couldn't. I no longer felt that I deserved any of them. I felt that I didn't deserve the regard of good people. These others were more suitable, because I was worthless and any old riffraff I ran into in some dive was good enough for me.

All the time we were working together at Reliant, I liked Rob a lot. He's a good bit older than I am, but we were congenial. He seemed wiser as well as older, and somebody you could look to for support when you needed it. He'd always get me cooled down if I began to get hot under the collar about some gumpy thing that happened at the office. He used to say, "Joe, you can't afford to lose your temper. You're too big. If you ever hit anybody it would be terrible." I never hit anybody then or any other time, but after the day he saw me punch out a card rack—better a card rack than Bill Zimmerman, the fellow who had burned me up—he was afraid I might. I suppose it was a possibility, but not much of a one.

Rob was kind to me in more ways than one. I was quite young then. I'd never seen a burlicue show, and I was selfconscious about this around the other men. I didn't want them to know how green I was. I told Rob about this, and he said, "We'll go see Rose La Rose." Some of the men belonged to the Rose Club, and she was supposed to be a powerhouse but in a nicer way than most. I was all steamed up to see her, but when we got there it was Blaze Storm. You could see at once why she had that name. She was flaming and storming all over the place, stamping and flailing about and throwing that long red hair all around. I was shook. I'm sure it showed, and I felt like a fool. But Rob was nice. He said, "She really is overpowering." It's a silly thing, but this one little excursion made me feel easier around some of the other men, I had seen Blaze Storm and I was no longer quite so wet behind the ears. I was grateful to Rob for that.

He was always so quiet. People said he got into all kinds of trouble, but I don't see how. It seemed to me he lived very quietly. Earlier in our acquaintance he used to go to shows once in a while. He loved theater and seemed to know a good bit about it, and he used to go whenever he could. He always had something interesting to say about what he'd seen. Then he sort of shrank down, and he just worked and went home as far as I could tell. But he did have lots of trouble later on about having places to live and go home to. Everywhere he went, something would go wrong. He moved all around. This was much later, after he was no longer at Reliant.

A time came when he got very flighty. He'd look at you while you were talking to him, but you could tell he was a thousand miles away. He'd hear you and understand you, and he'd answer you, but he'd answer briefly and he didn't show any of the responsiveness that he used to. Used to be he'd talk a blue streak. He got to where he didn't express much sympathy or interest or enjoyment or whatever, and this was a difference in him. This continued on. He got more and more remote and then he cracked up. Maybe from overwork. But who knows? Because even after the changes came, he really put out the work when he was more or less steady. At his best, he was outstanding; couldn't be touched by anybody else in the section.

He came on back to work after a while in the hospital, but it never was the same with him again. Soon he began to do all that moving around. He moved so often you'd have thought he was keeping one jump ahead of the sheriff. It got to where it was hard for me to keep up with him. I began to feel he didn't want me to keep up with him. Then when he lost out at Reliant, things went to hell in a handbasket. He went downhill fast. Not our friendship. That happened by degrees. There was no big bust-up, and I didn't dump him at the first sign of trouble, either. I was there for him when he let me know he wanted to be with me. Once I went and helped move him from one place to another. I piled all his gear in Mrs. Ritter's car. She drove him to the new place and I met them there and hauled all that stuff in for him. Then he was saying he couldn't bear to be alone just yet. He stood on the curb looking shaky and lost and said, "If I just had somebody to eat supper with." We didn't like to leave him that way, but she couldn't stay and neither could I. Her husband was coming back from a business trip and she had to go to the airport, and I had to do something I'd promised my mother.

Rob would say he couldn't bear to be alone, but generally he'd rig things so that he would be alone. When I would manage to get in touch with him, he was always friendly but somehow it always ended up that I wouldn't know how to get in touch with him again. He was always the one who could get in touch with other people. They couldn't find him. After so long a time, I got fed up with that.

I lost track of him, but not on purpose. He was a great help to me in the Reliant days and we were fast friends. But then everything seemed to get out of shape and break up. And then, to be honest about it, I did get mad with him.

For months, as long as I could halfway keep track of him, I kept up some kind of off-and-on contact. But it's hard, persevering at such a onesided thing, and besides it was taking too much of my time away from Jenny. This was before we were married. In fact, some of it was before we were engaged. But we were serious about each other and we wanted to spend as much time together as possible. Rob had never shown any real interest in Jenny and our prospects, and this bugged me. The deeper my interest in her, and the more inaccessible Rob became, the more the very idea of Rob began to fade. He drifted and drifted away from me, and I didn't know any more about him. Not where he was, not what he was doing, not how he was managing, nor anything at all. Any more, he was out of the picture. At first this worried me some, when I happened to think of it; but Jenny and I were making plans and looking at furniture, and I all but forgot him.

I remember the last straw. I knew he was having trouble on a new job, because he phoned me one day at work to tell me. And he told me where he was living. Up on Smith Place, just off High. Not long after that, when I hadn't heard from him again and figured I wouldn't, I thought, "All right. I'll do this one more time." So that night after I left Jenny, I went on by there. It was late, but I knew that wouldn't matter, and, after I thought of him, I had got a little worried about him. When I got to the house, the door to his room was locked and I couldn't get any answer to my knocking and calling; so I stuck a note under the door asking him to call me. I never heard a word from him.

I'm nobody's fair-weather friend. What happened, the whole thing petered out because I got tired of running around after him and trying to keep up a friendship with somebody who wouldn't hold up his end at all. Jenny thought I was a fool to hang on as long as I did. It wasn't everybody at Reliant liked him, I remembered. Some thought he was stuck up; and for the first time I began to think maybe they had a point.

Rob didn't have to be alone. He had me, he had the Ritters—Mr. Ritter was one of the higher-ups at Reliant, and he and Mrs. Ritter were very good friends to Rob—and he had Mr. La Roche, and he could have had others. But he treated every one of them the same way he did me. I know Mr. Ritter went over to Smith Place early one evening. It was summer, and Rob and a married couple who lived there were sitting on the porch. Mr. Ritter asked him if he'd like to come home with him for a little visit, and Rob said no, some other time. Next morning, Sunday morning, the Ritters found a tin can of daisies at their front door, holding down two poems.

Mr. Ritter came by one day at the office and showed me

the poems. One was called "Holiday." I was so impressed by it that I copied it down.

Saturday night and man takes holiday
From labor that was safer wine,
But on Saturday night—come Saturday night—
He knows himself, vacuous, cold,
Hunting the colors, filling the empty spaces,
No longer a king with a column of figures
A column of figures to be added and subtracted
And himself therefore
A man managing the affairs of the world.

But on Saturday night a guy has leave to talk to himself.
To reclaim his soul.
To hunt what he has wanted, or forget what he never had.
To chase the dream, or drown it in futility.

God, do you see?
Or are you too far away reclining on a star?
How about coming down and walking for a little
Where we are?
Do not tell me no one has asked You,
Over the cups in the dark of night
Saturday night
Do not tell me no one has cried to You
Lost in the dark and without a light
Saturday night.

Your stars are beautiful, but we
Need some nearer light to see.

This softened my anger against him for being so flib-bertygibberty and so impossible to get hold of, and I carried the copy around in my wallet until the paper started tearing in the creases. But the first impact wore off in time and I decided that he didn't want to be friends with me any more, and even if he did it had got to be too much trouble. I had my life to live. After that night I put the note under his door and never had any answer, I never tried to find him again.

The day after that night, I went out at lunch time to do an errand and I ran into Mr. La Roche outside the Reliant building. He said he'd been out to Smith Place looking for Rob too. He said he had gone on to the laundromat around the corner, but the man there said Rob hadn't been in, and there wasn't any other place in the vicinity to look. Nothing else for blocks around but a ratty looking bar and grill.

26
TWENTY-SIX

Several years back, a great change came up. There was an opening—for a really good job—at a downtown motel. It was completely outside my field of competence, but, through some connection of Mr. La Roche's, I had a chance at it. I had never done a lick of work in a motel in my life; but here was this opening, and for some unknown reason I felt equal to it. I never understood this in myself. Usually I felt shaky, even when the job was something I well knew I could do. But this unlikely time, like manna from heaven or any other miracle, a good measure of self-confidence came over me.

I made myself as presentable as my worse than seedy condition allowed, and I went to the interview with something close to high heart. I had my hopes up. Here was something wonderful, I thought, and all I had to do was to reach out and take it. I got the job. The manager seemed to like me, and he could see I was game. Still amazed at myself, I jumped in with all four feet, and next thing I knew I was having a second blooming.

It was at the Wayfarers' Inn, close to the heart of Columbus. It's a fair-sized motel, and I ran it. My title was special assistant to the manager, but I ran the place. I had caught on to things very quickly, and in short order the manager, Neil Keller, was sitting back and taking things mighty easy. I had soon found out that the hotel business was not for me. But there wasn't any choice; I had to make the best of it and be thankful. For one thing, the way it was then, I was in constant distress about the maids and the conditions they worked under and the pay they got. There were other drawbacks but, in spite of them, I almost loved that job. In a way. It looked like Convoy all over again—the biggest success of my life. My lack of training didn't seem to matter one bit; I saw things that needed to be done and I did them. Neil's secretary used to say, "Robby is everywhere and does everything."

This was true. I even kept the books. When I went there, the books were a mess. After I cleaned that up, I continued as bookkeeper. Neil liked me, and well he should have. I voluntarily took on more and more tasks until finally I was doing several jobs, including most of his. I couldn't have done this if they hadn't been losing employees right and left before I went there. I had actively sought additional work to do because overwork staved off the voices.

I was surprised at the way I got along without the help of pills. I got up early every morning and went to bed tired to the bone, so I managed to sleep part of most nights, and I learnt to live with the voices enough that it was only once in a while that They bothered me a lot. I felt lucky any day I got through without panic, but somehow I even handled panic too and all in all I felt I wasn't doing badly.

If the press of work made me put all my attention on what I was doing, that would fend off the voices. That's the thing to do. Crowd them. Dislodge them. Be stronger than They are. At least for the time being. It's impossible to keep this up every living minute; it takes huge amounts of psychic energy. Physical strength too. When you're overtired for too long, it's very hard; when you're sick, it's out of the question. So in the long run the voices are always stronger. But hard work helps. It always has.

Insofar as I still had any capacity for enjoyment, and I did still have a little, I enjoyed that job. After a long time of dragging the ground, I was treated as a person of some consequence, by the motel people and by the guests. It also gave my spirits a lift to be spruced up some. I had two charcoal gray blazers to wear to work. They were the first decent pieces of clothing I'd had for a coon's age, and one had pewter buttons. That one looked even better than it actually was. The Ritters gave me the set of buttons, a new-job present, and they made all the difference.

So I was sharp and snappy looking, everybody seemed to like me, the boss gave me a gold pen for Christmas, and one time Eudora Welty stopped over with us and I showed her to her room and carried her bags.

It was plain to see that the motel was coming up in the world since Neil took me on. Definitely, it began to happen after Neil took me on. In the past I had often reflected that my life was one straight shot to the hospital. Which it had been. But now I began to equate the motel's fortunes with my own, and I so far forgot myself that I even began to believe that maybe we both could be rehabilitated and hold on. I even wildly speculated that maybe, just maybe, I could cling to this job until retirement age. Retirement pay plus Social Security might give me enough to pinch through. This line of thought redoubled my efforts and before too long I had that place running like my uncle's railroad watch.

Soon after the end of my second year, the motel was cited by the national office as the unit in the chain showing the most improvement in management. This was due to me. It was accepted as that—although tacitly—by the staff, and I felt mighty good about it. When you're parched and nearly withered from a feeling of utter worthlessness, coming out first in a nationwide chain is like water that brings life. It was a shining hour for me, because before me the Columbus

Wayfarers' Inn really had a distinctly unenviable record. The home office was astounded at the change. Even though Neil got official credit, I got back my self-respect. And my dream continued. I thought I was on my way.

This was too good to last, of course. I was there for only a little over two years before it blew up in my face. I decided to walk over to Lazarus one night, the night the stores were open every week, and on the way I came up on some sort of demonstration on the State House grounds. I never knew for sure, but I imagine it was an anti-Vietnamese-War thing. I had no intention of getting mixed up in it. At that time and in that place, it's safe to assume that I would have been on the side of any demonstrators, but I couldn't take part in anything like that. I wasn't steady enough. I guess I was awfully tired and had lost some caution, and I got too close to the edge of the crowd. People came to join in and, as I was on the edge, they formed a small mass behind me before I noticed. When they pushed forward, they moved me along in front of them, and then I was in the crowd and they were on the edge. I was engulfed, and, after that, willy-nilly, I moved however the crowd moved. That's frightening. It's even more frightening to be beat over the head with a cop's billy club just because you're there. I wound up in jail with my head split open, and while I was there I caught flu.

That did it. Physical sickness drains me of my ability to fight off the voices in any degree. Any time I'm bodily weakened, They simply take over. Pile right in, in full cry, and I can't lift a finger or a brain cell against them. It was nearly a week before things cleared up and I was able to get back to the motel. When I got there, I found that I no longer had a job.

Neil's father had been critically ill in another town. He had died, and my absence had made a lot of trouble. I never did learn whether or not Neil got to his father while he was still able to see Neil, or what arrangements were made at the motel so he could leave, if he left. He didn't tell me anything. At least not anything like that. He told me a powerful lot otherwise, and it added up to, "Get lost. Drop dead."

This was a side of him I'd never seen. Of course I'd never seen it. Up until that time I'd never caused him even the slightest inconvenience. He yelled at me 'til he was hoarse. I never could cope with that kind of thing, so I didn't have any chance to explain. I don't suppose it mattered. Mrs. Ritter did explain to him later, but it had no effect. Neil was all right in his way, but he was too limited to get a grip on my situation and therefore he made no allowances. He had said when he hired me that he understood that at some point I might mess up. Still, when this thing happened to me, he couldn't deal with it. Or even understand it. I got the feeling that he didn't want to understand it. Besides, I think it was simply beyond him.

In a way, I don't blame him too much. All the same, he had hired me with knowledge of my situation. He'd had abundant opportunity to see that I did my dead level best. He had seen, and to his substantial benefit, that my dead level best was plenty good. And he had seen that I had sustained all that effort for more than two years handrunning. Of course on the face of it I was in the wrong. I didn't mess up from negligence, but I did mess up. Whether or not he was being fair didn't enter into it; I was held responsible. A lot of therapists think this is OK, but I disagree. How can you take full responsibility for a lapse when you have the lapse because you're not always fully responsible? If I had had a physical sickness, people wouldn't have had unreasonable expectations of me.

No matter how I try to see Neil's side of it, I had run that motel for him. What he did was sleep late, swim in the motel pool, and take his kid to that awful zoo where they kept having baby hippopotamuses that died almost immediately because the mother wasn't given the right kind of place to give birth. Neil would go off and leave that motel in my hands, and, if I do say it myself, I did very well by it.

None of that entered into his view of my mishap. All of it evaporated like this morning's dew, and he simply kicked me out. I feel wretched about his father, but I do not feel kindly toward him. I can't help thinking that it was small of him to figure that I'd made trouble for him, OK, he'd make worse trouble for me. Not only small but cruel, even savage. He'd forget my sickness and my contributions of the past more than two years and he'd throw me overboard without a qualm. And that's what he did.

Everything disintegrated, right then. I think it was enough to throw nearly anybody, but it devastated me because I had allowed my hopes to be raised. As long as you're pretty nearly without any hope, one thing you don't suffer from is disappointment. But I had been foolish enough to think that maybe things could be all right for me, even at that late date, that life might hold some little promise after all. And things went well for long enough that I had begun to think they'd keep on. And when my golden opportunity turned green on me, I was ground to a powder.

Nothing improved, and it's too late for improvement now. I'm irreparably damaged, way past any possibility of comeback. By now, in 1973, I'm not even physically able to work. It's the emphysema that's so rough now. When you can't take a really deep breath, or clean a room, or walk two blocks without gasping and stopping, you're unfit for much gainful employment. This factor even swallows up the matter of age. Fifty-three is not a popular age for new employees.

I keep trying to set forth the inner turmoil that made my life what it has been, all the while knowing that I can't do it as plainly as I want. I keep remembering something that George Eliot wrote in a letter. It was to the effect that nobody should complain about being misunderstood, since we are all totally unable to present ourselves accurately. I wonder if she was thinking about candor. I don't worry about failing in accuracy except as it involves complete candor. I most desperately want that, but there's my barricade to be reckoned with. Barricades like mine are like habit in a proverb Aunt Mozelle used to quote. "Habit is a cable. We weave a thread of it each day and at last we cannot break it." My barricade didn't begin like a thread, and it didn't grow by tiny additions until it was like a cable. At times I have thought of it as similar to a coral reef, but it wasn't that way in its beginning. As I've said, in early childhood it sprang up whole, like a goddess full-grown from her father's forehead. Sprang up whole, all at a thunder-clap, and was immediately effective. Then I involuntarily laid a rock on it every day of my life, and I've never been able to really clear it away. The best I ever could do with this barricade is to make a small breach in it here and there.

My life now is unrelievedly gray and dismal, every day and every night miseries to be endured. Of course that's nothing new, but with time the accumulation grinds on me heavier and heavier. I'm worn down by it. Eroded. There is some difference now, from my young years. It's not that I'm not still tormented. It's only that I don't get as wildly agitated as I did then. For one thing, I can't get out and rush around; I'm not able; I just grit my deteriorating teeth and do housecleaning and tough it out. It's still a desperate thing.

I live in poverty. Not genteel poverty; plain unvarnished poverty. For some years I've been sharing part of the down-stairs of a small duplex with Catherine Leonard. It's the same deal as with many aged people who live under the same roof, pretending to be married so they can combine their scant resources. Catherine is a widow around my age. When I met her, she'd been widowed for some time, and for several reasons she had great difficulty holding a job. She was living on nickels and dimes. Her husband's family sometimes sent her money, but at irregular and widely spaced intervals. I was already dirt poor myself, and later we got together so we could perhaps keep our heads above water. Alone, we were both going down. To avoid any possible hassles, we passed ourselves off to the landlord and neighbors as sister and brother. Neither of us was in any condition to be hassled.

Our arrangement does two vital things for me: It somewhat dulls the cutting edge of destitution, and it saves me from devastating loneliness. I have got to where I could not survive alone, entirely aside from money. Aloneness was always unmercifully battering for me, but now I just couldn't hack it, not for a day. The voices would pulverize me and keep me pulverized. I feel that, with age, whatever is awkward gets more pronounced, even little quirks and crochets, let alone mental disease. If I live to be old, I know I'll be awful. I'm awful enough now. I used to think that I'd never make old bones, but you never know. I hear that sometimes paranoiacs in their old age, if they go senile, get along better. The paranoia seems to ease up. Or so some people get the impression. But I'm only middle-aged, and even great old age doesn't necessarily bring senility, not by any means.

If anybody, anybody at all, is with me, I can somehow manage by the skin of my teeth. It's not a pretty setup Catherine and I have. I don't have any real liking for her, hardly much respect even, but I need her. I don't think she ever did like me, but she needs me. Ever since I've known her, she has taken advantage of me; and now she's able to call all the shots. She knows I could not bear to be alone, and she uses this like a gun to my head. Not that she ever openly threatens me. She doesn't need to, and she knows this.

She's always had the upper hand. She used to throw away my little dab of money like it was all hers and plenty more where that came from. Back a while, she used to invite neighbors in to dinner when that would wipe out our grocery money and leave us hungry, very hungry, for days before we laid eyes on a penny again. We live on welfare, and no taxpayer need worry about our being "coddled."

In anything that involves money, it's like Catherine has taken leave of her senses. Even now. She really acts crazy. She got hold of Willene's phone number once when we were both in better health, and she called her in North Carolina and asked her to give us a car. A *car*. One, Willene couldn't; two, she wouldn't; three, she shouldn't; and four, if she had, we couldn't have kept it up for a week. But Catherine was furious when Willene didn't give us a car.

One Christmas she insisted on giving her married daughter a cashmere sweater. I couldn't believe she was serious when she first brought that up, but she was absolutely singleminded about it. She won, of course, because I was afraid to cross her. She knew that I had a bit of money painfully held on to from way back. She steamrollered me and bought this expensive sweater. There went my tiny hoard, there went our grocery money, there went our coin-laundry money, and the rent went overdue.

We paid dearly for her grandiose gesture. We kept bodies and souls together with a little canned soup and sometimes stale rolls the bakery sells cheap. If her daughter had had a shred of decency, she'd have returned that sweater to the store and given me back my money. She very well knew how Catherine came by that sweater, and she very well knew that I was threadbare. I didn't say a word, of course, but I was boiling inside.

Since then Catherine has become bedridden. A diagnois of malignancy was made a good while ago but then, after right many months, she went into the hospital again and they could find no sign of cancer. This condition held for nearly a year and they were calling her the miracle lady, but then the cancer returned. To her spine. She says she doesn't have pain, and she doesn't seem to. I can't understand that, but I'd be afraid to question her too much; sometimes she stirs up quicker than a hornet. She puts a good face on things, and she's in better spirits than I would be. In one of her rare moments of speaking of what was likely in store for her, she made me admire her tremendously. She said, "Whatever other people have stood, I guess I can stand too."

For a time she could, with help, get out of bed for short periods, but no more. A visiting nurse comes twice a week and gives her a bath, and other than that I take care of her. I'm slow because of shortness of breath, sometimes because I'm clubbed by medicine, but I can do it. I don't mind. I feel sorry for her. Although it wouldn't do me any good if I did mind; I'd have it to do anyhow. I look after her the best I can, never keep her waiting for something she wants or needs, and all that. But I know that if our positions were reversed she'd find a way to get out of doing the same for me. It was all talk when she used to say she thought so much of me, would do anything for me. Then and ever after, she very aggressively made use of me. Even way back when I first knew her.

Jim Morehouse and I were living together (another arrangement of expedience), and Catherine was living next door. She had just delighted in Jim, and he used both of us. He'd go over to her place and they'd drink and laugh at me. Indirectly I paid for the liquor. Catherine was always "borrowing" from me and she bought it. Jim never could have. As a lowest-level attendant at the State School, he wasn't loaded down with pay. We didn't live far from the School, and he could walk to and from work. He buttered up Catherine, and for his pains he got a lot of little treats that made life a mite pleasanter. I'll say this much for him though: He was kind to those retarded children. Once he came home from work and said, "This morning I lined them all up, and I went down the line and hugged each one." He and Catherine weren't pulling any wool over my eyes, but there was no way on earth I could defend myself and I simply had to put up with them.

She was really set up about her thing with Jim. I think it bolstered her that she was involved with somebody as young as Jim, and he was rather nice looking. And, badly as he treated her eventually, he gave her life a little color and shine for a while. Catherine looked her age, and her eyes were too small and too close together, but she had great hair. It was chestnut, the most beautiful rich warm color, and it often made me think of Jo in *Little Women.* Mrs. March used to say Jo's hair was her "one beauty."

Jim was blond and looked even younger than he was. He had a kind of sweet-boy face. He was *not* a sweet boy, but he had a sweet-boy face. He was well aware of this, and he traded on it. He could take on the most ingratiating manner, and he'd use this in all kinds of situations—with tradespeople, with employers, with acquaintances—and it was astonishing how often it worked, especially with older women. If he'd had any chance at all, he could have been a successful con artist. He actually was a con man, in a narrow area and a picayune way. Catherine would spend whatever she had on him, and then she'd come crying to me. If I had anything at all, I'd have to share with her. She and Jim were very thick, and I couldn't risk her turning him against me. She was fully capable of trying this. I was already afraid he might leave me alone and go live with her. He could have, any day.

I think Catherine protected herself from noticing that Jim never went to bed with her except when he was half drunk. He told me that cold sober he couldn't. If that was true, it was true; but I don't think he should have told it to anybody. He had no loyalty or even gratitude in him.

They planned—or he let her think they planned—to live

in New York and get married. He was to go up first and get a job, then she was to join him. This was wildly impossible, less likely even than that my sister would give us a car, but Catherine swallowed it whole. Why Jim did this, I don't know, except that it was his nature. Of course he skipped out on her, and on me too. Went to New York or somewhere, left us both high and dry, and that was when Catherine and I cast our lots together and moved to the duplex. We never ever heard a word from Jim or knew anything about him.

They were some pair. The same types I had always got embroiled with. When I had a therapist once, he told me Jim was a sociopath, and I had seen it demonstrated time and time again. I couldn't help feeling sorry for Jim, though. I felt sorry for all three of us.

I don't know what pushed him over the edge, but once he cracked up and had to be hospitalized. And this is how deprived a life he had led:

When he was discharged from the Psych Institute at OSU, Mrs. Ritter and I went to pick him up. He had checked out earlier than we'd expected, and he'd gone to the barber shop near the hospital. Left word for us to find him there. He had gone to get a manicure. Didn't have but seventeen cents on him when we got there, but he'd had that manicure. He said he did it because he'd never had his nails done and he desperately wanted some nice thing, right that minute. Mrs. Ritter thought that was understandable and so did I, but it was sad.

It was also sad to be getting out of a mental hospital on his birthday, but that's how it was. Mrs. Ritter drove on up High Street and out Route 161 and took us to lunch at Green Meadows. We had coconut cake for dessert and we called it birthday cake, and Jim told me later that it was the first time in his life anybody had ever done anything for him on his birthday. Of course I wasn't ever sure how much truth was in what he said, but I know he'd had a thin time.

Well, that's all behind us. Now, with Catherine in bed all the time, I'm housekeeper and practical nurse and body servant. We're within walking distance of a supermarket. Not easy walking distance for anybody as short of breath as I am, but I take it slowly and I manage. Lord knows I'm not heavy laden with bags to bring home, not on what I have to spend. We do without a lot of things, and I'm very close with what we do have. I have to be. Last week I didn't even have money to get the chocolate Catherine likes in her milk. That was awful, because chocolate milk is about all she can handle now.

I do the cleaning, the little cooking and the washing up, the whole thing. I don't feel all this only as oppressive; it's also a queer misshapen kind of blessing. I can't say I have any morbid fondness for it, but it keeps me busy and that puts a cushion of sorts between me and the voices. No, not anything as softening as a cushion. A partition. The work builds a partition between me and Them. I go on hearing my voices, and I see a clinic doctor every three weeks. Pills often make things hard for me. Nothing helps like Mellaril, but a strong enough dose to help keeps me half asleep. On that dosage, I can hardly walk when I haul myself up in the morning. The doctor keeps changing my medicine, and he insists that sooner or later he'll find something. Lately I have terrible headaches too.

The partition that the housework builds, even though fairly flimsy, is something of a shield. While the partition holds, it makes it a little harder for Them to get at me. For this reason, I work more than would otherwise be absolutely necessary; so we live in a clean place. Once when the voices were giving me a monstrous hard time, I cleaned and polished that antique of a refrigerator, inside and out, until it was dazzling. It wasn't in need of quite that elaborate attention and I felt guilty about using the cleaning materials, but I had to do it.

There's always somebody to say, "No matter how poor you are, you can be clean." A lot they know. That takes a person who has never known poverty or even observed it at close range, and such a person is all unaware of how stupid and cruel a remark it is. When you live in bitter poverty, it's *hard* to keep clean. We stay clean, but it takes a tremendous effort. If it weren't for my special needs to keep busy, I couldn't do it.

Of course I buy the lowest-priced products, but all cleaning materials are expensive. When I buy the large economy sizes, we're painfully pinched somewhere else that go-round; and sometimes I have to waste money buying smaller sizes because I don't have enough to buy the big ones. Paper products are nearly all out of reach. About the only paper we use is toilet paper, and we use as little as humanly possible. I don't buy paper towels; I use rags. We don't use paper napkins; we use old scraps of cloth tht I can throw in with the clothes at the laundromat; in a word, rags. I don't use cellulose sponges that fall into crumbs in no time; I use rags. And rags are OK to work with, it's just that they're a great nuisance to keep washed out.

Praise be for wash-and-wear clothes, but I save up what does have to be ironed and do it all at once. I can't be turning the iron off and on and using up power that way. Once the iron gets cold, it takes more to heat it up again. I have to be aware of things like that.

I go a long time from one haircut to another; mostly I hack at it, or Catherine does. She has long done-up hair and doesn't have to worry about that. But she does need an emery board once in a while, and so do I. People don't think, but being as poor as we are means, for one small thing, you can hardly keep your nails clean and at a reasonable length. We don't dare to lose the nail file. Usually I have newspaper in the bottoms of my broken shoes. It's a rare and memorable day when I get new half-soles. We don't buy regular deodorants; we use baking soda.

Just the very act of observing all these severe economies is an additional misery and an aggravation to the main misery. It won't let you forget for a minute just how abysmal your condition is. It keeps you quiveringly alive to your poverty.

We have one luxury. TV. It's an old color set left over from better days and, balm to my soul, it works. When it breaks down, we'll be without it. I could never pay for TV repair. I worry about the televison the way a less poor man would worry about his jalopy. For me, television is narcotic and analgesic. I can look at TV when I couldn't read to save my soul. All my life I've read, ever since I learnt how, but now I never crack a book. There's a branch library right around the corner, and this would give me some solace if I could only make use of it. I get books for Catherine. Some time back I tried to read *Eleanor and Franklin* and, over and over, I'd find myself at the bottom of a page and I wouldn't know a word I had read. When this happens all the time, you're not reading. A couple of years ago I tried again, with a book by a Russian woman, about World War II. I couldn't keep to it, couldn't really read, only skip and skim. I saw some passages that made me want to read it all, but I couldn't.

TV can still hold me. I think that's because of the moving images. Also, you don't have to bring anything to it; you don't have to put out any mental exertion at all. Reading takes mental effort; and if your anxieties are strong enough, they take over from the book. Even simple housework calls for some attention to what you're doing, not much but some, and it's active. TV is passive. You just sit there and let it dump on you. For whatever reason, it's a mercy that I can watch TV. It doesn't work for everybody. One person I knew at the hospital, whose trouble was the same as mine, was later a shut-in and lonely and really needed TV for the "company" it is. But he had to quit because of the talking. He got the dialogue mixed up with his voices, and he thought the people on the screen were talking to him and about him.

That's a thing paranoia does. It cuts you off from one thing after another. There was one woman whose small pleasures kept getting lopped off. Hats were becoming to her and she had always enjoyed wearing them, even when hats weren't being worn too much. Something happened, though, something to do with her voices, I feel certain, and she suddenly quit and never put a hat on her head again. She used to like to wear earrings. Same thing. This sort of attrition keeps up, and eventually you have nothing of even the simplest and tiniest gratifications and all has gone gray for you.

I'm pretty much a shut-in myself, going out of the house only when there are necessary errands to be run. Recreation is not to be even thought of. Social life is non-existent. I couldn't go anywhere even if I had anywhere to go; I have no money for bus fare. We see nobody except Catherine's daugther and her husband once in a while. The Ritters have moved to another state. And, since Mr. Ritter is no longer on the board of the Schizophrenia Research Institute, Mr. La Roche doesn't know my name. His job never did require him to take special interest in the likes of me, but he did as long as Mr. Ritter was here. He was enormously kind and helpful to me over a period of several years, even sometimes at his own expense. I looked on him as a saint. I'm still grateful for all he did, and it was a lot. But I couldn't help noticing how it all went glimmering as soon as the Ritters moved away. Mrs. Ritter wrote to him in my behalf a few years ago, and he never even acknowledged receipt of her letter. I can't so much as go walking in good weather, because of the emphysema. And Catherine, of course, is stuck in bed. So here we are.

My world has shrunk to our small living quarters and the

places of business I can walk to. I've reached the age and condition where I can't avoid knowing that my life can't amount to more than it already has. I've had very few good things. And whatever good things I haven't had, I'm not going to have. In this fix, with no rational hope for better, all I can do is will myself toward some degree of not caring, toward the ultimate giving up. And wait.

I'm doing all I can, and that's no more than holding on. I keep "going," to the extent of my ability to go, but I'm often going like an automaton. Pick up one foot, put it down before the other, this foot, that foot, this foot, that foot, until somehow each day winds down to an end and somehow I live through the night.

Always there are the voices. Of course I don't ignore them. That's manifestly impossible. But I stay tired—the housework is taxing because of shortness of breath, and trying to beat off the voices takes it out of me—and I don't get wrought up the way I used to. Not even about the most terrible of the voices. They hurt me, They upset me, They infuriate me, sometimes They scare me. But I don't fly up because of them. I think I'm not able. I think the point I'm groping toward is that I'm still tormented but now I'm suppressed. That's probably not just right; I don't know how to say it.

Often I think back to two comments that have stuck in my mind for many years. I think back to Ken Rockwood at Reliant saying, "That boy looks like he lives in a shadow." I did indeed live in a shadow, and as time went by the shadow steadily deepened and the one I live in now is gray-black. I think back to one of the early astronauts, when he was beaming descriptive messages back to the listening earth. At one point he said, "We are moving toward darkness all the time." Unlike him, I am not moving anywhere. Darkness is moving toward me all the time.

HOLIDAY

Saturday night and man takes holiday
From labor that was safer wine,
But on Saturday night—come Saturday night—
He knows himself, vacuous, cold,
Hunting the colors, filling the empty spaces,
No longer a king with a column of figures
A column of figures to be added and subtracted
And himself therefore
A man managing the affairs of the world.

But on Saturday night a guy has leave to talk to himself.
To reclaim his soul.
To hunt what he has wanted, or forget what he never had,
To chase the dream, or drown it in futility.

God, do You see?
Or are You too far away reclining on a star?
How about coming down and walking for a little
Where we are?
Do not tell me no one has asked You,
Over the cups in the dark of night
Saturday night.
Do not tell me no one has cried to You
Lost in the dark and without a light
Saturday night.

Your stars are beautiful, but we
Need some nearer light to see.

—by the real Robby Wilde

327

Elizabeth Kytle

SATURDAY NIGHT

Broken calla lilies, cathedral altars,
Magnolia petals, ermine coats, debris,
Weddings, dances, drinks, bottles, perfume,
Disgust, clear eyes, uniforms, madness, war,
Upheaval, bedlam, starry dark, snow, red wine,
Gold wine, bleary eyes, colored lights.

Mostly I think it is the colored lights,
Always the lights.

Moths, we are all moths.
All men are moths, all women are moths,
And whether we drown in the red, or the gold, or the blue—
All of the lights are promises, mostly broken.

Cool sky
Where is the light that does not lie?

Broken calla lilies.
We are like that—we who drown in wine.
Moths after a light
Saturday night.

God, wherever you are,
Cool, lighted, far on the rim of a star—
If You have not forgotten
Look down and You will see Saturday night.

Spin out Your web of white stars in Your sky—
So far away from men who die
On Your mad muddy earth—
Spin out play airy graces on the flutes of our eyes.

You sing.
A quick ear will not escape Your singing.
We have heard Your tunes up there, have seen Your
Crystal facets dancing—

But why play on a stage so far it's hard to see or hear?
You made man a moth for light
And these lights are so near,
Wine red, wine gold, wine,
Colored lights!

Synthesis of color—white.
You make so far a light
For mortals seeking colors in the night
Saturday night.

—by the real Robby Wilde